CW01083597

DIENER & DIENER

DIENER & DIENER

JOSEPH ABRAM
ROGER DIENER
SABINE VON FISCHER
MARTIN STEINMANN
ADAM SZYMCZYK

Thanks and acknowledgments

The oeuvre of Diener & Diener is the work of many. My most sincere thanks goes to all my inspring partners in design, with whom I have collaborated for many years.

This monograph is a response to the curiosity brought to our work by Richard Schlagman as well as to his friendly patience, and also to the energy and the wise council of Emilia Terragni and Sara Goldsmith. Without their efforts, this monograph would not have come about.

Jean Robert and Käti Durrer were responsible for the design. They guided us in selecting images and texts in a manner far beyond mere professionalism and mutual friendship.

Isabel Halene worked closely with the designers and Phaidon Press to develop this project and with Annina von Planta in realizing it. For their work, long-standing partners of Diener & Diener, I am deeply grateful.

Finally, my thanks go to Joseph Abram, Martin Steinmann, Adam Szymczyk and Sabine von Fischer as well as to Helmut Federle and Peter Suter for their contributions to this book. Our conversation is dear to us.

Roger Diener

7   **Diener & Diener: The beauty of the real, Joseph Abram**

34   Apartment Buildings Hammerstrasse, Basel

40   Apartment Buildings Riehenring, Basel

46   Apartment Buildings St. Alban-Tal, Basel

56   Office Building Steinentorberg, Basel

64   Showrooms and Administration Building for Manor, Basel

68   Administration Building Hochstrasse, Basel

76   Training and Conference Centre Viaduktstrasse, Basel

84   Administration Building Picassoplatz, Basel

90   Gmurzynska Gallery, Cologne

98   Office Building Kohlenberg, Basel

102   Vogesen School, Basel

106   Housing & Office Buildings Warteck Brewery, Basel

112   Apartment Buildings Parkkolonnaden, Berlin

118   Extension to the Centre Pasqu'Art, Biel

126   Hotel Schweizerhof, Migros Supermarket, Migros School, Lucerne

132   Apartment Buildings KNSM and Java Island, Amsterdam

140   Swiss Embassy, Berlin

149   **Architecture beyond design, Adam Szymczyk in conversation with Roger Diener**

157   **Firmitas, Roger Diener**

166   Masterplan for the University Harbour, Malmö

170   University Building, Malmö

178   Frankfurt Book Fair, Frankfurt am Main

182   Apartment and Office Building Bäumleingasse, Basel

188   Collection Rosengart, Lucerne

192   Ruhr Museum at Zeche Zollverein, Essen

198   Extension to the National Gallery of Modern Art, Rome

202   Extension to the Pergamon Museum, Berlin

206   Residential Buildings Ypenburg, The Hague

212   Masterplan for the Maag Areal Plus, Zurich

216   Mobimo Tower, Zurich

222   Stücki Shopping Centre, Basel

230   Novartis Campus Forum 3, Basel

246   Casa A1 at the Olympic Village, Turin

250   Westkaai 1+2 Apartment Buildings, Antwerp

258   Convention Centre 'ZürichForum', Zurich

262   Shoah Memorial Drancy, Drancy

266   Music House for Instrumental Practice and Choral Rehearsal, Einsiedeln

272   Kunsthaus Zürich Extension, Zurich

276   Swiss Re Headquarters, Zurich

282   Kunstmuseum Basel Extension, Basel

286   New East Wing Expansion of the Museum of Natural History, Berlin

299   **Architecture engagée: Diener & Diener, Martin Steinmann**

314   Project chronology, 1976–2011

318   Biography and Bibliography

319   Index

Diener & Diener: The beauty of the real

Joseph Abram

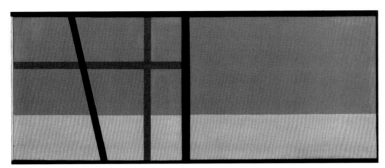

Window, Museum of Modern Art, Paris, Ellsworth Kelly, 1949

In October 1949 at the Museum of Modern Art in Paris, I noticed the large windows between the pictures interested me more than art exhibited. I made a drawing of the window and later in my studio, I made what I consider to be my first object, Window, Museum of Modern Art, Paris. *From then on, painting as I had known it was finished. The new works were to be painting/objects, unsigned, anonymous. Everywhere I looked, everything I saw became something to be made, and it had to be made exactly as it was, with nothing added. It was a new kind of freedom: there was no longer the need to compose. The subject was there already made, and I could take from everything; it all belonged to me: a glass roof of a factory with broken and patched panes, lines of a roadmap, the shape of a scarf on a woman's head, a fragment of Le Corbusier's Swiss Pavilion, a corner of a Braque painting, paper fragments on the street. It was all the same: anything goes.*

Ellsworth Kelly, 1969[1]

It might seem strange to open an essay about Diener & Diener with a quotation from the American painter Ellsworth Kelly recalling, twenty years after the event, how his work had undergone a radical transformation into 'painting/objects'. Strange and even dubious, given that much of Roger Diener's architectural practice is premised on an affirmation of architecture's autonomy from other artistic practices, and from any other reference that might distance it from its own traditions. For Diener, architecture must continue exploring its own discipline, as opposed to attempting to reflect what is happening elsewhere in the plastic arts, literature or cinema. He distances himself from expressive approaches that claim there are equivalences of form between different artistic practices, as well as those that attempt to represent architecture's contemporaneousness. But this does not mean Diener is uninterested in being contem-

porary, or that, for him, architecture's continuity as a discipline transcends other historical processes. His architecture does maintain an organic relationship with its own present but it does not attempt to represent this relationship. The problematics that it addresses take place in an intellectual climate inherited from an earlier – postmodernist – crisis. As is well known, this crisis did not put an end to modernity,[2] but it did correspond to the development of a greater breadth of objective understanding of the historical foundations of modernity. In addition to the chaos in meaning caused by the collapse of the idea of the 'metanarrative',[3] this crisis also illustrated the complex conditions that are inherent in the development of modern societies, a theme explored as early as the 1950s by Hannah Arendt. In her view, by extending man's technical dominion over all natural processes, the modern age brought about a fluidization of the real and a loss of widespread meaning.[4] As the conceptual apparatus of 'history' has exploded into critical thinking over the last few decades, it appears Arendt's theories have been strikingly confirmed. How can cultural practices avoid becoming isolated from their context when their frame of reference is now a history that is entirely self-referential? How can they create significations of universal value in this new order of fragmentary reality? Trying to think about Diener & Diener's work outside of signification requires a clarification of the recent debates in history. In order to understand the contemporaneousness of Diener & Diener's work, it has to be placed right within the centre of its own paradoxes. This requires an exploration of the process by which the work takes form and also a verification of the validity of the positions it selects during this process: among others, these include a re-centering around the core discipline of architecture, a porosity towards other practices, a rejection of any identifying signs, the dissolution of place into non-place and a fusion of the universal and the ordinary.

From the Urban to the Banal

During a conference in Zurich, in 1996, Diener recalled Aldo Rossi's impact on his generation.[5] He recalled his student admiration for Rossi's Gallaratese housing project (which, for him, merited 'iconic' status) as well as the influence of Luigi Snozzi, his professor at the Eidgenössische Technische Hochschule (ETHZ) in Zurich, whose work during the 1970s provided Diener with encouragement. This encouragement was due not only to the intrinsic quality of both men's projects in the Ticino region, but also their commitment to the architectural profession. The dissemination of Rossi's ideas on the city offered a solid referential framework to eager students, while the arrival of Snozzi and the Ticino school onto the international architectural scene heralded a return to building.

In *L'architettura della città* (*The Architecture of the City*), 1966, Rossi illustrates the problematic relationship between architecture and the city:

Thus there is a direct relationship between the formulation of certain proposals and the buildings that arise in the city ... But it is equally obvious that this relationship can also be considered in its separate terms. The world of architecture can be seen to unfold and be studied as a logical succession of principles and forms more or less autonomous from the realities of locus and history. Thus, architecture implies the city; but this city may be an ideal city, of perfect and harmonious relationships, where the architecture develops and constructs its own terms of reference. At the same time, the actual architecture of this city is unique; from the very first it has a characteristic – and ambiguous – relationship that no other art or science possesses. In these terms we can understand the constant polemical urge of architects to design systems in which the spatial order becomes the order of society and attempts to transform society.[6]

We can hear here what would become the intellectual challenge for a younger generation: an architecture that is capable of slotting itself into a city, but that does not entirely submit itself to a city's order, or, conversely, attempt to simplify the problem by erasing the city's contradictions. In his 1973 comment on the German edition of his book, Rossi provides us with some precious information:

This book is an architectural project. Like all projects, it depends less on the material it draws on than on the relations it establishes between facts. An investigation of the meaning of the relationship between the singularity of form and the multiplicity of functions was the principal objective of this study. I still believe today that this relationship constitutes the meaning of architecture. Some of the elements analyzed in this books have subsequently become elements of a design theory: urban topology, the study of typology, the history of architecture as the material of architecture. In these elements time and space are constantly intermixed. Topology, typology and history come to be measures of the mutations of reality, together defining a system where gratuitous invention is impossible. Thus they are opposed theoretically to the disorder of contemporary architecture.[7]

The system of values defined by Rossi can be considered one of the theoretical foundations of Diener's work. Topography, typology and history all allowed Roger Diener to construct his own vision of the city as well as supplying him with a first set of three-dimensional design tools. However, while Rossi and the Ticino school provided the initial impetus for Diener &

Apartment Buildings St. Alban-Tal, Basel

Administration Building Picassoplatz, Basel

Diener, the firm's practice soon developed a critical distance from their built work. The Apartment Buildings Hammerstrasse (1978–81) and the Apartment Buildings Riehenring (1980–5), both in Basel, have very little in common with Italian or Ticino experiments of the time.[8] The only genuine precedent one can find is Livio Vacchini's school building in Losone (1973–5),[9] which displays a similarly neutral relationship to structure. However, the ideas Diener absorbed from Rossi and the Ticino school, and the methods he used to inscribe his projects into the surrounding urban reality provided him with a way out of the widespread formalism of the time. As a result, the design approaches he put in place helped to protect him from a prevailing ethos concerned with a historicity that worshipped notions of 'context', 'memory' and 'place'. These approaches would also provide him with a solid theoretical base for his work, which he could then proceed to address and to endlessly perfect over a period of thirty years.

In an earlier essay on Diener & Diener's work,[10] I situated their beginnings in Basel's tradition of modern architecture, focusing on the firm's history (founded by Roger Diener's father, Marcus Diener) and the rich seam of a local Rationalist tradition present through the works of Karl Moser, Otto Rudolf Salvisberg and Hans Bernoulli.[11] I underlined certain similarities with the poetic Functionalism of Walter Gropius[12] and Hannes Meyer, and I also theorized about an original contribution that this firm made: their extension of a form of Rationalism – itself a product of the New Objectivity movement – into the contradictions of the contemporary period. In this way, the firm's creative attitude could be linked to the 'pragmatic realism' described by Jean-François Lyotard in his book, *The Postmodern Condition*.[13] I also remarked on how Diener's Basel projects of the early 1980s had possible connections with the Rationalist part

of Robert Venturi's ideas.[14] All these crossovers in thinking demonstrated the strength of Diener & Diener's theoretical position and the ability it had to surpass the limits of the referential framework within which it was originally constructed.

As opposed to the many architects who saw Venturi's writings as a providential sourcebook for architectural composition, Diener & Diener were not interested in Venturi's renewal of ways to define form. Instead, they were interested in the ethos of ordinariness that his books heralded. If we remember Venturi's comments on what other critics have called his 'ugly and ordinary' images of American cities, we see that he actually delights in their beauty: 'But the pictures in this book that are supposed to be bad are often good. The seemingly chaotic juxtaposition of honky-tonk elements express an intriguing kind of vitality and validity, and they produce an unexpected approach to unity as well.'[15] By valorizing disordered spaces, complexity theories were registering an inexorable slide from the notion of an urban culture to the idea of an urban landscape.[16] It is this tendency within modernity, which can be understood as including both a floating sense of identity and a dispersing appropriation of space, that reveals the connection between Diener & Diener's and Venturi's theories.[17] An aesthetic of banality was beginning to appear as the ultimate form in modernity's process of integrating different levels of culture. It began to develop as early as the 1950s, following contact with Brutalist architecture and the propositions of British Pop Art.[18] By taking an anti-normative stance, Roger Diener could take up the tradition of extending high culture into the world of the ordinary in a way that was wholly his own. He seems to have taken on the task of realizing the anti-normative programme behind Venturi's ideas[19] but only by freeing himself from their actual content. He needed to find a springboard that

Office Building Steinentorberg, Basel

a new understanding of the real could provide him with, and he found a critical path that allowed him to reconcile three non-heroic ideas of architecture: Rossi's typological and urban conceptions, Venturi's embrace of the ordinary and, finally, a Rationalist, constructive approach inherited from the New Objectivity movement.[20]

Design Approaches

Right from the beginning of their work, Diener & Diener persevered in their chosen experimental path. The studio focused its energy by defining a limited set of problems to which it could systematically apply itself. A retrospective of Roger Diener's work reveals a pattern of distinct buildings: the Office Building Steinentorberg (1984–90), the Administration Building Hochstrasse (1985–8), the Administration Building Picassoplatz (1987–93) and the Office Building Kohlenberg (1992–5), all in Basel, and the Gmurzynska Gallery (1988–91) in Cologne. Although different in form, these objects all have unusual appearances that seem to refer to a single set of fundamental principles, applied with genuine consistency. Their quiet presence produces a strange sense of timelessness. They are there, calm and present, as if they have been standing since time immemorial.[21] The eye is able to fall upon them without actually seeing them or having to continue looking at them. These buildings are able to create a stable urban image of themselves through a kind of controlled absence, a relational invisibility achieved through a long process that places them at the centre of an imaginary web upon which the real seems to hang. Existing within this network of different energies, the projects are able to absorb the surrounding urban substance, while halting any kind of preconceived determination – i.e. strict architectural programming, typological values, a geometrical tradition, any relationship with its own materials –

that could be projected onto it. The resulting architecture achieves a kind of appropriateness through the sequence of actions it has taken to construct its identity. It rejects the idea of the city. The actual undertaking of the 'project' overcomes the city, using the illusion of a centrality of design, which is then decentralized as it moves inexorably towards oblivion. Place becomes non-place. The edifice leaves the world of thought for the world of objects, but still keeps traces of its alternating transitions between the two.

As a vessel for these contradictory values, Diener & Diener's architecture establishes a particular relationship with urban culture. This relationship has constantly evolved in spite of the stable principles that underpin it. Four phases [22] can be distinguished in its development. Initially, the studio focused on a pragmatic inventory of its own methods of architectural intervention. The order of classification for this first period included the description, enumeration of these methods, as well as making them readable. Their architectural undertakings of this period (Apartment Buildings Hammerstrasse, Apartment Buildings Riehenring) prioritized hierarchies of scale, type and usages. Their design processes adopted the articulating principles used to organize urban space, while simultaneously revealing the joints in these principles. Their approach already included the main elements of the studio's working method, including collective decision-making, limited use of representational devices, a preference for well-established typological classification, an open, generous attitude towards the ordinary.[23] This phase could be described as the beginning of their architectural problematic. In the next stage of development, as a result of client demand, their work focused on one particular entity, the building, which appears as an ambiguous space in which the surrounding fabric of the city intermingles with the

Administration Building Hochstrasse, Basel

building's internal configuration. As an object in a landscape, the building works to achieve equilibrium between the principles that have produced it and the characteristics of the urban fragments that will receive it. The city penetrates the building, traverses it and imposes its order upon it. Using a design approach incorporating analytical drawing, as in the Apartment Buildings St. Alban-Tal (1981–6), in Basel, the studio created an equivalency between interiority and exteriority.[24] In the third phase, the studio began a powerful system of densification. Managing complexity took another form, no longer a process of assemblage but a one of compaction.[25] This is the heroic period of the Gmurzynska Gallery and the Administration Building Hochstrasse, the Office Building Steinentorberg, and the Residential Building Allschwilerstrasse (1984–6) in Basel. In these projects, existing urban tensions are managed by the structure. In the Gmurzynska Gallery, the device of analytical drawing persists, but the volume produced exists at a point of near fusion.[26] Space flows between the building's adjoining volumes, which remain distinct even under the structure's smooth enveloping surface. Interior and exterior have been given the same value.[27] The wealth of semantic richness provided by this mode of creating architecture is also evident in the legibility of the structure of the Administration Building Hochstrasse. Situated near Basel train station, alongside the railway tracks, this block accepts any logical overlay its environment might suggest. Anything goes. It channels the forces that are around it with a plastic vigorousness, which, in turn, identifies it as both a part of and a witnessing object for the neighbourhood. As for the Office Building Steinentorberg, the viaduct that runs along it has such a solid facade that building and viaduct become indissoluble. Through this immersion in urban complexity, the architecture is able to reinforce the fragments of reality it identifies, in order to infiltrate itself

into the mental images of city-dwellers.[28] In the studio's final phase we see a radicalization of these design approaches and their export into vaster areas. By now, the studio had defined its methodology for architectural intervention. Traditional blocks of buildings are substituted with more open configurations better adapted to actual needs. A new way of dealing with the built substance begins to emerge, in which the building itself starts to play an original role. We see a pacification of contradiction. The Administration Building Picassoplatz appears as a compressed block of buildings. Its rectangular outlines, the repetitious sequence of its windows, the stacking of floor levels and the dimensions of the building's concrete elements all consolidate the building's presence, and it is able to give form to the surrounding empty space. The building weaves invisible links with the city. The surrounding context is sucked into this 'block of buildings as object', but in a mediated and considered way. Other projects around this time base their structure on differentiation of different wings of a building and the positioning of these pieces in relation to each other. In the project for the extension of the BWB (Berliner Wasserbetriebe; Berlin Water Company, 1993) and the Apartment Buildings Parkkolonnaden (1994–2000), both in Berlin, built blocks annex empty adjacent spaces to create an open-plan site where each subset of space is defined.[29] The projects for the Nancy School of Architecture (1993), the masterplan for Baden Nord (1994–8) and the École Polytechnique Fédérale (EPFL) in Lausanne (1993), implement this kind of approach. The introduction of these modes of design into a project of larger urban scale can be seen in the Apartment Buildings KNSM and Java Island (1995–2001), industrial wasteland projects for the dockland areas of the KNSM and Java islands in Amsterdam.[30] The two buildings created for these projects, one conceived as a square courtyard structure and the other a massive horizontal block,

Housing and Office Buildings Warteck Brewery, Basel

New York Office, Edward Hopper, 1962

bring together disparate entities. By harnessing the site's elements together (big or small, near or far), the project stabilizes their presence within the remodelled landscape of the port. The Biel Gas Works (1992) and the Masterplan for the University Harbour in Malmö, Sweden (1997), also display the use of this kind of intervention right within the organizational fabric of a city.

Through these different approaches to the architectural project, Diener & Diener have opened up new territories for architecture as a discipline. Their body of work appears as one of the most coherent of the last few decades. By insisting on the limits of architecture, Roger Diener acquired an authentic project strategy: 'It is not about asking an object to express something outside of itself and making it responsible for representing it, nor is it about giving a building meaning through an artificial device that is projected externally onto it.'[31] Architecture enters into contemporary reality by using the methods that properly belong to it. Through its own internal workings, it is able to capture some of the unstable configurations that have come out of the infinite relationships created by our many historical practices. The more a work identifies itself with an approach that empties it of concrete meanings, the more energy it is able to produce as a result. By eliminating all that is incidental, it is able to use its own actual concrete reality to show the rigorous sequence of its architectural deductions. Through its own processes, it contributes to collective representations that cast immediate history into contemporary narratives.[32]

The Inhabited Window
Roger Diener talks about a painting by Balthus showing a young girl looking out of a window. The window opening appears out of scale with the rest of the painting:

The relationship between the person and the window is important. It shows a situation distorted to its limit. How far can we expand the window before it is no longer a window? We manipulate the window opening but we want it to remain a window. Generally, we want to stay within the register of traditional space, but transform it to the point just before it gets lost.[33]

The window is an inhabited space.[34] Along with other architectural elements, it constitutes a spatial type defined by usage. Like the hall, the bedroom or the office, it belongs to a collection of life spaces. It is an element whose character can be imperceptibly varied by playing with its dimension, the amount of light it transmits, its view on the outside world, etc. The window is not just a simple functional opening. It offers a particular interface between the interior and the exterior. It is also about the ordinary. One could make a study of Diener & Diener's projects by just looking at their use of the window in terms of scale, proportion and placement on a building's facade. Diener & Diener's windows are large and generously reflective. They are able to capture, mirror-like, images of the buildings opposite, or the trees and other objects on a street. Their frontality devours, seeming to absorb elements in the surrounding landscape and just leave empty space – which can be understood as distance in relation to other objects,[35] and so the building's facade seems to turn inwards into a virtual interior. Inside the buildings, the city colours a living space with its fluid presence. The bedroom, the living room, the kitchen become cubes of space bathed in urban light, evoking certain paintings by Edward Hopper, including *Morning Sun*, *Rooms by the Sea*, *Conference at Night*, *Office in a Small City* and *Western Motel*.

Office Building Kohlenberg, Basel

In Diener & Diener's residential buildings, the windows take on meaning through the apartments' overall design schemes: they become a series of rectangular volumes attached to each other. The window does not fit into a rhetoric of construction. It only communicates its presence as a window: a banal form common to both architecture and the city. For Diener, construction is not the object of representation:[36] 'We like to make use of current technical possibilities, but we are not trying to represent them. We are not looking for a language to express construction.'[37] Construction is able to produce abstract rules for the organization of matter and space, which help to remove a project's superfluous determinants. The design process tends to structure the inherent features of a plan around its usages, the materials and the site, without any prior hierarchization. By following traditions of established typological classification, architecture can be understood as a form of mental ordering. It puts its trust in conventions set down by a long history of use. For Diener, the orthogonal space is such an archetype:

We can thank it for the creation of our most beautiful urban spaces, but also our most beautiful sacred and secular interior architectural spaces throughout the centuries. The orthogonal space defines the underlying principle in our design during a project's development, which, in a sense, is a process of repeating the same fundamental elements. The comprehension of a space, a building's structure, the organization of an architectural plan and the ordering of its windows create an indissoluble system of elements that we repeat while, at the same time, we try to redefine in different ways. The right angle leads to a simple, constructive physical form, a mental ordering of elements and a notion of the ideal, through to the creation of a signifying and symbolic space.[38]

And it is an archetype that underlies much of our way of life, as Diener explains in discussing an installation that Hannes Meyer created for a photograph: 'simple paper surfaces, simple angles ... The installation really expresses the dimension of the "lived". How the "lived" can be conveyed by space and objects. Everything is there in it because of the orthogonal space's primordial states. What we are interested in today is not exceeding these states, but continuing to explore them.'[39] By testing to see where its limits lie, Diener & Diener's strict application of the right angle has been proven through an endless verification of its possibilities. Its longevity can be explained by its capacity for inventive use, even its capacity to induce experimentation. In Diener & Diener's work, it appears as the operator taking them through assembled buildings (Apartment Building with Bank, Basel, 1982–5) to compact blocks (Administration Building Hochstrasse), open-plan blocks of buildings (Housing and Office Buildings Warteck Brewery, Basel, 1992–6), and sequences of increasingly dense buildings (Apartment Buildings Parkkolonnaden). An assertion of the rectangular unit of space (and its links to real usage) is the thread that runs through the studio's projects. Within interior spaces, residential rooms are fused together as segments within a rigid organization of space, a sequence of identifiable volumes held together between a building's concrete plates. Diener's internal plans for apartments are not free or open-plan. Instead he adapts traditional architectural typology to a site's potential, through the control of elements including an apartment's internal volume, and the assembly of its rooms and proportions.

Fresco cycle in the Scrovegni Chapel in
Padua, Giotto, 1303–06

Volume and Tension

Even if it is not immediately obvious, the primacy of internal
volume is always an important part of Diener & Diener's work.
As opposed to the Gmurzynska Gallery, where cubic structures
are pressed together to the point of fusion, the Administration
Building Hochstrasse is a solid block that seems to be twisting
on its axis. This rotation is created by the use of a referential
cube that seems to frame the building and creates a persistent
sense of duality, as a duplicate mental image is created alongside the built volume. On the one hand, there is the concrete
edifice; on the other, the virtual volume that contains it.
Writing on Diener & Diener in 1991, in order to make this effect
of torsion/duplication more explicit, I referred to certain
paintings by Francis Bacon, which use a series of outlines
around figures' heads to suggest the emergence of cube-like
space: *Head VI*, *Study for Portrait*, *Pope II*, *Triptych Inspired
by T. S. Eliot's 'Sweeney Agonistes'*, *Three Studies of Lucian
Freud*, *Water from a Running Tap*.[40] In these paintings, space
is pressed against the surface, without any visible decrease of
this space. Volume is constructed in a desperate inter-space
existing on the painting's surface. It manages to have neither
surface flatness nor the homogeneity of perspective. In order
for this inter-space to break free from the painting's surface,
it has to exert considerable violence towards it. In the play
of these internal energies within a painting, it is possible to
see the archaeology of an ancient practice, the works of both
Giotto (*The Death of the Knight of Celano*, 1297–1300, Assisi;
The Last Supper, 1320–5, Alte Pinakothek, Munich) and Fra
Angelico (*Annunciation*, 1434, Diocesan Museum, Cortona; *Birth
of Saint Nicholas of Bari*, 1437, Pinacoteca, Vatican) being
remarkable examples. Both painters used volume as an instrument for creating depth. According to Erwin Panofsky, Giotto
conceived of three-dimensionality 'not as quality inherent in an

ambient medium and imparted to the individual objects but as
a quality inherent in the individual objects as such'. He strove
to master the third dimension 'by manipulating the plastic
contents of space rather than space itself', and Giotto painted
this way right into his late period, in works such as the Peruzzi
Chapel's *Resurrection* in Santa Croce, Florence, 'where space is
generated by the solids instead of pre-existing before them'.[41]
For a contemporary viewer (used to both visual perspective
and its pictorial demise), these contradictions of volume and
space add to the beauty of the works. Giotto's frescos (cycles
illustrating the *Life of Christ* and the *Life of the Virgin*, executed
around 1303–5) in the Scrovegni Chapel in Padua can be seen
as non-transparent windows within which the interior space
has been entirely given over to these antagonistic forces. The
scenes' energetic volumes seem to press against the chapel's
walls and into the central emptiness of the space. The regularly
positioned 'opaque windows' also seem to scale down these
energetic volumes. And, yet, all the forces within these scenes
(which are sometimes juxtaposed, sometimes superimposed)
end up cancelling each other out on this pictorial surface
(with its virtual relief of pictorial volume) as they are ultimately
absorbed back into the wall's material primacy.

Twentieth-century artists became particularly interested in the
contradictions of volume and space. Whereas Renaissance
artists used volume to suggest an invisible interstitial depth,
without attempting to create a uniform space, modern painters
– weary of perspective's homogeneity – used this contradiction as a powerful tool to reintroduce chaos into the pictorial
space. We can see this debate around volume developing at
the very beginnings of Cubism, in Braque's paintings (*Houses
at L'Estaque*, 1908) and also Picasso's (*Houses on the Hill,
Horta de Ebro*, 1909).[42] It then disappeared, overtaken by other

Annunciation to St. Anne, Scrovegni Chapel in Padua,
Giotto, 1303–06

Houses on the Hill, Horta de Ebro,
Pablo Picasso, 1909

Women Running on the Beach,
Pablo Picasso, 1922

developments in pictorial representation, only to reappear again in Picasso's paintings of the 1920s, when he reinstated objects within the depth of a picture: *Three Women at the Fountain*, 1921, and *Women Running on the Beach*, 1922, for example.[43] The bodies in these pictures seem to have frozen gestures, like sculpture. It seems as if Picasso is now transcending the destruction of perspective within the domain of the pictorial surface. And in this 'surface depth', represented objects acquire a surreal presence.

Antagonism between space and volume might seem incongruous in architecture, given how the discipline allies itself solidly with the three-dimensional. All buildings can be translated into a volume, which, in principle, can be inserted into a surrounding space without any distortion. In reality, an object's final form and how perspective relates to it (or not, as the case may be) can be played with at the design level. One senses this has happened with some of Diener & Diener's buildings when one stands in front of them. Even as they appear calm and serene to the eye, they also have a slightly disturbing feel. This effect is clear at the Administration Building Hochstrasse and continues with the later buildings. The origins of this effect have to be searched for at an earlier point in the conception of Diener & Diener's buildings, in the way that they are designed to locate a particular tension in their peripheries. Suspended between the forces of interiority and exteriority, the facade wall is subjected to the myriad energies of these two different universes. This bipolar tension is very apparent in the early works. Although it is somewhat more hidden in the later buildings, the effect persists, inserted into the robust envelope of the building, which acts as an interface between interior and exterior. Like the Scrovegni Chapel (where Giotto frescos seem to stretch the walls horizontally), Diener & Diener's buildings

absorb considerable forces into the depth of their walls. But this depth is not a virtual dimension; it is profoundly linked to the volumes that occupy the space inside the walls. The integrity of Diener & Diener's facades is often interrupted by a regular placement of window bays, which create a grid to which the transparent volumes of glass can be attached. Their designs consolidate an isotropic arrangement of urban space, and they use the stacked rectangular volumes of windows to create static forms. We can see this effect in the Housing and Office Buildings Warteck Brewery. Three blocks make up this set of buildings built on the site of a former brewery. The first building is made up of offices organized around a closed patio. The structure's envelope, made from green concrete slabs, creates a sense of movement through the variation in placement of the horizontal panels of windows. The second building arranges housing around an open court. The facade, of polished brick, stacks smaller and larger windows in columns. The third building, in industrial brick, contains general facilities and commercial premises within the old brewery's renovated building. The brewery's tower, with its original company markings, has been kept as an integral part of the neighbourhood's history. The three buildings are differentiated by the materials used in their facades and the schema of their windows, but all of them make use of an equivalency between the built and non-built in order to create a large, open block of buildings that is able to integrate itself within the pre-existing scheme. The play of openings on the surface underlines the primacy of the wall: the horizontal flow of the glass panels on the green building and the stacked window bays on the polished brick building (which are indifferent to the building's internal organization) make the surfaces of the building's envelopes into readable entities. As they come into contact with these solid blocks, the internal and external spaces around the buildings are transformed into

Residential and Office Building Elsässerstrasse, Basel

virtual but still legible cubes. Some of Diener & Diener's other buildings also show this play of window and surface, which demonstrates a novel approach to the relationship between interiority and exteriority.

In a lecture in Paris in 1997, Diener underlined the strict way in which his Office Building Kohlenberg in Basel is linked to the city. 'Situated on a narrow plot, the building just has two large windows on each floor, one on each side of the building's angle. In a certain way, the gentle flow of the window bays projects the building's substance into its surface volume.' But as Diener explains, the facade does not make use of movement, but of immobility: 'We tried to avoid creating an image of meaningful rhythm. There is no particular movement. The building is not trying to underline the corner in an urban planning context – it is the corner.'[44] It is interesting to compare this modest structure with the Residential and Office Building Elsässerstrasse in Basel (1996–7), as the design of this facade works in a different way. Windows are placed over each other to form a regular grid, without any kind of visual flow. The concrete sections between windows are narrow – just wide enough to suggest a traditional system of pillars and window bays. Three design actions consolidate the building's volume: first, the removal of the windows that are closest to the corner creates a wider section to stress the surface quality of the block; second, the narrowing of the windows on the left side of the facade enlarges the width of the last concrete section just before the corner divides the building into two facades; and third, the window bays on the ground floor are transformed into larger glass shop-fronts, creating the sense of a plinth and simultaneously underlining the corner of the building. These three design features transform the facade into a surface volume. The edifice becomes a solid entity capable of creating empty space around it. Through this process, architecture indelibly moves into a different kind of representational space.

On the Threshold of Image

'For us, architecture is first and foremost a work on a frozen object. Architecture is essentially static. It is not about movement. Dynamism exists, but this is the result of perception. Above all, an architectural project is a reflection upon an immobile object.'[45] Referring to Erich Mendelsohn, who underlined the impossibility of trying to reflect movement in architecture, and instead suggested a definition of 'architectural dynamics' as 'the expression of a tension innate to elastic building materials, of movement and counter movement within the immovable stability of the building itself.'[46] Diener explains why a building's expressive gestures should not try and convey its character, and why images should not be grafted onto a building: 'We want to stay in the reality of expression'.[47] Diener & Diener's structures create a purified language. Their sequence of words appears as simple volumes: a bedroom, an apartment, a building, a courtyard, a part of a street, a square, etc. Within these volumes, the endless process of everyday life occurs, and it is the city, through the infinite variety of urban life, that infuses them with an intangible beauty. As Pierre Sansot has written:

The city is made up of un-owned places and objects that have accumulated a wide range of presences (a telephone box, a boulevard, the metro: all collective locations of interiority and exteriority). It would be impossible to try and possess them. In the same way, we feel we are both ourselves and everybody else, irreplaceably unique but also part of this collective mass of others who, like us, cannot limit their own individual understanding of a world that constantly invites different approaches and visions.[48]

Sansot suggests a definition of the urban that not only classifies different locations (a railway station, a square) but also covers objects related to the way of life linked to the 'dazzle of cities'. As opposed to places, which the city creates, and which by implication are 'made from the same clay', objects, by definition, can separate themselves from their context. Sansot examines these manufactured objects and their capacity to create, beyond their actual use, an urban poetry around themselves: how can an object without a known past, unrooted in the particular reality of a single observer, create a world of meaning around itself and have a real poetic existence? For these objects to radiate meaning – and they do – the surrounding landscape must have somehow required it.[49]

Diener & Diener's architecture creates this 'urban object', which is also a 'landscape object'. In their immobile journeys, these strange objects take with them some of the city's essence. They have a non-localized relationship with their setting, which is both real and unreal. They don't take root in their cities, but instead imply the rootlessness of the whole urban expanse. Diener & Diener's buildings are placed in a signifying space. Their relationship to the city around them is very complex: they seem to listen attentively to the narratives of the spaces within which they crystallize, or perhaps it would be more accurate to say that they detach themselves almost imperceptibly from these narratives while simultaneously absorbing their substance. All the givens registered during the design process solidify into the magma that then solidifies into the building. And the meaning they take on is universal – an interpretative meaning that abstracts the realities it encounters. Diener & Diener's design process does not reject anything, nor does it sort that which it encounters into preconceived hierarchies. It proceeds from that same opportunism that Ellsworth Kelly

described as 'anything goes'.[50] Architecture explores the act of non-composition in its own particular way. It transfers fragments of the real into strange objects that express nothing, and which do not respond in a clear fashion to the multiple referents of this fragmentary reality. The building is not eliminating composition through the density of its design approach – it is radicalizing the act of composition by fusing all previous information into a multi-signifying block. The tension inherent in this approach may short-circuit the sense of unified intent that would result from a more traditional, perspective-based design approach, but does not get rid of this intent; it displaces it into a more abstract space. As a result, it is legitimate to talk about 'non-composed' architecture here, although this kind of concept only has meaning at the theoretical level of aesthetics, as it relates abstraction's ultimate effort to rid itself of perspective. To acquire speed, an architectural practice has to employ materials that have already become 'givens'. And, like language, not all of architecture's ordering principles can be compressed, which mean efforts at non-composition eventually become composition. This is why we see the use of standard typologies in Diener & Diener's repeated efforts to create elemental blocks capable of being transformed into resistant urban entities. Architecture cannot sacrifice itself to a utopian ideal of a 'language without syntax',[51] although it can, through its own processes, attempt to find what is essential, in order to make language anew. The product of radical strategies, Diener & Diener's buildings take their place within the urban landscape in a new way. Their novelty does not necessarily translate as excessive visibility. Their presence is both majestic and discreet. They possess dignity within the spaces they occupy while also relating to the natural flow of the surrounding areas. The built and the non-built, the pre-existent and the now, the empty and the occupied – all these meanings disappear through a series of equivalences. The architecture cancels itself out in a continuum of signification by exhausting the relationships it establishes, here and there, with the surrounding city. Diener & Diener's buildings allow the real to flow in, then in one go disengage themselves from all possible referents, divesting themselves of any expressive intent. They are never monumental. Their solid presence recalls the ordinary presence of silos and warehouses and the peaceful relationship these structures have with the landscape. (This is true even for the buildings with no visual resemblance to industrial structures.) As necessary agents of production, industrial buildings are often regarded as the structures furthest removed from what is generally classed as 'architecture'. They are free from architecture's normative machinery; one has to look at the expression of their form in terms of an aesthetic of non-composition. They are born and die in a rhythm determined by the economic considerations that define the topology of an urban landscape as a whole, transcending the buildings within it. It is precisely this detachment that creates their beauty.

Diener & Diener's buildings are placed within an urban landscape with the same peacefulness. The presence of their volumes seems to fade into a floating state that borders on emptiness. Like industrial buildings, their architecture conveys images that have no location. But their implacable sense of being is not founded in the necessary and labyrinthine functions of industrial production. Instead, it comes as a result of the tension in Diener & Diener's design process, which itself results from their complete immersion in the intellectual culture and the valuable resource of rigorous analogy that culture provides. Freed from regressive ideologies about identity, Diener & Diener's architecture allows urbanity to be revealed as the surface of an isotropic space. Their buildings move towards detachment; a logical move in the contemporary world, where location is a non-location, paradoxically both unique and standard. The identity of the architecture, like the identity of the cities it occupies, has become fluid. They both dissolve into universal space, like blue ink in water. And the cities it which in is located become all cities, real and imagined. Although highly complex in its cultural determinations, Diener & Diener demonstrate their intellectual work using the obviousness of the banal; the finality of their forms can be achieved only through the prism of our collective values.

Diener & Diener's Roquette Residential Buildings in Paris (1992–6) are built in a working-class neighbourhood. Two L-shaped edifices are placed in a zigzag to create a courtyard and passage. The window layout on each facade is identical.[52] A walk along the boulevard de Ménilmontant clearly tells you about the characteristics of the nearby buildings: elevations, shop-fronts and warehouses follow each other in a simple way. The windows are large: more or less tall in height, more or less wide, but identical in each facade, with each having its own unique sequence of windows. On the boulevard's ground level, boutiques create an unpretentious plinth for the structures. All of the construction speaks a common language. Diener & Diener's buildings have learnt this language. They use its words, without trying to mimic their surroundings in order to be accepted by them. They articulate their own specific identity through the play of the project's internal decisions, without distorting the accepted mode of construction, or undermining the values set by usage. Their double-aspect apartments make full use of their position. The architecture offers fundamental values to the neighbourhood drawn from that same neighbourhood's history, without giving them an over-emphasized significance.[53]

Swiss Embassy, Berlin

Memory and Oblivion

Because it exists just this side of an image, in the space of iconic pre-signification, Diener & Diener's architecture demands active perception. It triggers images that are both precise and non-determined, taking shape in our minds through a fluctuating, almost dream-like relationship to the real. This relationship to the real employs the same type of hazy, extended analogy we use in our minds when we read a novel.[54] A simple evocation of places (known or not known), even a basic cataloguing of street names, squares, boulevards and avenues creates a kind of loose system in our minds where presence and spatial movement can take place.[55] Imagination follows an invisible line. As we read a novel, a window opens onto a reality whose continuous landscape is connected to the novel's every word.[56] Through this, we discover the treasures of spatiality ingrained in the written word. This is the kind of spatiality to which Diener & Diener's architecture aspires. Its essence is very close to the essence of language. It is close to that feeling of uncertainty you have when trying to think of a word that eludes you and which eventually escapes you altogether. A chasm opens up at the centre of a phrase that nothing can fill. The fluid space into which meaning should enter, now appears as emptiness, an unoccupied space. This gap creates an imperceptible sense of suffering. All your efforts come to nothing as you try to locate this missing piece, but as we all know, this piece will eventually reappear, in a roundabout way, right at the moment you least expect it. To get to this point, you have to think about something else – forget your forgetting – and not try to force the word to come back. But this absent word, in a flash, has created a tear in the fabric of language, suddenly revealing the presence of those subtle mechanisms through which memory is tethered. When it reappears later, in another context, the retrieved word creates a sense of relief,

as if we have been given a signal that the incredible machine of language and memory has invisibly started to work again.

The order of things is restored but this abrupt experience of the void has, for a moment, left us free to perceive the mnemonic apparatus that lies at the heart of our identity.[57] Diener & Diener's architecture has worked its way into these complex mechanisms. It has learned how to forge intellectual links between an object and the various strata of a territory, weaving into reality the threads of a spatial and temporal web around which intellectual thought can move freely. By exploring the surface of things, it arrives at depth. It acts in the world of objects and by manipulating these objects, it is able to produce structures that can receive meaning.

Diener & Diener's building for the Swiss Embassy in Berlin (1995–2000) demonstrates this process.[58] The structure was built to complement a former palace, whose urban context had been destroyed during World War II and which was now a solitary object near the Reichstag gardens. Rather than attempt to re-create a new facade, Diener & Diener decided to underline the mass of the whole palace. They made use of a photomontage to show what they envisaged for the project: a smooth, cubic structure with large vertical windows is positioned next to the Neo-Classical edifice and its engaged Ionic columns. Seen together, the two buildings create a single contradictory entity. Initially, the new extension appears as a comparable volume to the palace, creating a sense of commonality as well as a strange choreography between the two. It evokes an archetypal relationship about 'the pre-existent' and 'the new' – an almost universal language that shows how external decor and its absence underline the distinction between the two. Through a kind of visual contamination with the new structure, the old

Untitled A, Helmut Federle, 1992
1992, Private collection, Therwil

West facade of the Swiss Embassy, Berlin,
Helmut Federle

building becomes the essence of its own construction. The extension acts as pivotal force on the palace. It plays with its volume and meaning, returning the palace back to its original significations. The two structures seem to support each other spatially and semantically. A sense of rotation that appears to lift the buildings off the ground can be felt. The extension's western wall, on which Helmut Federle has created a large relief, presses the new extension's volume against the old palace.[59]

While working towards the competition for the project, Diener & Diener used three images as references: Paul Baumgarten's photomontage of the palace (1911), a photograph of Gunnar Asplund's Gothenborg Law Courts extension (1937) and a photograph of Adolf Loos's Tzara House (1926) in Paris. Relating these three images to the new extension provides a compact project device. Baumgarten's photomontage shows us the palace within the context of a Berlin urbanity that no longer exists. Asplund's enlargement shows us an image of a new facade as an extrapolation of an older facade, which creates an overall effect of folded architecture and which is the most explicit reference for the extension. The Tzara House shows how this effect of folding would work, if we consider it, like the Viennese master architect Loos did, as an external surface revealing the outer shape of an interior volume.[60] Diener & Diener's project suggests those unconscious mechanisms at play below the surface. Images, which are linked here to the problems found in the project, follow on one from another until they merge into a hyper-dense object.[61] Acquiring physical solidity through a set of rigorous architectural operations, the building is able to project its duality from its theoretical origins into the world of ordinary objects.

The Poetics of Co-presence

There are other Diener & Diener projects for extensions to existing buildings, like the Centre Pasqu'Art in Biel (1995–9) and the Stuker Auction House in Bern (2001–3), that have also played their part in renewing the problematic of how to treat duality. Because these projects bring into focus how contiguous objects with distinct identities relate to the real, they help us to look at complex theoretical questions such as otherness and historicity. In Biel, the practice was asked to enlarge a former hospital to house a contemporary art centre. Located at the foot of a valley's steep angle, the project juxtaposes two heterogeneous elements: the Neo-Classical edifice of the former hospital, with a universally regular arrangement of windows, and a new greenish, concrete, and rather austere block.[62] Linked at the rear by a stairwell, each building contains a range of differentiated spaces. The cube's first floor houses three exhibition rooms with lateral natural light, and its second floor has a single room, lit from above. The rooms' dimensions complement those of the two smallest rooms in the hospital building. Now renovated, the older building houses an exhibition office and a row of rooms that receive daylight from the front facade's sequence of vertical windows. The new design creates a homogeneous relationship with the verticality of the older building. It also uses the steep incline against which the museum is built, integrating it into the overall logic of the project. The way in which Diener & Diener project an interior space into the surrounding geography is one of the most remarkable aspects of the project,[63] and equally, the topography of the land features inside the extension. Although the rear facade of the extension links it to the existing building, from the front it appears to be an independent object – a concrete volume separated from the old hospital by an empty space. This new volume is supported by a playful use of a cantilever, which in this

Centre Pasqu'Art, Biel

project almost seems to be an oversized corbel. Underneath this projection, an entirely glass wall on the structure's ground floor becomes the entrance for the museum – one which the city is able to penetrate. Inside, the ground floor becomes a fragment of an urban zone. This topographical effect remains throughout all the levels of the building, but develops differently on each of them. Through the control of light and space, the structure creates a museum atmosphere, but one that is cut out by giant windows, which turn into living paintings as they absorb the real from outside. The museum's generous use of space gives the window openings a particular meaning. Each of the three rooms on the first floor has two large windows, one looking onto the street and one onto the steep slope of the landscape at the rear. In their repetitive sequence, the windows endow the project with an intrinsic order. At the rear, they reveal the hill's steep flank and the way in which the site's architecture handles the interstitial space between itself and the hill. The bays of the window are too vast to properly frame what can be seen outside. Their huge surface rids them of their presence as windows, obliging one to choose what objects to look at through them, creating a synchronistic apprehension of the exterior reality outside of a framed perspective.[64] From the outside, despite its opaque character, the concrete box structure appears light and limpid. It has a relationship with the existing building that suggests the textures of the city's ground and its adjacent empty spaces, introducing a new kind of duality. The cube projects the old hospital into a representational space. It is able to crystallize its essence through a system of equivalences that free it of any weight or narrative. Historicity is treated as a material. The juxtaposition of volumes creates a lateral interaction between the structures, releasing a new form of conjunctive space where the former hospital can emerge as a new object.[65]

This lateral interaction between buildings can also be experienced at the Stuker Auction House in Bern.[66] Located in a park situated on the city's heights, the gallery is made up of two contradictory elements: a nineteenth-century, Neo-Baroque villa and a modern cube made out of copper and glass.[67] The cube's elevation consists of six large bays (corresponding to a row of three large windows on the first floor), which form a structural grid that functions as a set of coordinates for the villa.[68] The two entities engage in a dialogue through the analogy set up by their facades and their outlines. However, one soon becomes lost in the conspicuousness of the juxtaposition, as if the villa's classical composition tries to elude understanding in order to let the cube's non-composition float free.[69] Each of the two axes within this dual structure serves as a point of reference for the other. In the interior of the extension, the windows' vertiginous bays create an intense relationship with the nature that surrounds the structure. The cube's windows give the work-space a kind of dignity. One can feel a sense of logical design. To conjugate the 'pre-existent' and 'new', the cube reuses the villa's dimensions. This choice determines the cube's plan, but not its height; however, the height is not an arbitrary feature, but one which serves to underline the original architectural programme of the villa which, as a result, acquires a specific scale.[70] The villa represents a force of positive inertia for the cube. The new does not adapt to the old. It is conditioned by its contact, the product of a rigorous design processes.

Ruhr Museum at Zeche Zollverein, Essen

New East Wing Expansion of the Museum of Natural History, Berlin

The Readymade as Strategy

Relating a building to a contiguous object is just one of the many forms Diener & Diener has used in the treatment of historicity. As demonstrated by the unrealized project for the Ruhr Museum at Zeche Zollverein (Essen, 1999), certain types of design approaches can work across the scale of a landscape. In this project, Diener & Diener came up with a strategy suited to the requirements of this vast piece of industrial heritage, winning an international competition.[71] Positioned between industrial buildings and machinery, the museum is perched on top of the pre-existing buildings, making it a lighthouse-like superstructure that dominates the whole mining territory. During the day, the volume's glass surface captures natural light; at night, it transforms into a beacon visible across the whole region. Despite being a newly inserted object, this large rectangular structure is able to preserve the site's authenticity by creating a distance between itself and the past, and a concomitant overall effect of distance in the way the site is perceived. It changes the usual relationship between the pre-existing and its surroundings, by creating a new architecture within which the industrial landscape emerges as a 'readymade'.[72]

Although situated within a very different physical context, a similar attitude towards heritage can be noted in Diener & Diener's renovation of exhibition space and New East Wing of the Museum of Natural History in Berlin (1995–2010), which involved the rehabilitation of a monumental ensemble of buildings damaged in World War II.[73] Confronted with the site's densely woven historical backdrop, the project accommodates the necessity for a unified urban design by linking the old and new through a variety of different procedures combining restoration and new construction. The aim of this pragmatic approach is to ensure the physical and cultural continua-

tion of the institution. The new wing is located and positioned over the site of several demolished buildings. As a result, the older architecture remains part of the coherent whole.[74] The restored, repaired and fully completed ensemble achieves unity in a diachronic way, enabling the museum's identity to be constructed for its users as they explore the site. In another museum project nearby, Diener & Diener's unbuilt Extension to the Pergamon Museum (2000) invites both the visitor and the city's inhabitants to discover the museum's analogical preoccupations. This great didactic machine presents fragments of antique architecture, replicas of sculptures and monumental entrances detached from the interiors they once led into. Diener & Diener's proposed intervention embeds itself within the physical mass of this Neo-Classical complex in order to display these fragments, but also to consolidate the structures and significations of the museum building and its programme. This linking building joins the museum's two historical wings, improving how the overall 'museum experience' is spatially organized without compromising the edifice's integrity or its aspect of openness to the city.[75]

In addition to the synchronic unity of a 'readymade' device and a more generalized form of diachronic intervention, Diener & Diener make use of other design modes to integrate historicity within contemporary reality. Their as-yet unrealized extension to the National Gallery of Modern Art in Rome (2002–) adds a new layer of construction onto an original 1911 building and its 1933 extension.[76] The new wing runs along the 1938 extension, which now takes a central position in the gallery's overall structure.[77] The new construction's transparent facade opens up the museum's contents to passers-by. Inhabited with statues, this space reveals to the outside world the gestures and details of a usually hidden-away population. The museum thus invites its own expansion to be read as a controlled proliferation of recomposed temporal strata.[78] The Collection Rosengart in Lucerne (1999–2002) has a different relation ship to history. In this project, Diener & Diener redeveloped a former bank to house one of the most beautiful collections of modern art in Switzerland. Situated in the centre of the town, the Neo-Classical edifice (1924) stands imposingly in its surroundings. Four facades with identical windows support the building's solid volume.[79] The names of artists represented in the collection are listed in gold along a discreet frieze: Monet, Renoir, Seurat, Signac, Cézanne, Picasso, Braque, Matisse, Léger, Klee, Kandinsky, Miró, Chagall, Modigliani, Dufy, Rouault, Soutine, along with the name of the collection itself. The entrance hall leads immediately led into the exhibition rooms, a rapid transition between the street and the collection. Running along the length of the facade, the rooms link in a kind of continuum. This sequence is arranged as a series of cloisters, divided by partition walls with vertical opening slots, leading the visitors forward and allowing their vision to precede their movement. This design approach creates an experience of the whole floor as a single block of space made up of a series of large adjoining volumes. The original support structure (beams and pillars) has been retained, but the ceiling fixtures, slate floors and a liberal use of large rugs transform a bank's solemn universe into a warm interior.[80] An oblong space in the basement houses the works of Paul Klee. There is an easy progression through the space. The visitor is guided through by the plan. The Diener & Diener studio's precise architectural intervention makes no attempt to talk about the present's relationship with the past. It avoids employing architecture to signal contemporary reality as a way of guaranteeing historical integrity.[81] By distancing itself from this kind of posture, it finds a way to genuinely respect what is already in existence.

The Real as Material

Despite the knowledge that has been accrued about conservation across most of Europe, especially given the precision of knowledge available, there is no consensus on the system of values that should direct heritage projects. Diener & Diener's experiments in these history-laden environments provide us with interesting possibilities about handling heritage projects in a contemporary way. Each of these possibilities represents a new development in the treatment of the past: converting old buildings (Collection Rosengart); enlarging and restructuring buildings (Centre Pasqu'Art, Stuker Auction House, Swiss Embassy); completing a monumental complex with a new building (Museum of Natural History, Pergamon Museum, National Gallery of Modern Art); adapting an industrial landscape (Ruhr Museum at Zeche Zollverein). Together, these approaches reveal an overall problematic that sees a building's relationship to history inscribed in a wider vision of the real as an actual material and end in itself. Certain of Diener & Diener's works convey this complex theoretical universe, in which new construction is seen as only one of the supports underpinning a far greater system that is working towards the reconstitution of city fragments with an attached historic value through a handling of empty and occupied space, materials and their usage. Diener & Diener's Migros Supermarket, part of a project that also includes the Hotel Schweizerhof and the Migros School (1995–2000), is a cubic structure in oxidized copper built in the centre of Lucerne. Positioned behind a luxury hotel, between a church and a row of houses, the supermarket's dimensions confirm its authority over adjacent empty space. It does not take inspiration from the built context.[82] It asserts itself as an autonomous element, by using references drawn from an earlier point in the city's memory. Its site, next to the church, occupies the traditional location usually given over to a town's covered

Apartment Buildings KNSM and Java Island, Amsterdam

market. This position gives it a kind of benevolent legitimacy. The building enlarges the public space and substitutes itself within it. It establishes a system of presence and distance with the surrounding structures. An old hall attached to the hotel plays a determining role in the overall effect.[83] Painstakingly restored as part of the project, this historic building reinforces the semantic value of the whole ensemble, creating an effect of otherness as it crystallizes historical meaning.

Taking the past into account is done in a more abstract way in some of the firm's projects, by reworking some of the characteristics of a condemned historical building. The firm took this route with the Hotel Bellevue in Rigi Kaltbad (1999), using the existing building and its visual domination over a mountain village as the model for the project. In order to safeguard the integrity of the exceptional landscape,[84] the studio reduced some of the hotel's dimensions. It reinterpreted the hotel's corner towers as projecting volumes, and used the signage on the upper part of its facade as a fundamental element of the site's identity. Because it was necessary to react sensitively to the landscape, the structure had to fit into the tradition of alpine construction. The team's response was to make these constraints the actual project material. In this project, the transfer of values from the past is managed in an informal way, but it is done from an actual existing object, which is defined and located. In other cases, a looser relationship with historicity is established. The Migros Supermarket Eglisee building on the Riehenstrasse in Basel (1994–6) reconstructs a local cultural model through a process of abstraction. Built near a tram station, on a route towards a park, the building is a simple cubic structure topped by a flat roof with a generous overhang. Endowed with this emphatic cornice-like roof, the building stands like a little pavilion in its urban surroundings.

Its simultaneously rudimentary and elegant classicism becomes the factor that defines its presence in the public space, and which also endows it with a kind of authority in relation to the surrounding residential towers, normal-sized buildings and car park. This privileged status results from a sophisticated knowledge about the usage of the box form, employing a vocabulary borrowed from Basel's modern tradition. The smooth concrete and glass surfaces, large forecourt and generous cornice give this commercial building a particular character and evokes the architectural works of Otto Rudolf Salvisberg.

Other examples within Diener & Diener's practices corroborate a non-formal relationship with memory. The Apartment Buildings KNSM and Java Island, as discussed earlier in this essay, are composed of two structures: a 'courtyard house' type structure and a massive, horizontal block with cut-out sections, both of which draw their meaning from the industrial past of the site. The buildings integrate some of the characteristics of the now-demolished warehouses and hangars, including the density of their walls, their materials and their relationship with the quays. This non-formal relationship with memory can be found both in the interior of this project – the unusual configuration of the living quarters in the 'courtyard house' follows on from a particular allocation of space linked to a memory of the building's industrial use – and in its exterior: the massive cut-out horizontal block appears to emerge out of the water, offering its inhabitants an intense relationship with the surrounding port basins. Diener & Diener's Masterplan for the University Harbour in Malmö also involved the conversion of port wasteland.[85] The winners of a town-planning competition for the project, Diener & Diener were inspired by the pre-existing structures (silos, hangars, warehouses) to reconstruct an open-feeling town plan made up of generously dimensioned

Model, Maag Areal Plus, Zurich

blocks. The project's masterplan envisaged various units of buildings around the port's basins. The University Building that Diener & Diener then built within their masterplan (2003–5) is characterized by smooth mass and an unusual silhouette. The green building envelope consists of large transparent, translucent and opaque sections, which help transform the port's appearance while retaining its essential spatial features.

Industrial Wastelands

Over the last few decades, reclaiming industrial wastelands has elicited a particular kind of investment from architects, most of whom use urban architecture as their source material for these projects. One of the most sensitive aspects of reclaiming an industrial space is the process of diagnosing its redevelopment potential, which should ultimately include how culturally relevant a project will be. Abundant examples can be found that confirm a conversion's success in terms of its own architectural programme, but these might turn out to be cultural failures because the site's industrial memories have been erased or treated too simplistically. It is exactly in relation to these difficult questions of diagnosis that Diener & Diener's work throws up some interesting elements. The firm was asked to work on the ABB complex in Baden Nord (1994–8), within the context of an architectural programme that proposed the demolition of a former factory plant to make way for a sizeable housing and office development. In opposition to this proposal, the studio was careful to insert new structures alongside pre-existing structures.[86] The plan made explicit the original structure of the complex, so as to ensure that the referential relationships of all future buildings on the site could be evaluated. Treated as autonomous entities, the new buildings were positioned around older buildings that had been saved from demolition, taking up their imposing dimensions in the process.

Diener & Diener's approach, when confronted with an industrial wasteland, can be interpreted as a poetic reading of the site as a grid, in order to determine the scope of its urban potential. Given the responsibility for drawing up the Masterplan for Maag Areal Plus (2000), a mixed-use development destined for the former Maag complex in Zurich, the studio put in place a variety of strategies to create a coherent fabric for the project: the renovation of existing buildings, the insertion of additional structures and substitution of old buildings with new ones. Located by the side of railway land, the complex contained industrial buildings of real quality. By outlining the future neighbourhood around the pre-existing buildings, the studio sketched out a large public space as well as visualizing a way in which the residential sections could weave together given the site's existing characteristics. For each sector of wasteland, rules were set out for the height and mass of buildings, as well as for their density – both how they could be grouped and the treatment of interstitial space between them. Their plan for the first sector defined new buildings in relation to pre-existing heights (only at certain points within the urban fabric would new heights be allowed to exceed older buildings). In the second sector, the plan called for the parallel placements of existing warehouses to be echoed; and for the third sector, space for movement and access was enlarged, and building mass was treated in a sculptural way (cantilevered structures, cut-out sections). As this project demonstrates – and as the Baden, Amsterdam and Malmö examples that have been mentioned do as well – Diener & Diener work in two stages. Following a sensitive analysis of an industrial wasteland, they develop a kind of map of the pre-existing state, which allows them to comprehend its substance and potential. Over the course of the work, diverse images and fragments of intent are laid down on this canvas. In the second phase, this grid analysis turns into an active project grid: chosen materials now begin to condense into volumes and lines, occupied and empty spaces, and they begin to exhibit characteristics drawn from the pre-existing context. This 'open' design process does not impose a hierarchy on the givens of a project using predetermined criteria; it leaves itself open to possibilities. Paradoxically, as a result of its total immersion in an urban and industrial reality (spaces, volumes, materials, colours), the project is able to fully remain within the imaginary and the abstract realm.

The Urbanistic Form

Diener & Diener were immersed – like all European architects coming out of the intellectual context of the 1970s – in the culture of urbanity that had supplanted urbanism. Unlike the majority of architectural firms, they did not invest their energy in designing 'urban forms' – at least, not in the sense that this notion is generally understood. Their practice was not limited to renewing the traditional form of a block of buildings. Nor was their practice informed by traditional rhetoric concerning the hierarchical structure of different urban levels. This hierarchy, which is generally assumed to be consubstantial with the idea of the city, gives way in Diener & Diener's projects to a more synthetic vision, which tends towards linking all the aspects of a site into a solid form encompassing the project. Rather than 'urban forms', it is more relevant to talk about ' urbanistic forms', in that the 'quality' possessed by the architectural ensembles of Diener & Diener results as much from an idea of their physical aspect as from the result of the method used to produce them. Referring to an idea of Marcel Duchamp, one could say about them that they make use of his 'plastic approach to method'.[87] Duchamp spoke about how the game of chess produced, through the minds and hands of the players, 'mechanical sculptures' that were essentially plastic in nature. The physical execution of a project can likewise initiate, by the rigour of its sequences, aesthetic effects of this same order. The complexity of the situations encountered in a project by Diener & Diener is compressed through abstraction into just a few large objects, which can integrate long-held values about the formal arrangement of both urban spaces and blocks of buildings. In Diener & Diener's 'urbanistic forms', these values are projected into another space of the city or, more accurately, into another temporal point of the city's development. They link disparate aspects (abstraction and concreteness, presence or absence) in order to engender meaningful fragments. Everything occurs as if Diener & Diener have decided to transform the historic, centred, delimited city into a vast, open decentralized territory. Their projects appear as block-like structures in this universal territory. They construct an isotropy of gradual approach, outside any centrality.[88] Their works' expressive neutrality becomes the determining factor in their objective presence. Today, it is abstract sculpture, and not painting, that informs the theoretical model for architectural abstraction.[89] The old pictorial strategy, which was anti-perspective, planar, expressive[90] and tended towards proliferation, has been supplanted by a new, spatial approach that refers to volume, compression and silence.[91] This radical transformation – correlating with the slide from space to landscape – leads to new approaches about the real. Diener & Diener's experimental role in this arena has been of primary importance. It opened up many avenues as a result of its pioneering practices.

This approach is demonstrated by Diener & Diener's projects for Berlin (Apartment Buildings Parkkolonnaden; Extension of the BWB; Office and Residential Buildings 'Quartier 110',

Apartment Buildings Parkkolonnaden, Berlin

1996–2004), for Munich (Hypo-Bank Theatinerstrasse, 1994), for Cologne (Gerling Residential and Office Buildings, 1995) and for Zug (Residential and Office Buildings Gartenstrasse, 1999–2009) by showing how this territorial apprehension of the city calls for block-building as the basic unit of construction. This basic entity does not imply any kind of prior scale. It can be retracted or dilated according to the project. It can combine with other similar units, to create solid-appearing empty spaces able to integrate into the three-dimensional continuum of a city. The Apartment Buildings Parkkolonnaden, between the Potsdamer Platz and the canal, consisted of a sequence of buildings of roughly similar height, which delineated quadrangular empty spaces between them. This chain of buildings, which consists of a train station, shops, schools and accommodation, creates a linear mechanism, which amplifies in effect as one approaches Potsdamer Platz. A different use of the block-structure appears in the two other Berlin projects, which link up various spatial volumes behind older buildings, to create a system of courtyards. The Hypo-Bank Theatinerstrasse defines a formal shape (made up of three buildings) which establishes itself in the centre of a large block of buildings, creating an interior space, not closed off, but still protected from the street. In the Gerling Residential and Office Buildings in Cologne, four single blocks of different heights create an open group of buildings, which is punctuated in the centre by a tower. The density of this architectural composition generates a powerful sense of urbanity. The Residential and Office Buildings Gartenstrasse insert three single blocks between three older houses. Using scale and positioning, these new buildings transform the entire plot into an isotropic fragment of territory, out of which the original houses emerge forcefully, unusual objects laden with history.

This practice of interrelating blocks has shown itself to work equally well in some outlying urban monofunctional zones, such as university campuses. In order to integrate the Lausanne School of Architecture's new premises into the Federal Institute of Technology's complex in the Lausanne suburb of Ecublens (1993), Diener & Diener developed a network of large 'courtyard residence' type buildings. Positioned next to pre-existing buildings in a continuous sequence around the university's circulation network, these massive objects create a system of buffer zones that stabilize the public space. It is interesting to compare this project with the one designed for the Bocconi University in Milan (2002). While in the Lausanne project the thickly-set blocks create a dense and open ensemble that contains but does not erase the outlying complex, in Milan, where the university campus is set in the middle of the city,[92] Diener & Diener's work enriches the pre-existing environment without destabilizing it, by drawing on subliminal images from history's unconscious. The auditorium resembles an amphitheatre, the faculty a tower, the space around the great hall is likened to a theatre. Using latent images to identify architecture is part of Diener & Diener's concern with locating and differentiating urban space, but in certain circumstances their work takes on a more abstract appearance by allowing images to float more freely. This can be seen in the Novartis Campus Forum 3 in Basel (2002–5). The project required a new building that could complement the pre-existing buildings, but also symbolically identify the whole pharmaceutical complex. The reference that became immediately apparent to the design team was the National Library of Mexico at the Universidad Nacional Autónoma de México in Mexico City. Over and above any other discourse, its artistic dimension seemed to embody the cultural identity of an important university.[93] It was this particular kind of density, able to confer a place with an archi-

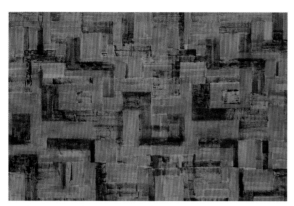

4,4 The Distance (Desviaciones de), Helmut Federle, 2002
collection Novartis AG, Basel

tectural form that could both absorb and irradiate referential meaning, that Diener & Diener wanted for the Novartis Campus building. The building appears as a long abstract volume endowed with a three-dimensional envelope of coloured glass. Designed by Helmut Federle, this interlinking screen has no formal structure and gives the building a homogeneous, undivided and rupture-free appearance. In the interior, each floor is envisaged as an urban plateau, with its own monuments (stairs, escalators), residential areas (offices and their system of loggias) and relaxation spaces (cafés and tropical conservatories). A multi-coloured monolith, the building's overall plasticity forms a variety of relationships with the campus, giving the whole ensemble a new image.

Art / Architecture

At the time of his collaboration with Helmut Federle on the Swiss Embassy, Roger Diener commented:

We decided on a collaboration with Helmut Federle the moment we realized the project's complexity meant traditional methods would not be sufficient to create our vision. We thought Helmut Federle could contribute in a much more precise way than we could have managed ourselves. I went to Vienna to meet him. At that point, we had just one general vision, not an exact vision, nor one about the frieze wall in particular, or even our building. Helmut probably had an idea about our work together on the building in his head, in the way we both had one about our potential work on the frieze wall. These two slightly speculative ideas encouraged us both.[94]

For Federle, the work could only be possible if there was implicit agreement:

Our era is one where we shouldn't do things on our own. We have the opportunity to work communally and this gives rise to much more interesting situations ... Roger Diener would not have come to see me if he had not been able to relate to my state of mind and, conversely, I would not have said yes if I could not relate to his state of mind. From the outset there was a mutual respect and we knew there was agreement.[95]

However, as Federle explains, he had complete autonomy over his work:

I was only interested in the form my part of the work would take. I knew from the start it would be a relief ... Roger never came to me with suggestions or directions. I was given a free hand in my design for the wall and I took advantage of that... The relief has no function, it has no openings; it suggests substance on its surface through a structuring of the horizontal and vertical. The grid gives it surface body. Its corporeality suggests something like weight or permanence.[96]

Speaking about the project, Federle evokes Egyptian, Khmer and Asian architecture. Looking at the finished building, the artist's specific contribution is clear. Federle's relief presses the old palace into the new volume to create a composite whole of the two entities.

For the Novartis Campus Forum 3 in Basel, the collaboration between the architect and the artist took a new direction. The building's coloured carapace is not presented as a regular pattern of lines. Instead, a thick, informally patterned screen is produced through the superimposition of different sizes of glass panes. The origin for this system of proliferating plasticity can be found in Federle's paintings. These do not belong to a

View through coloured glass facade, Novartis Campus Forum 3, Basel

tradition of geometric abstraction; Federle's work turned away from the purity of colour and form to move towards depicting emotion and memory. As described by Gottfried Böhm, they develop a particular environment dominated by the phenomenon of transition: 'Somebody who enters a space containing Federle's paintings now exists in an in-between world, a temporal interval that becomes an elapse.'[97] The artist has remained faithful to the notion of composition:

For me, composition remains ... an essential element in painting because the picture, within an environment, lives from this dialogue, from the energetic relationship between the picture and surrounding space, between its mass and colour and the physical materiality of its support. I don't think you can have an entirely non-referential form of painting ... It's clear a picture's essence can exist as such, but unless the picture directly stimulates a viewer, it generally offers a way into a pivotal experience that will eventually lead into the heart of memory.[98]

In Basel, Federle's bright, rareified colours are used in a measured way. The precedents are a 1963 painting and his stained-glass window for the State Central Bank in Meiningen in 1999.[99] Even though the Novartis Campus Forum 3 building facade contains glass panels in bright colours (navy blue, turquoise, green, yellow, red and orange among many others), light passing through it remains fluid and clear. Paradoxically, although the building is wrapped up in this multi-coloured mosaic, it does not feel closed off. Its carapace retains a wide, open feel. Air seems to circulate around it, as does the movement of one's eye. Underneath its transparent envelope, the building appears like a vast window. Federle's artistic intervention, although constrained by the functional issues of the project, could be described as architecture just as much as art. It creates a

plasticity right at the frontier of the two disciplines, bringing into play barely tinted colours (pale green, pink, pastel blue) alongside the stronger ones. The glass envelope perfectly fulfils the normal functions of window-sill, balustrade and sun filter, while dissolving these functional elements in its textural continuity. Looking at it from within, through the pattern of its cut glass panels, the surrounding area seems even more imbued with urbanity. One inevitably thinks of Edward Hopper, but also of Fernand Léger.[100]

The Wider Landscape

Projects from their most recent period show how the Diener & Diener studio has moved from the world of buildings, and blocks of buildings, to a larger urban scale, without losing its theoretical stance. Despite the considerable scope of their territories, their designs for Baden or Malmö have the same qualities of construction as the more isolated interventions in Bern and Lucerne. Their treatment of larger industrial facilities demonstrates a similar precision. Despite the constraints that such buildings present, the studio has never resigned itself to regarding these structures as simple functional entities to be passively placed within a landscape. Instead, they regard these structures as a section of a city, set apart. Their unrealized Athletics Stadium Letzigrund (2003) in Zurich anchors itself in the reality of the neighbourhood that will use it. As well as the specific function of hosting sporting events, it offers a public park to the surrounding inhabitants. The permeability of Diener & Diener's architectural objects underlines their relationship to the wider environment.

In the Residential and Cultural Buildings 'Streichhan-Kaserne' (1997) in Weimar, Diener & Diener positioned three buildings opposite an old barracks to create a gem-like space that appeared almost inlaid into the landscape. In the Residential Buildings Wasserstadt (2001) in Berlin, they devised a sculptural tower by the side of the Spandau Lake. The choice of a polygonal shape becomes clear in the panoramic views it provides apartments. Covered in copper sheeting, and situated in a natural area with greenery and water, the tower looks like a strange object moulded by the landscape. Their project for the Hochberger-platz (2002) in Basel links the two banks of the Wiese river to create a kind of esplanade. An open rectangular space arranged over an artificial base, the site transforms the view of the river, presenting it as a current moving through an immobile frame. The foliage covers the space in a protective veil. Through these devices, the public space is able to assert itself between the movement of both water and traffic. Normal activity (market, second-hand stalls, bowling) and the use of lighting at night weld the space into its environment. This poetic approach to the city is evident throughout Diener & Diener's practice – from the physical reality of the buildings to the fluidity of the studio's practices. It works to bring different levels of urban reality together and fundamentally characterizes the work of the firm. The attention paid to context in each of their interventions turn each of their projects into an investigation of public space, and one that works to dignify that space. This is true all the way through into the residential projects, including the Row Houses Isteinerstrasse in Basel (1997–2003). Situated within a block of buildings, a courtyard planted with trees allows the residences enjoy terraces that can be accessed on both sides. They do not express a juxtaposition of separate constructions, but the unity of a flattened, spread-out block of buildings, which signifies that they are part of the collective space of the city. Even with structures not built on a determined site, Diener & Diener's architecture always includes a context, or at least a future premise for one. Their 'Twogether' Prefab study for prefabri-

cated housing (1996) demonstrates this paradox.[101] The search for a form of mass-produced housing has inspired a number of modern architects, and Diener & Diener's design for a wooden house demonstrates the studio's inheritance and questioning of these investigations. Simple but complete, the structure is made up of two offset cubic structures, punctuated with identical openings.[102] Independent of any landscape, it engenders a context of well-defined external spaces. Through its building envelope (in plain or coloured wood), it weaves links with a future environment.[103] Given the attention paid by Diener & Diener to context, it might seem incongruous that a prefabricated house, non-situated and without a use, could embody the values of civility and sociability that the studio strives for. And yet, through the equilibrium it establishes, this residential structure suggests a future appropriation of an outside space. Through its spatial structure and its ability to respond to need, it appears as a kind of archetype – a quality seen in most of Diener & Diener's projects. In this sense, all of Diener & Diener's buildings are houses, whatever their scale or chosen location: the Gmurzynska Gallery, the Centre Pasqu'Art, Hochberger-platz, Novartis Campus Forum 3, and all the others. Placing the house right at the heart of architectural practice underlines, better than any of the discourses attached to their projects, the ethical dimension of their work.[104]

In the tradition of Adolf Loos and Louis Kahn, Diener & Diener take on the implications for the discipline's universal application in its relationship to society. Through exploring the universe of possibilities, the practice defines the scope of its responsibility, and emphasizes the fact that architecture's nobility resides in the way it can formulate meaningful spaces.

Installation at the Frankfurt Book Fair, 1998

One last project by Diener & Diener, far removed from prefabricated housing, demonstrates the measure of this approach. For a temporary installation at the 1998 Frankfurt Book Fair, the studio, in collaboration with Peter Suter, chose to fit out a pre-existing hangar instead of building an autonomous pavilion between the esplanade's exhibition halls. Coloured curtains (red, green, cream and yellow) divided the volume into seven rooms of different dimensions. The seven rooms housed the exhibition pavilion's usual zones of activity (library, restaurant, television studio, etc.). Defined by their fabric envelopes, the rooms were separated by a series of hallways that acoustically sealed them off from each other. The library was set up as the central space of the exhibition. In it, long tables were arranged with rows of books covered in coloured paper. Each of the books' monochrome jackets displayed only the title of the book it wrapped, blocking the cover's other visual distractions. The device worked to intrigue visitors, inviting them to open up and look through the books. By blocking out the elements that obstruct a book's primary message, the installation seemed to reduce all books down to their common value: a material organization of printed pages, which, through the magic of language and writing, can liberate a person. As Theodor Adorno has reflected, a writer lives in his book in the same way that he lives in his home: 'Just as he trundles papers, books, pencils, documents untidily from room to room, he creates the same disorder in his thoughts. They become pieces of furniture that he sinks into, content or irritable ... For a man who no longer has a homeland, writing becomes a place to live.'[105] The rows of coloured books at Frankfurt represent an ephemeral memorial to the abstract house that is thought. The installation's seriousness and universality revealed its heightened sense of history. Here, as in all their work, Diener & Diener create architecture that brings an ethical dimension to spatial reality through their manipulation of objects – whether those objects are existing, unreal or vanished. Their architecture offers a way to experience the essence of things. This essentiality gives it its dignity.

1 Ellsworth Kelly, quoted in: John Coplans, *Ellsworth Kelly* (New York: HN Abrams, 1972 or 1973), 30.

2 See Joseph Abram, *Patrimoine Architectural et Production Comtemporaine. Tome 1: Modernité et Postmodernité: La Question de l'Héritage* (Nancy: Ecole d'architecture de Nancy, 1981).

3 The notion of the 'metanarrative is taken from Jean-François Lyotard, *The Postmodern Condition: A Report on Knowledge* (Minneapolis, University of Minnesota Press, 1984).

4 See Hannah Arendt's discussion of 'The Concept of History' in Hannah Arendt, *Between Past and Future: Six Exercises in Political Thought* (New York: Penguin, 1961), 51.

5 Roger Diener, lecture at the Eidgenössische Technische Hochschule in Zurich (ETHZ), 29 October 1996.

6 Aldo Rossi, *The Architecture of the City*, translated by Diane Ghirardo and Joan Ockman (Cambridge: MIT Press, 1982), 113. Rossi's book was first published in Italian [*L'architettura della città* (Padua: Marsilio Editori, 1966)] and like Robert Venturi's *Complexity and Contradiction in Architecture*, also published in 1966, Rossi's work created quite an international stir.

7 Aldo Rossi, 'Comment on the German Edition' in *The Architecture of the City*, 179.

8 For more information on these building projects, see Ulrike Jehle's articles in *Progressive Architecture* ('In the image of the city', October 1982) and in *Werk, Bauen+ Wohnen* ('Hofraum als Ergänzung der Stadt', no. 4, 1985, and 'Tradition der Moderne in der Gegenwart', no. 12, December 1983).

9 This school building represents an important point in Livio Vacchini's work. It is interesting to note how this form of construction influenced his definition of space.

10 Written in 1991 and published in English in 1992 as: Joseph Abram, 'From New-Objectivity to Contemporary Realism', in *Diener & Diener, From City to Detail* (London: The Architecture Foundation, March 1992, 8–21).

11 Roger Diener joined his father's practice in 1976. Marcus Diener's firm benefited from forty years of experience, with a number of important projects already to its name. The name 'Diener & Diener' was first used for the Apartment Buildings Hammerstrasse and the Apartment Buildings Riehenring.

12 With reference to Giulio Carlo Argan, *Walter Gropius e la Bauhaus* (Torino: Einaudi, 1966), 22. Analyzing the foundations for Gropius's activities, Argan writes: 'The work of art should not preach, exhort, make use of emotion, or exhibit idealistic aims: its reason for being is itself and nothing outside of this'.

13 Jean-François Lyotard, *The Postmodern Condition: A Report on Knowledge* (Minneapolis, University of Minnesota Press, 1984), 18–23.

14 These include Apartment Building with Bank in Basel (1982–5); Apartment Buildings Saint Alban-Tal (1981–6); Residential Building at Allschwilerstrasse (1984–6). See 'From New-Objectivity to Contemporary Realism'.

15 Robert Venturi, *Complexity and Contradiction in Architecture* (New York: Museum of Modern Art 1966), 103.

16 The slide towards landscape is evidenced by Venturi in his second publication: Robert Venturi, Denise Scott Brown and Steven Izenour, *Learning from Las Vegas: The Forgotten Symbolism of Architectural Form* (Cambridge MA: MIT Press, 1972). Regarding the issue of contemporary landscape, see Joseph Abram, 'L'actualité de Venturi', AMC, no. 19 (March 1991), 26–7.

17 See Joseph Abram, 'Objets de pensée, objets de culture. L'architecture de Diener & Diener aujourd'hui', *Faces*, no. 41 (Summer 1997), 22–5.

18 These propositions were particularly evident at the 'This is Tomorrow' exhibition (London: Whitechapel Gallery, 1956), in the works of Richard Hamilton, John Voelcker and John McHale. See Reyner Banham, *The New Brutalism: Ethic or Aesthetic* (London: Architectural Press, 1966).

19 The agenda aimed to link popular culture with high culture by widening the field of contemporary architecture's references. Venturi was inspired to do this in part by the movement of Pop Art.

20 This reconciliation rests on a rigorous articulation of contradictory theories. It can be opposed against a kind of referential eclecticism that would just amass architectural points of view without trying to exceed them.

21 I would suggest that this sense of atemporality comes from the fact that actual space and representative space coincide in Diener & Diener's work.

22 A division into four phases is clearly an arbitrary device. The way in which Diener & Diener's design methods developed during concurrent projects is not a linear phenomenon, unlike a critical discourse's exposition of this development, which must necessarily be so.

23 The studio's method of working accords an important place to discussion. It avoids sketches, which would subtly displace a project into an individual's visual universe.

24 For further information on the St. Alban-Tal project, see Ulrike Jehle, 'Wohnhäuser im St-Alban-Tal in Basel', *Werk, Bauen + Wohnen*, nos. 1–2 (1987).

25 For composition based on assemblage, see Ulrike Jehle, 'Komposition aus Fragmenten', *Archithese*, no. 1 (1986) and Ulrike Jehle, 'Modernism of a Most Intelligent Kind: A Commentary on the Work of Diener & Diener', *Assemblage*, no. 3, 72–107.

26 See Joseph Abram, 'Galerie Gmurzynska in Cologne, 1991', *Werk, Bauen + Wohnen*, nos. 7–8 (1991), 46–9.

27 This strategy is somewhat different from that used in the Residential Building Allschwilerstrasse, which presents a violent contradiction on the exterior surface, explained by the internal organization of the building.

28 Even when 'just' a block structure (Administration Building Hochstrasse, Residential and Office Building Elsässerstrasse, etc.), Diener & Diener's objects are 'landscape-objects'. The way in which their field of design has been enlarged gives them this landscape dimension.

29 The Perret architectural practice foreshadowed the use of an opened-out block of buildings in Le Havre. But its content is radically different. Diener & Diener's use of the design involves the mass of the block structure, the adjoining spaces linked to the structure's surface and the isotropic base of the urban area.

30 For further information about these projects, see 'Edificio de viviendas en Java Eiland, Amsterdam', *a+t: arquitectura+tecnologia Density II*, no. 20 (2002), 2–13, and Jan Perneger, 'Choses sans parti pris. Logements sur l'île de Java/KNSM, Amsterdam', *Faces*, no. 52 (Summer 2003).

31 Roger Diener in conversation with Joseph Abram, Basel, April 1996.

32 I use the term 'narrative' here with reference to Paul Ricoeur, *Time and Narrative*, Volume 1, trans. Kathleen McLaughlin and David Pellauer (Chicago: Univeristy of Chicago Press, 1984), 400.

33 Roger Diener in conversation with Joseph Abram, Basel, April 1996.

34 I have borrowed the expression 'Inhabited Window' from the title of 1987 exhibition by Roger Diener and Gilles Barbet. Exhibition catalogue: Roger Diener and Gilles Barbet, *Fenêtres habitées / Die Wohnung im Fenster* (Basel: Architekturmuseum, 1987).

35 Like Auguste Perret, Roger Diener is one of the rare architects of the twentieth century to have developed a theory of the window. For the French rationalist Perret, the vertical window 'frames man' and represents a 'complete space'. In a similar way to the paintings of Édouard Vuillard (*Place Vintimille*, 1908–10, Guggenheim Museum, New York; *Rues de Paris*, 1909, private collection, New York) and Pierre Bonnard (*Au travers des vitres*, 1910), Perret describes how the vertical rectangle captures the Parisian landscape – from the street to the tree tops to the sky – as if it has been organized by the frame of the window. Diener & Diener's tall and wide windows also have this same quality of everyday life but, like Edward Hopper, their relationship with the city is expressed through a uniform rectangle able to capture the volumes of space and objects. Hopper manages to create these hermetic cubes of luminous space even when the painting's scene takes place outside. He uses the way light hits the ground (on either a terrace or concrete platform) to create the depth of volume. 'My desire', said Hopper, 'was to paint the light on a house wall.' See *Edward Hopper* (Marseilles: Muse Cantini, 1990). See also *Les Réalismes 1917–1939* (Paris: Centre Georges Pompidou 1980), 258–9.

36 Diener & Diener's architecture avoids the historical tradition of Constructive Rationalism (including figures like Eugène Emmanuel Viollet-le-Duc, Joseph-Eugène-Anatole de Baudot, Auguste Choisy, Julian Guadet and Auguste Perret) as well as all rhetoric about representation, in order to develop an objective approach to construction able to serve spatiality.

37 Roger Diener in conversation with Joseph Abram, Basel, April 1996.

38 Roger Diener, lecture at the Centre Culturel Suisse, Paris, 21 January 1997.

39 Roger Diener in conversation with Joseph Abram, Basel, April 1996.

40 I noted in 1991 that the building on Hochstrasse links a road and a landscape: 'Its device is related to the depiction of rapid head movements one finds in some of Francis Bacon's portraits (for example, *Three Studies of Lucian Freud*, 1969). Like Bacon's pictures, the building brings into play space, geometry and a body, but here the building's 'face' does not break apart at the building's angle ... It draws the eye of passers-by coming from the train station, or the railway tracks' industrial landscape, towards the street. Time seems to go by here within a cube of space. Like the three portraits, time has stopped ...' See Joseph Abram, 'Diener et Diener: un Réalisme contemporain', *AMC*, no. 24 (September 1991), 35–44.

41 Erwin Panofsky, *Renaissance and Renascences in Western Art* (Stockholm: Almquist & Wiksells, 1960), 119.

42 It is precisely this treatment of volume within the pictorial space that determined the works being qualified as Cubist by the critic Louis Vauxcelles.

43 The 'space/volume' relationship established by Picasso is different to the one created by axonometric projection (see, for example, El Lissitzky, the *Proun* projects, 1919–24). By rejecting a vanishing point at infinity, axonometric projection favours flat, two-dimensional surfaces over volume. When painting renewed its links with perspective, it started formulating new questions about volume. It is interesting to note the possibility of an intermediary form of representation, which asserts volume against space by using a form of axonometric projection but not its rules. This approach to volume can be seen as a valid approach through an observation Marcel Duchamp made in *The Green Box*: 'The hanging figure is the form, using normal perspective, of a hanging figure, whose real form, we could perhaps try to find. This comes down to the fact that any kind of form is a representation in perspective of another form, using a certain vanishing point and pictorial distance' (Duchamp quoted by Jean Clair in *Marcel Duchamp*, Paris, 1990). A cube that is represented using a form of quasi-axonometric projection is a prism whose 'real form' we have tried to find. This prism reconstituted as a cube through our perception releases a kind of voluminal energy against space.

44 Roger Diener, lecture at the Centre Culturel Suisse, Paris, 21 January 1997.

45 *Ibid*.

46 Erich Mendelsohn, *Letters of an Architect* (London: Abelard-Schuman, 1967), 166.

47 Roger Diener in conversation with Joseph Abram, Basel, April 1996.

48 Pierre Sansot, *Poétique de la ville* (Paris: Klincksieck, 1988), 16.

49 *Ibid*, 387.

50 See note 1. 'For Kelly, the whole world becomes a reservoir of already-composed "compositions". The impulse originates with the spectacle of urban existence, which interests Kelly perhaps more than any other because it is at once non-intentional and non-natural. We see the painter's fascination with the stains and volutes left on a cement pillar by a mirror that has been torn off, which he scrupulously sets down and copiously annotates as if to ridicule the rhetoric of the *informel* movement. We see him fill up his sketch pads and note down, pell-mell, a ventilation cover from the Métro, balustrades, the cut of the stones on old Romanesque walls, billboards plastered with posters of all sizes and colors ...' Yves-Alain Bois, Jack Cowart and Alfred Pacquement, *Ellsworth Kelly, The Years in France 1948–1954* (Washington: National Gallery of Art, 1992), 18–9.

51 'The monochrome panel as a color sample is an index of colour as such, designation its own color without any transformations. There may be an Edenic dream at work here, a utopian desire for wholly motivated language in which the linguistic map would perfectly cover the terrain of things (and isn't there discernible allusion to language, to Western alphabetic writing, in the linear horizontality of Kelly's polyptychs, as if colors constitute the words of a language with syntax?).' *Ibid*, 28.

52 The windows have a different set of dimensions for each building (1.30 x 2.03 m for one and 1.50 x 1.71 m for the other). The self-bearing hewn stone facing is 10.5 cm thick. See Joseph Abram, 'Un caractère intemporel', *Faces*, no. 41 (Summer 1997), 20–1.

53 The sculptor Dani Karavan was commissioned to design the interior court within the block of buildings.

54 In 1991, I spoke about the relationship Diener & Diener had with this type of spatiality referring to the novel by Patrick Modiano, *Missing Person* (Cape May: Cape, 1980), first published in French [*Rue des Boutiques Obscures* (Paris: Gallimard, 1978)].

55 I am thinking of the novels by Patrick Modiano, *Honeymoon* (London: Harvill, 1992), first published in French [*Voyage de Noces* (Paris: Gallimard, 1990) and *Vestiaire de l'enfance* (Paris: Gallimard, 1990). See Joseph Abram, 'La spatialité dans les romans de Patrick Modiano', seminar at École des Beaux-Arts de Metz (1993–4).

56 'I walked along the Boulevard Soult. The apartment blocks were silhouetted against the light. Occassionally there was a big patch of sunlight on one of their facades. I noticed some too, from time to time, on the pavements ...' Patrick Modiano, *Honeymoon*, 12.

57 Chris Marker's description of the complexity of memory's texture is apposite. At the beginning of his film *La Jetée* (1962), the voice-over includes the following phrase: 'Nothing tells memories from ordinary moments. Only afterwards do they claim remembrance on account of their scars.'

58 Regarding the Swiss Embassy in Berlin, see Joseph Abram, 'La memoria del olvido: la embajada suiza en Berlin', *a+t: arquitectura+tecnologia*, no. 17 (2001), 112–25; Catherine Dumont d'Ayot, 'Un bâtiment, un dialogue', *Faces*, no. 50 (Winter 2001–2), 62–9; Marta A. Urbanska, 'Neutralnosc emocjonalna', *A & B* (2003), 26–39.

59 On Roger Diener's collaboration with Helmut Federle, see Catherine Dumont d'Ayot's interview, *Faces*, no. 50 (Winter 2001–2), 67–9.

60 Asplund's extrapolation consists of a simplification of the older facade, which is extended and freed of decor. Creating a fold in the facade would be the equivalent of creating a break in the right-angled extension of the old Law Courts. This operation would liberate the building's interiority around the break. Closing this internal gap with a new membrane would solidify the periphery of the internal space into a minimal surface. Loos's facades are built surfaces that define the primacy of the wall. Diener & Diener's surfaces are built membranes that define the primacy of their essential volume.

61 The building's abstraction does not result from a plasticity drawn from the pictorial space, but from a sculptural aesthetic inherent in the sequence of images and reasoning lying at the heart of the building's design process.

62 The old and new create a contradictory whole: the old hospital is long, the extension compact. One is decorated, the other stripped down. As Paul Klee suggested, the whole has to be dismantled in order to be re-created anew. See Paul Klee, *On Modern Art* (London: Faber & Faber, 1966), 55.

63 From 1935, the painter Jean Hélion insisted on the necessity for architecture to install its interiority in the surrounding geography of a location. In his studio, Hélion would map out the cardinal points and outlines of adjacent structures, in order to mentally reconstruct the surrounding space. See Jean Hélion, 'Termes de vie, termes d'espaces', *Les Cahiers d'Art*, nos. 7–10 (December 1935).

64 One can also experience this way of capturing the real synchronously in a remarkable picture painted by Moïse Kisling while in the United States during the war: *Hotel Beverly Hills*, 1942, Musée de Lodève, France.

65 This new object, instantly freed of its entire past, works as a readymade. I use this term in the way it was originally intended and not, as critical theory often has, as a synonym for the notion of 'already there'. On the issue of the readymade, see Rosalind Krauss, 'Forms of Ready-Made: Duchamp and Brancusi', in *Passages in Modern Sculpture* (Cambridge MA: MIT Press, 2002), 69–104.

66 About this building project, see Joseph Abram, 'Stuker à Berne', *Giornale dell'Architettura* (October 2003) and Joseph Abram, 'Extension et rénovation de la galerie Stuker à Berne', *d'Architecture* (February 2004), 57–9.

67 The Villa Rosenberg was built in 1872 by Johann Karl Dähler.

68 The cube's structural grid is mechanically derived from the classical facade of the adjacent villa. It is non-composed, not only because it is homogeneous, but also because of this mechanical transposition of its exogenous facts. About the modern signification of the grid, see Rosalind Krauss, 'Grids', in *The Originality of the Avant-Garde and Other Modernist Myths* (Cambridge MA: MIT Press, 1985), 8–23.

69 This appearance of this solid entity right at the heart of the park changes the natural space's substance.

70 The internal volume is not part of the design programme but comes from the neighbouring villa's dimensions. The audacity of this type of creation opens up an unusual type of space, using space the way a loft does.

71 The complex was designed at the beginning of the 1930s by the architects Fritz Schupp and Martin Kremmer. Initially protected as a heritage site by the German government, UNESCO eventually made it a World Heritage Site in 2001 as an example of modern industrial architecture. The Zollverein Coal Mine Industrial Complex includes the complete infrastructures, both historical and modern, related to coal mining.

72 Here, the readymade is the landscape itself, which implies an inversion of the usual 'painting/object' device.

73 Building started on the complex in 1875. The Museum of Natural History as it exists now is both a home for academics and researchers and a public museum.

74 Diener & Diener's projects are almost always founded on the urban logic of the monumental complex. It does not try to oppose this logic at any point.

75 This linking building, housing the section on Egyptian temples, also creates the effect of a kind of a door into the museum's main entrance, but one which does not alter the openness of the museum's forecourt.

76 The museum was designed by Cesare Bazzani, who also carried out the 1933 extension.

77 The proposed extension involves a complete restructuring of the museum. It would give the museum a diverse set of rooms, new flexibility and additional space for the long-term growth of the collections.

78 The museum presents a form that represents symmetry/asymmetry as well as this proliferating stratification. In the interior, the three levels of the building retain their historic identity, but they now work in a unified way. The exterior of the project establishes a form of unstable equilibrium between the monumental gable and the transparent wing populated with statues.

79 Zurich's city architect, Hermann Herter, gave this building a safe, reassuring quality suited to a bank. Diener & Diener softened this original character to create an atmosphere better suited to a museum.

80 The plan's simplicity and the character of the overall organization create a sense of proximity with the paintings, which aids an appreciation of them. One moves around the museum as if one were moving around a large apartment.

81 The dogma of historical authenticity can lead to a play of forced articulation between a representation of the past made sacred and a set of purely incidental contemporary gestures. This sort of play of elements can turn an edifice into a superficial jumble.

82 The supermarket has a self-referential aesthetic. Creating its envelope as a system of greenish-bronzed copper panels and large windows, which seem to emerge from its surface, helps to establish a sense of equilibrium between its dual qualities of irradiation and absorption that is comparable to Minimalist sculpture.

83 This beautiful hall (1863-5) was designed by Leonhard Zeugheer.

84 The Rigi Kaltbad site is located high up in the mountains, accessible via a rack railway.

85 The decision to create a university on the site of the old naval building docks was made by the Malmö city council to help counteract unemployment and create training possibilities. The city had been stricken by industrial decline. The council acquired the port wastelands for the building project.

86 The design study for the ABB complex was followed by the construction of an ensemble of buildings (ABB Power Tower Engineering Building, Baden, 1999–2002), which took up and reinterpreted the configuration already laid out on the site.

87 Marcel Duchamp, interview with Michel Sanouillet, 'Dans l'atelier de Marcel Duchamp', *Les Nouvelles littéraires*, 16 December 1954, 5. See Yves Arman, *Marcel Duchamp: Plays and Wins* (Paris, 1984), 87.

88 See Joseph Abram, 'Ici-ailleurs I. Tectonique et paysage', *Faces*, no. 50 (Winter 2001–2), 80–7.

89 I am thinking here of Minimalist sculpture: Donald Judd, Robert Morris and Carl Andre. For an exploration of the Minimalist problematic, see Rosalind Krauss, *The Originality of the Avant-Garde and Other Modernist Myths* (Cambridge MA: MIT Press, 1985), 8–23.

90 See Theo van Doesburg, 'L'évolution de l'architecture moderne en Hollande', *L'Architecture Vivante* (Autumn/Winter 1925), 14ff.; Piet Mondrian, 'L'architecture future néoplasticienne', *L'Architecture Vivante* (Autumn/Winter 1925), 12–13.

91 See Joseph Abram, 'Perspective et paysage. La construction d'un espace problématique', in Jacques Lucan et al., *A Matter of Art: Contemporary Architecture in Switzerland* (Basel: Birkhauser, 2001), 178–89.

92 The buildings for this campus were designed by Giuseppe Pagano, Ignazio Gardella, and Giovanni and Lorenzo Muzio.

93 The library is part of the Central University Campus of the Universidad Nacional Autónoma de México, which UNESCO made a World Heritage Site in 2007.

94 Roger Diener, interview with Catherine Dumont d'Ayot, *Faces*, no. 50 (Winter 2001–2), 64.

95 Helmut Federle, interview with Catherine Dumont d'Ayot, *Faces*, no. 50 (Winter 2001–2), 67–9.

96 Helmut Federle, interview with Catherine Dumont d'Ayot, *Faces*, no. 50 (Winter 2001–2), 67–9.

97 Gottfried Böhm, 'Dunkles Licht', *in Helmut Federle,* XLVII Biennale Venedig (Baden, 1997), 55–69.

98 Helmut Federle quoted in Erich Franz, 'Gespräch mit Helmut Federle', in *Helmut Federle,* XLVII Biennale Venedig (Baden, 1997), 7–33.

99 *See Helmut Federle,* Musée des Beaux-Arts de Nantes (Arles, 2002), 28–9.

100 See Fernand Léger, *La Grande parade*, 1954, oil on canvas, 299 x 400 cm (Guggenheim Museum, New York). For more about the notion of a relationship between art and architecture, see Fernand Léger, 'Colour in architecture', in *The Function of Painting*, trans. Alexander Anderson (New York: Viking Press, 1973), 150.

101 This paradox has also been explored by Pierre Sansot in his notion of an 'urban object'. See Pierre Sansot, *Poétique de la ville* (Paris: Klincksieck, 1988), 387.

102 The house's duality also relates to the contemporary ambivalence about the private space, the result of professional and living space seeming to coalesce in contemporary life.

103 The house's envelope, in solid larch, gives it a natural appearance, with a slightly rough and painted render (which can be left alone or painted).

104 In connection with this, see the Louis Kahn interview in John W. Cook and Heinrich Klotz, *Questions aux architectes* (Brussels, 1974), 263–318.

105 Theodor W. Adorno, *Minima Moralia: Reflections on a damaged life*, trans. E. F. N. Jephcott (London: Verso, 2005), 87.

Apartment Buildings Hammerstrasse Basel 1978–1981

Client **Basellandschaftliche Beamtenversicherungskasse, Liestal** *Structural Engineer* **Léon Goldberg**

The Hammerstrasse subsidized housing project encompasses half an urban block on the northern outskirts of Kleinbasel. It is an early example of an urbanization programme in a formerly industrial area. The drawings for the site represent the entire block, half of which consists of existing buildings; the U-shaped volume of the newly built half-block leaves a tree-lined passage through the lot. Along this alleyway, a row of atelier houses continues the tradition of light industry and artisan production on the inner side of the pre-existing nineteenth-century blocks. The passage also adds a level of transparency to the urban structure, a move indebted to Modernist urbanism, and one which ties the inner, semi-public space to the overall urban fabric. Traces of a legendary exhibition of installations by contemporary artists, which took place here at the end of the 1970s and the beginning of the 1980s, are still visible on the firewalls. For example, one can see Ben Vautier's text, which is inscribed where film screenings and other events took place: 'on this podium, do anything, say anything, sing anything'.

The varying levels of openness on the facades are specific to the site conditions and activate the public and private spaces of the exterior, as well as the life inside. The rental units combine row houses, which are individually accessible from the street, with apartment units on the upper floors. The apartments vary in size to accommodate families and single people as well as elderly people. The units of each type and size are grouped together; the half-block forms a complete whole. The entrances of the row-house-type maisonettes, arranged along the street and emphasized by cornices placed over the doorways, contribute to the street life of the neighbourhood. The masonry walls above the two-storey base faced in concrete are painted with white mineral pigments. The window-frames introduce colour: the wooden ones set into the white masonry walls were originally painted in a pale blue-green tone.

A cylindrical volume accentuates the corner of the housing block. Here, smaller apartments for single-person households are placed behind the fully glazed, rounded facade segment, for which standard wooden window-frames were combined to make larger elements. The south-facing courtyard facade also features generous openings, which accommodate winter-garden-like balconies that project from the volume and are constructed of metal frames. The southern end walls, with wooden french windows and metal shutters, display a third type of facade construction.

An innovation that is evident in the plans is the combination of fourty-five and ninety degree wall configurations, which creates a through-space from north to south. The apartments are interlaced spaces in a dense and efficient layout, and the diagonal lines in the apartment plans emphasize the symmetry of the houses, which are equally wide and deep. Of the overall depth of 14 m (46 ft), 7 m (23 ft) is devoted to the living room. The roof terrace, a collective meeting zone for the residents, adds another intersection between the public and the private.

Clockwise from top right:
Courtyard
Roof terrace
Alleyway with live-work 'atelier houses'
Interior hallway
Winter-garden balcony

Opposite:
Northwest corner of the housing block

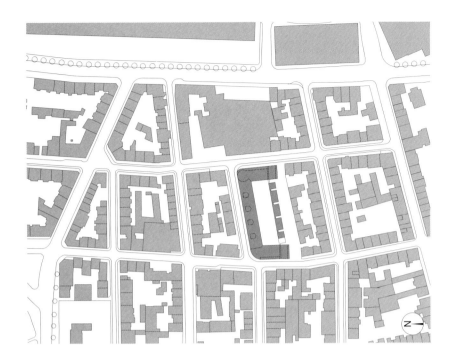

Clockwise from top left:
Site plan
Cross-section
Typical floor plan, four-bedroom apartment
Typical floor plan, two-bedroom apartment
Ground-floor plan, row-house-type maisonettes

Opposite:
Typical floor plan, housing block

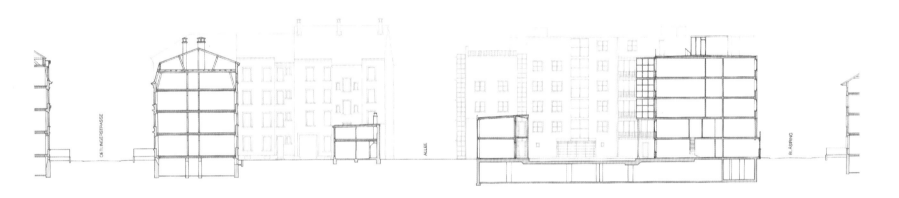

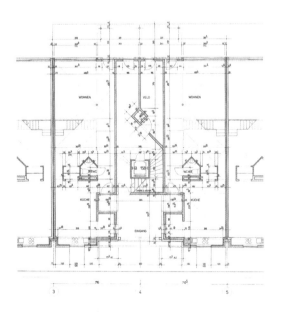

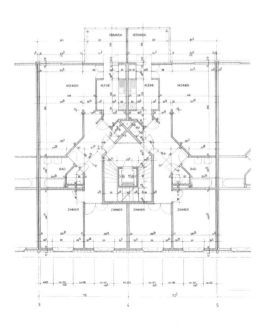

EFRINGERSTRASSE

BLÄSIRING

ALLEE

OETLINGERSTRASSE

HAMMERSTRASSE

Apartment Buildings Riehenring
Basel 1980–1985

Client **Basellandschaftliche Beamtenversicherungskasse, Liestal** *Structural Engineer* **Léon Goldberg**

As is the case with other apartment buildings in the immediate neighbourhood, the Riehenring project is based on a programme of subsidized housing. The tree-lined passage of the Hammerstrasse project situated on the adjacent block is continued as a narrower path through the Riehenring courtyard, ending next to a basketball court.

The ground floor is dedicated to retail and commercial functions, which makes the block a busy commercial and community centre at all times of the day. The public character of the project continues in the wide courtyard, which serves as a recreational space for the entire quarter. During the 1980s and 90s, film events were staged here, with a projector mounted on the terrace and directed onto one of the gable walls of the older buildings to the south. The roof terraces of apartment buildings are sun decks, providing hideaways high above the busy city and counterbalancing the collective space of the courtyard.

As a response to the surrounding urban fabric, the changing articulation of the facades coheres to, rather than disguises, the large scale of the project. Along Riehenring, a busy main street, three building units are structured around inner courtyards. The courtyard facades are clad with horizontally-mounted corrugated metal, and continuous lines of balconies emphasize the building's length. The street facades, where the living rooms are placed, are comprised of a frame of concrete filled with metal and glass. The street corner is the site of a unique moment on the block, where the pattern formed by the lines of the concrete frames and corrugated metal sheeting of the building's Riehenring facade is continued, but in the form of horizontal metal slats. Around the corner, along Amerbachstrasse, the compact volume is continuously clad with enamelled corrugated aluminium above a fully glazed ground floor. On Efringerstrasse, the four building units with stucco-finished fronts above a concrete base are separated by passages into the courtyard.

Although it has the appearance of a commercial building, the block primarily accommodates residential uses: the upper floors contain seventy-four apartment units of various types. The sizes (from two to five bedrooms) allow for a diverse range of residents.

Aerial view

Opposite:
Corner at Riehenring

While each of the three sides of the block has a specific configuration, all the floor plans follow a logic of three highly permeable layers and create a middle zone that is not only for circulation, but for living. The layout of the freestanding bathroom units and the diagonally-set open kitchens establish a spatial relationship between the entrance area and the generous, street-facing living spaces. Daytime functions are not defined by separate rooms, but by space-making elements that introduce a dynamism to the apartments.

RD   **Where the Apartment Buildings Hammerstrasse established a typological and architectural relationship to the ideal city, the Apartment Buildings Riehenring developed from an engagement with the biography of the site, which was previously a galvanizing plant. The freedom that an industrial location offers should inform not merely the building's spatial organization, but also its expression.**

Courtyard

Opposite, clockwise from top left:
Facade facing Efringerstrasse
Inner corridor facing Amerbachstrasse
View from the living space to the entrance area
of an apartment facing Riehenring
Balconies facing Efringerstrasse

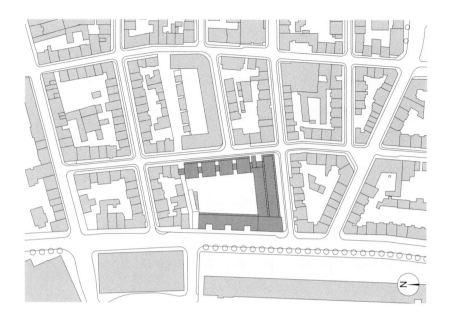

From top:
Site plan
Typical floor plan, two-bedroom apartments
facing Riehenring
Typical floor plan, three-bedroom apartments
facing Efringerstrasse

Opposite, from top:
Cross-section
Ground-floor plan

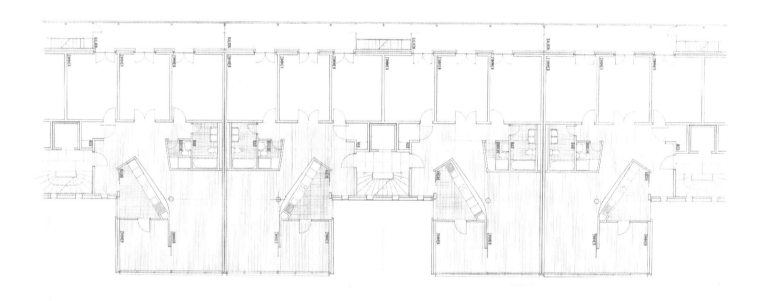

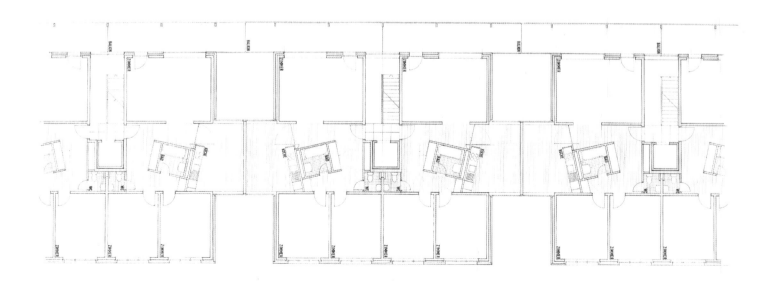

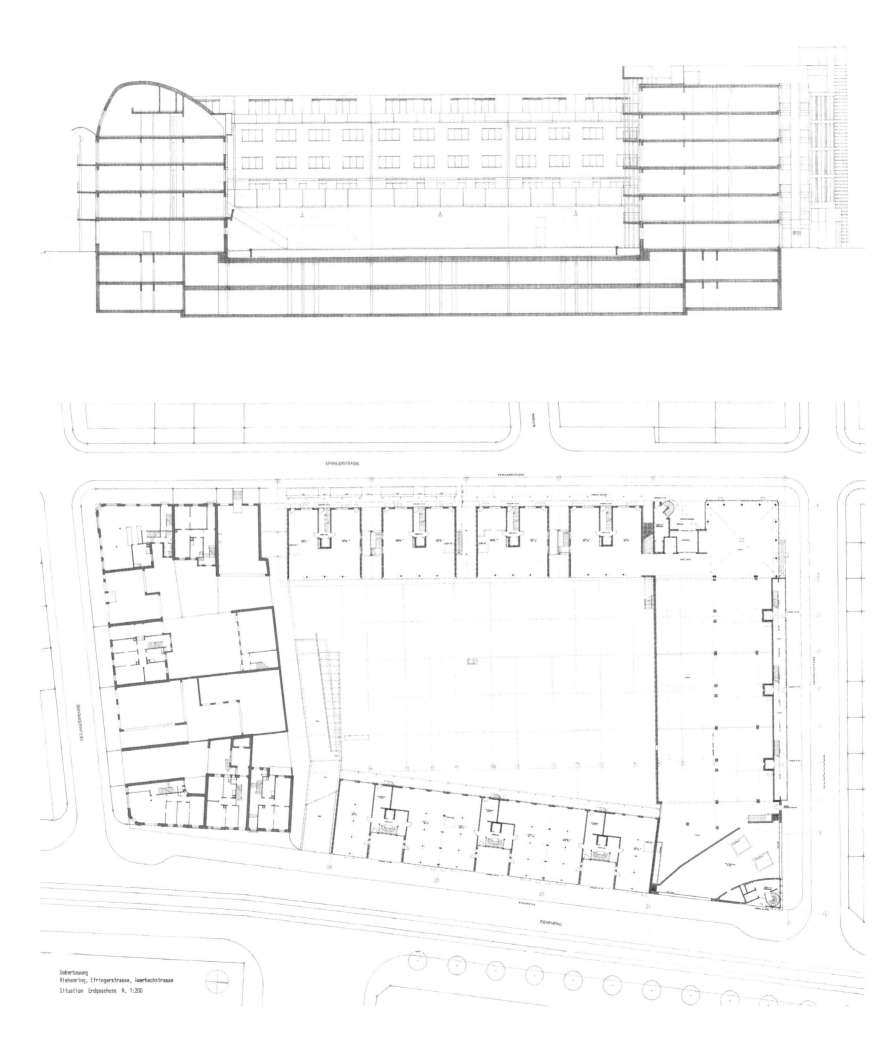

Ueberbauung
Riehenring, Efringerstrasse, Amerbachstrasse
Situation Erdgeschoss M. 1:200

Apartment Buildings St. Alban-Tal Basel 1981–1986

Competition **1st prize** *Client* **Christoph Merian Stiftung** *Structural Engineer* **Léon Goldberg**
Mechanical Engineer **Bogenschütz & Bösch**

The St. Alban-Tal quarter in Basel, which is adjacent to the restored former city wall by the river Rhine and a tributary canal, is one of the city's few early industrial areas. The architects mapped all the ground-floor plans in this quarter, in the tradition of Aldo Rossi's project to map the inner city of Zurich. Through these analytical drawings, which revealed the history of the site from its inner structure, they came to understand the industrialized character of the place.

The two apartment buildings, which replace two paper mills, stand perpendicular to each other, one aligned with the river and one with the canal. The easterly building faces the bank of the Rhine, and the building to the west relates to a square. The two buildings form a pair, yet are counterparts: their inner structures explore the principles of load-bearing walls versus *piloti* construction.

The larger building, next to the old city wall and parallel to the river, has four studios with entrances to the street, and seven apartments above. One layer of rooms runs behind each of the northern and southern facades. On the northern facade, ribbon windows of different lengths reflect the constant flow of the Rhine and express the sequence of living-room and kitchen spaces. The garden facade with its regular rhythm of horizontal windows echoes the bedrooms of identical size behind it, and the wood cladding mediates between the site's history and today's residential use. Between these outer layers a circulation area connects all the functions and repeats the sensation of spatial generosity and flow of the apartment interiors.

The smaller building on the square, with its back facade along the canal, contains six apartments. The apartments, which were conceived as variations of the free plan, were inserted into this volume. The arrangement of *pilotis* liberates the plan from the rhythm of the facade. On the canal side, the skeletal grid is filled with large windows that evoke a warehouse frontage. Towards the street and the square, the composition of the windows in their lean, elegant steel frames was designed by applying a *tracé régulateur*, a set of geometric rules based on the golden section and often used in the Modernist tradition.

View of both buildings from across the Rhine

Opposite:
View of the west building from the square

On the corner between the two facades of sandy white plaster over concrete, the construction method changes again. While along the street the facade is load-bearing, towards the square it is detached by virtue of the *pilotis* and stretches across the building like a fabric. Each facade addresses the site specifically and is constructed using a different structural system. However, while each explores the freedom allowed by the structures, the plans and facades remain mutually dependent.

Although controversial among local residents for its radical interpretation of the site, the St. Alban-Tal project, in the context of the architectural debates of the decade, was judged as a revalidation of Modernist architectural grammar and a counter-thesis to the prevailing use of historicist elements. However, a contrary view contextualized the ensemble within the architectural discourse of the 1980s by suggesting that it could be seen as 'a collage of signs, which establish a relationship to the surroundings', as Martin Steinmann pointed out in a public conversation with Roger Diener in 2009.

RD   The typological organization of the Apartment Buildings St. Alban-Tal can no longer be characterized as a traditional Modernist housing design, as was the case for the Apartment Buildings Hammerstrasse. It is also different from the Apartment Buildings Riehenring. In the residential buildings in St. Alban-Tal, the different structural layers were composed first, and only after this process were they filled in with floorplans. The resulting combination has been dramatized nether spatially nor architecturally. Rather, the impression is of a cooling-down process, a sedimentation occurring over a long period.

From left:
The rear facades along the canal,
looking towards the St. Alban-Tal quarter
View of east facade of the east building,
showing the roof terrace
The east building next to the old city wall

Opposite:
The rear facades along the canal,
looking towards the bank of the Rhine

RD   It is about the elements of building in their sheer form. These are employed according to strategies best compared to those of the Neue Sachlichkeit, but without removing them from the context of their use. This results in an experience that is perhaps comparable to a film still, an unmoving image that can suddenly convey something which is imperceptible within the moving flow of film.

Clockwise from top left:
Roof terrace of the east building, looking towards the old city wall
Backyard, to the south of the east building
Ribbon windows, with view to the Rhine
Interior of an apartment facing the Rhine

Opposite:
West facade of the west building, facing the square

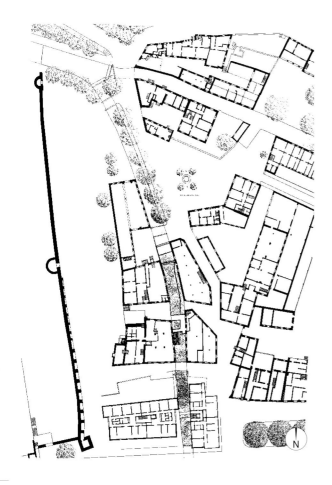

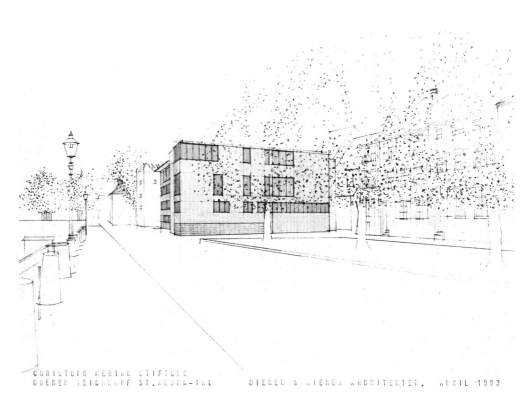

Clockwise from top left:
Site plan
Perspective drawing
Ground-floor plan

Opposite, from top:
First- and second-floor plan
Top-floor plan

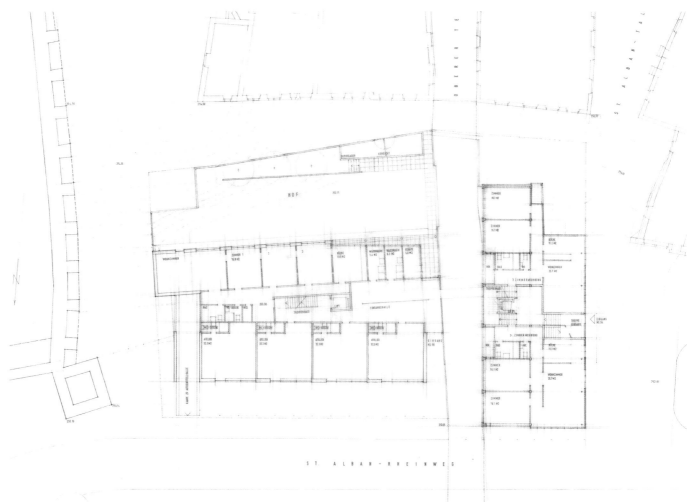

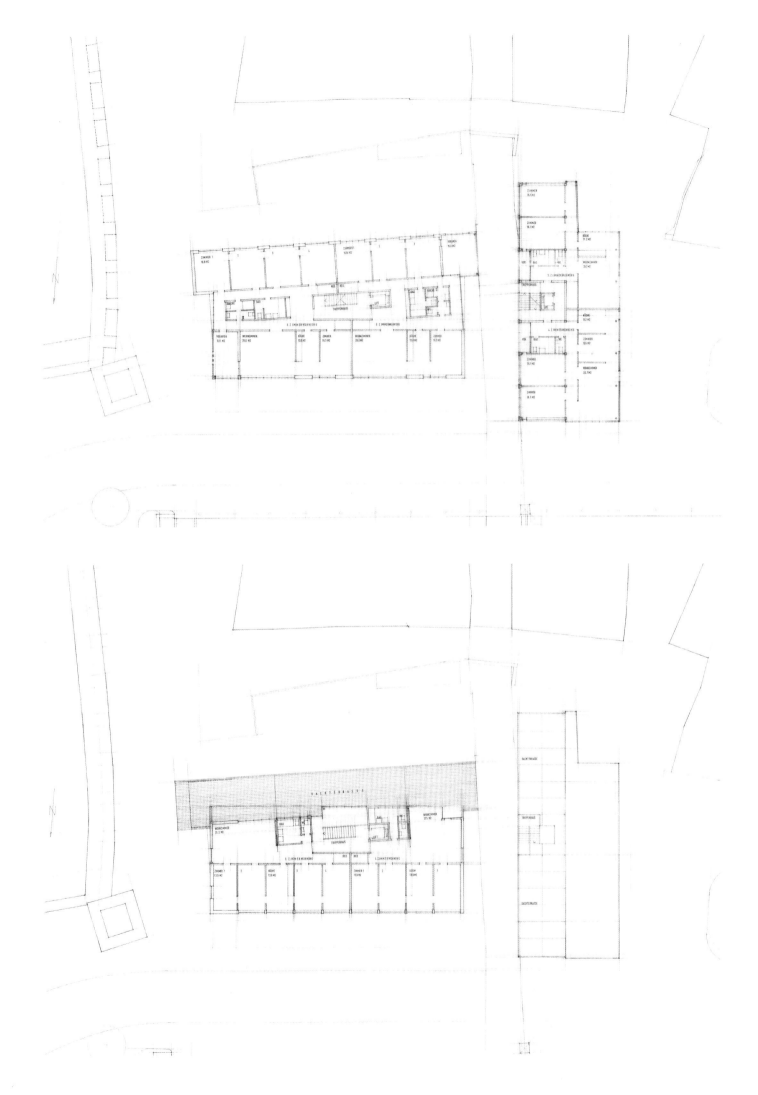

East and west elevations of the west building

Opposite, from top:
Detail of the east window of the west building
Details of the north-, south- and west-facing
window of the west building

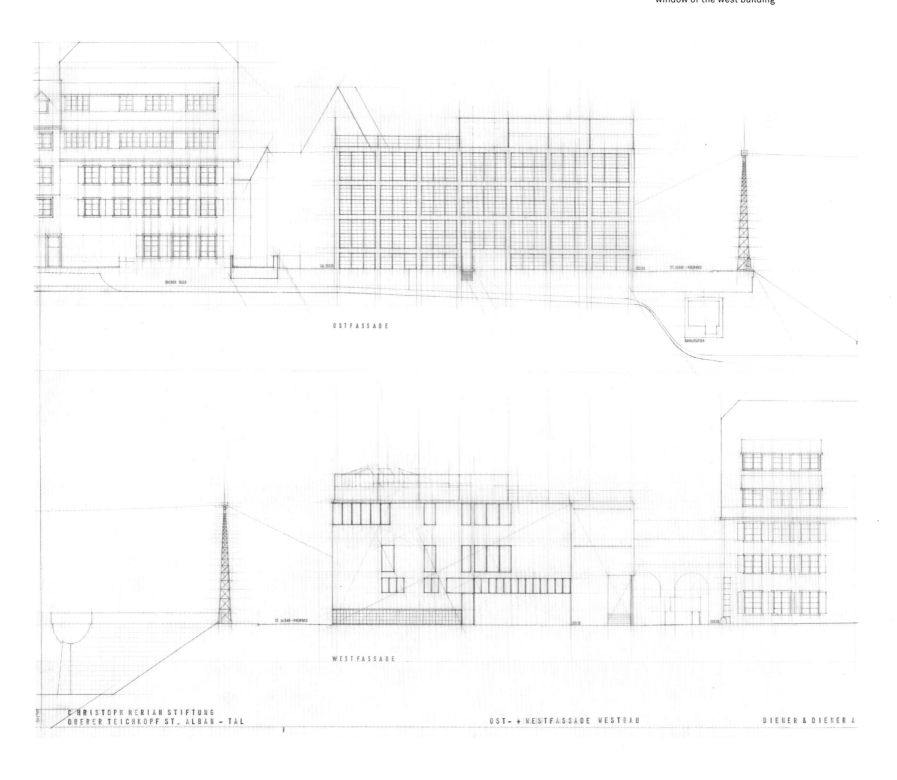

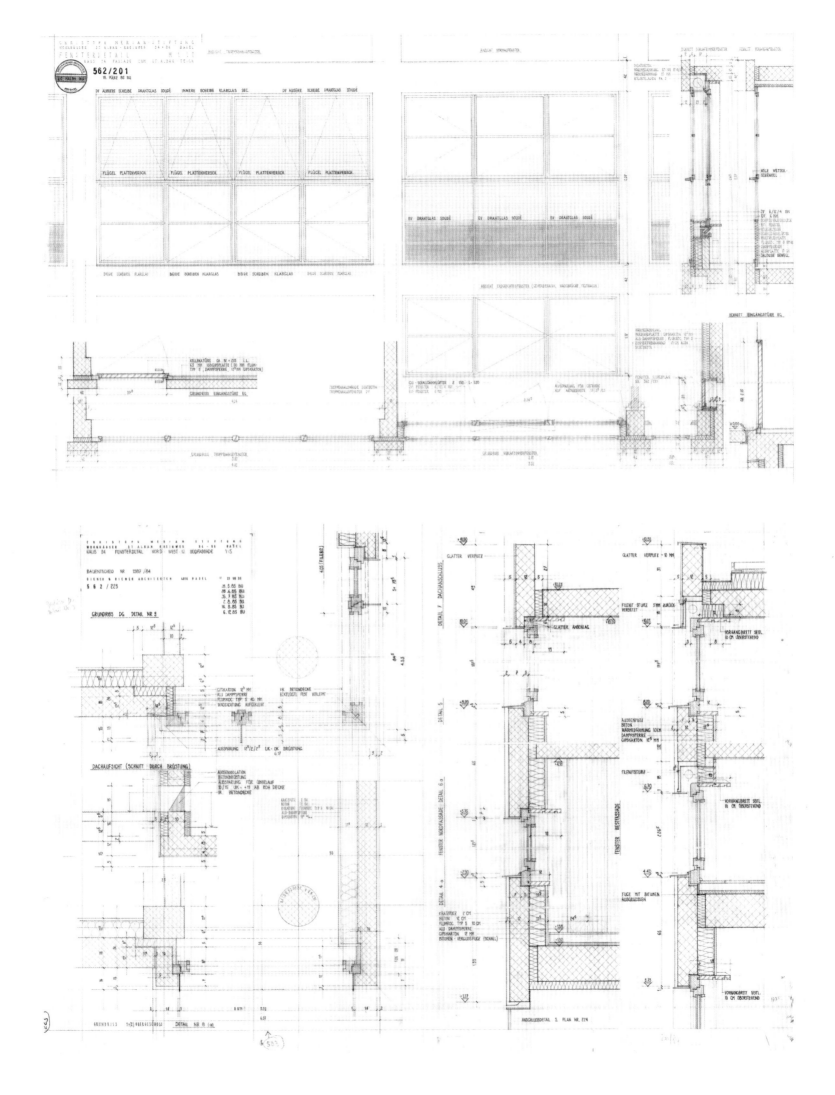

Office Building Steinentorberg Basel 1984–1990

Client **Steinentorberg Consortium** *Structural Engineer* **Léon Goldberg** *Mechanical Engineer* **Waldhauser Haustechnik, Bogenschütz & Bösch, Selmoni**

In Basel's inner-city Heuwaage area, the trust and treasury services company Fides commissioned a new office building. It replaced several smaller nineteenth-century neo-Gothic and older buildings. The composition is dominated by a long facade measuring almost 150 m (500 ft), made of greenish stone. The building sits on a wedge-shaped site that bends round the corner and faces the Heuwaage viaduct. This overpass was constructed in the 1960s in the midst of a cluster of smaller historic city buildings. Another large-scale landmark is situated up the hill, on the same block: the market hall with an octagonal cupola, a bold construction of reinforced concrete from the late 1920s. The office building introduced a new building scale at Steinentorberg while, at the same time, manifesting an urban, inner-city quality.

A base of red-stained concrete, which seems to absorb the resistance of the site, embeds the volume in the slope of the street. Three storeys are completely buried underground; a fourth level peeks out of the ground only at the bottom of the hill and, together with the ground floor, forms the base. Above this, the five storeys of the building are faced with stones that are coloured green by the addition of porphyry rock from Andeer. These large elements of the facade measure 140 by 40 cm (55 x 16 in), are 12 cm (5 in) thick, and weigh an average of 150 kg (330 lbs). Their size clearly indicates their industrial origin and it can easily be inferred that they had to be manoeuvred into place by cranes. The thin cement joints seem compacted by the weight of this outer wall of sandblasted, artificial blocks, which are bonded to the structural wall with mortar. The horizontality of the windows, each of which has five casement frames made of wood and faced in sheet zinc, and of the large stone blocks, underlines the steady flow introduced by the building into the urban fabric, and the rhythm of the stones and the windows together give serenity and a tranquil order to the steep street.

Opposite:
View from the Heuwaage viaduct to the northern corner of the office building

Next page:
The facade facing the Heuwaage viaduct; the market hall is to the left

On the rear side, which faces a courtyard, the reinforced concrete is plastered with an ochre-coloured stucco and the building is set back at each of the three floors until it meets the larger volume of greenish stone. The window-frames and the doors on this terraced volume are painted in olive green, which sets up a subtle tension with the green stones of the front-facing volume, but also communicates with the landscape architecture of the courtyard, where irregular lines form multi-level gardens. This stepped-back volume enters into dialogue with the many different buildings on the inner side of the block but, rising above, the building's overall figure can be seen to its full extent, announcing the larger scale of the city outside.

Terraced rear facade

Opposite:
The large opening of the two-storied hall has been furnished with lettering 'Fides'

RD   The Office Building Steinentorberg is made up of a number of individual elements whose straightforward relationship to one another is readily perceived. These include the load-bearing structure and the modular organization of the office space, as well as the structure of the 'skin' – the masonry, which is made up of concrete ashlar and windows.

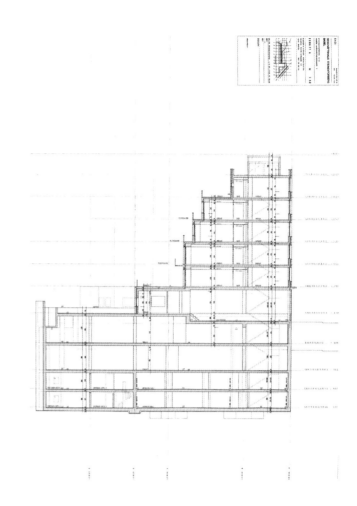

Clockwise from top left:
Site plan
Cross-section
Partial east elevation showing
the northern corner

Opposite, from top:
Third-floor plan
Second-floor plan
First-floor plan

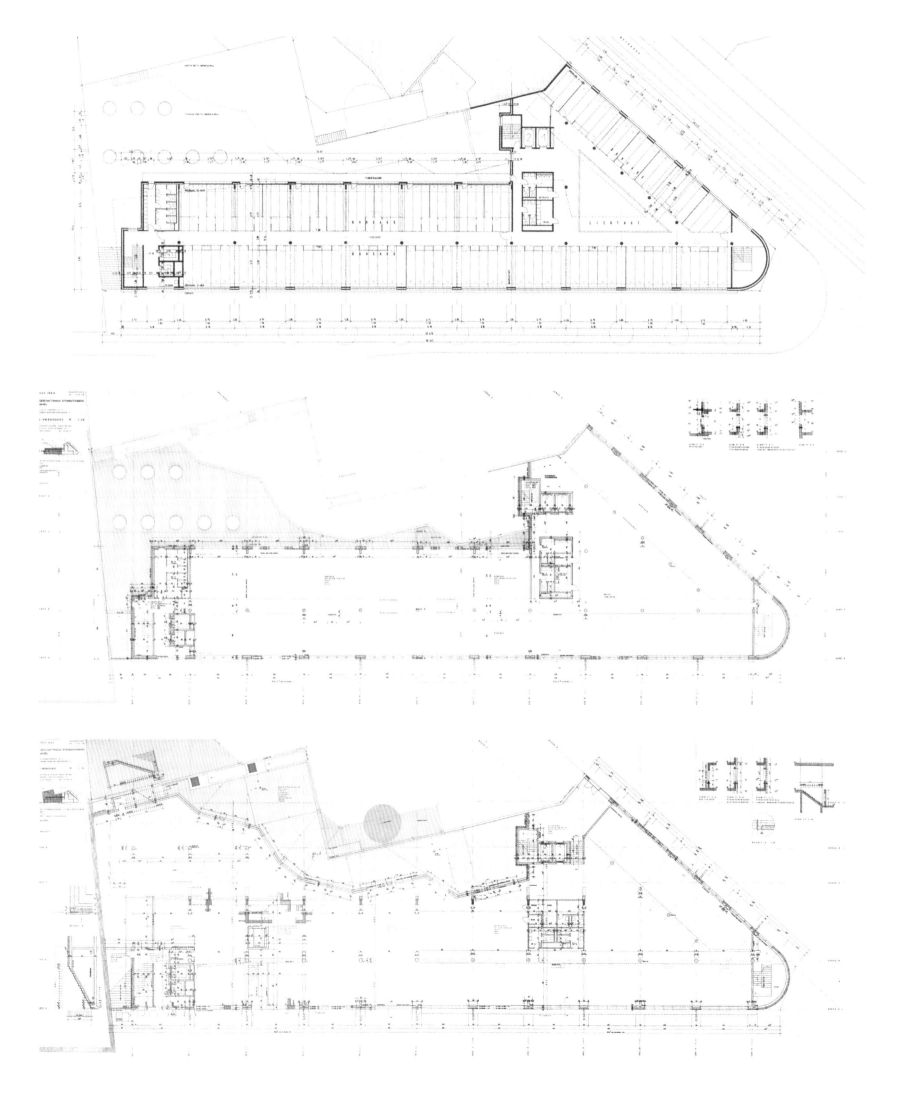

Showrooms and Administration Building for Manor, Basel 1984–1990

Client **Maus Frères** *Structural Engineer* **Léon Goldberg** *Mechanical Engineer* **D. Studer**

Once the garden of a Neo-Classical home, this site later became a courtyard surrounded by tall firewalls. The building, which houses showrooms and workplaces for more than 300 employees of the purchasing department of the Manor department store chain, now occupies three of the four quadrants of the plot. The lower right quadrant contains a courtyard as well as the garden building that serves as the employees' cafeteria and seminar building.

In the volume that occupies three quarters of the site, workers are located in open office spaces surrounding the courtyard; adjacent to these spaces, the sample rooms are arranged along the party walls at the back, forming an outer layer to the workspaces. With this configuration, the samples can be moved in and out of the rooms as they are being worked on. The geometric operation that underlies the 'intercept theorem' (by which the ratio between segments of two different lines is proven to be the same) is used here to create the required larger areas of the outer layer; as a result, the outer rooms are proportionally larger than the centre workspaces. In this dense and highly efficient organization of the plan, all spaces receive vast amounts of daylight: the work desks in the open-plan layout receive light from the side, and the sample rooms have skylights. A unique figure occurs at the inside corner of the open office space where a column is deliberately omitted; the resulting void in the column grid enhances the continuity of the space between the two wings and around the courtyard.

On the courtyard facade, massive concrete frames tinted a greenish-grey colour form an expansive tissue of large, staggered, horizontal openings that contain green aluminium windows. The thin stone elements framing the glass appear almost as fibres, giving the facade the character of woven fabric and making this heavy stone-framed window wall seem weightless. Behind a 3.45 m (11 ft 4 in) incision in the courtyard paving, which brings light into the administration workspaces, the facade begins at underground level, thus omitting a traditional facade base and underlining the idea of weightlessness.

Opposite:
Setback with water fountain in the east facade

Above the merchandizing department, two floors of offices faced with clinker brick are set back from the main volume. These floors follow the geometry of the rectangular column grid. This slight deviation from the shifted geometry of the site, which determined the angles of the facades of the main floors, creates a dynamic that makes the woven pattern of the artificial stone window-frames appear even lighter.

The closed front facade on the inner city street of Rebgasse in Kleinbasel is a counterpoint to the open wall in the courtyard. Three sculptural elements form a sequence: a setback with a bench, a niche with a water fountain, and two mosaics from 1954 by Basel artist Carlo König that have been reinstated in their original location. While the street facade has no entrance, its geometric elements welcome the passer-by. The bench, of the same white concrete as the window elements above it, invites the pedestrian to sit down and to contemplate the street, the artwork and the water fountain, a characteristic typical of Kleinbasel.

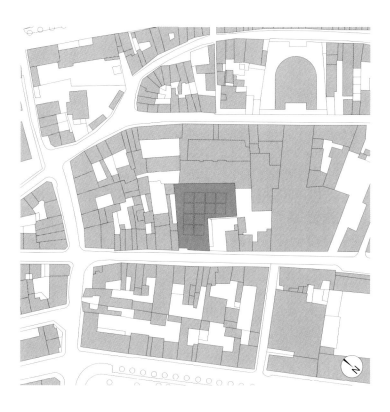

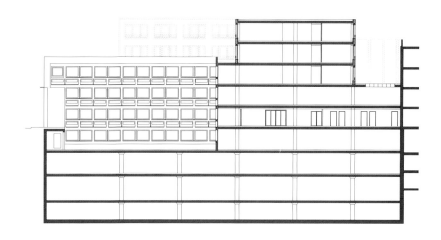

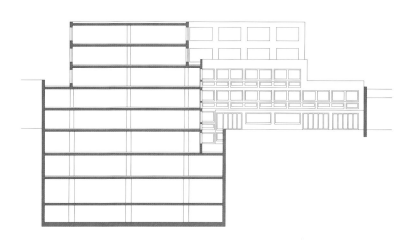

Clockwise from top left:
Site plan
Cross-section, east wing
Cross-section, west wing
Fourth-floor plan
Ground-floor plan

Opposite:
Courtyard

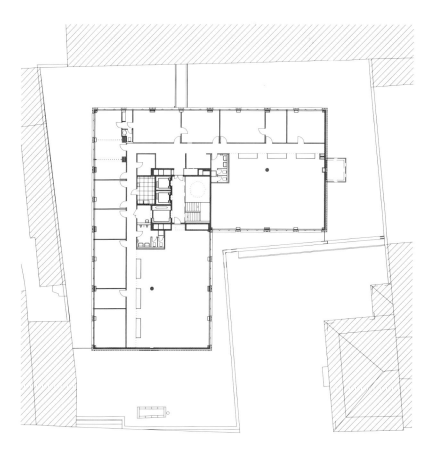

Administration Building Hochstrasse Basel 1985–1988

Client **Schweizerischer Bankverein** *Structural Engineer* **Aegerter & Bosshardt, Paul Weber, Suiselectra**

Immediately adjacent to the railway line, this office building is situated in a nineteenth-century area of Basel. In spite of the walls stained by the rust from the railway, blown here by the wind, the area south of the main station had become increasingly attractive for service industries, and in this case a bank commissioned a building with high-end office space. The six-storey building follows the established building lines exactly. Three deviations from a straightforward cube form the figure: a diagonal cut-out of the corner along the curve of the street, a smaller cut-out in the cantilever above this void, and a setback on the top floor. These interventions on the monolithic block generate sculptural qualities. The space of the street is drawn in under the volume's overhang and confronted with a windowless wall, which is clad with vitrified black clinker bricks.

As an allusion to the industrial origins of the site, the robust, monolithic body has incorporated the rough spirit of the place. The concrete of the outer shell is tinted anthracite, achieved by adding four percent iron oxide, as though the building had inhaled the carbon emitted from the railway. The concrete cavity wall that combines thermal insulation with a solid exterior shell 18 cm (7 in) thick is carried down to the street, where no plinth mediates between building and ground. The treatment of the concrete is refined throughout: the casting was done using large plywood panel formwork with a Bakelite finish, the window sills were prefabricated, and the reveals were sanded. Another characteristic feature of the building are its windows, which have frames made of bronze. They each have the same form and size, with 1:2 proportions and two wings.

Opposite.
Detail of the facade corner at Hochstrasse

Next page:
West facade and the railway tracks

To the south, the building marks the end of a row of predominantly residential buildings on Hochstrasse. The northern facade looks down over the railway tracks: at once both elegant and uncanny. The order of the facades incorporates both the vertical facade structure of the residential buildings on Hochstrasse and the horizontal movement of the railway tracks to the north. Facing the tracks, a lower level with conference rooms, lit by skylights, is concealed by an existing retaining wall.

Repeating the darkness of the building's shell, the interior of the upper floors bears dark colours, with large panes of polished black marble ennobling the eight heavy reinforced concrete columns. The columns structure the space in a regular grid and determine the position of the large windows.

RD   The building has been cut from the urban space, just as this urban space gives the building its final shape. No architectural gesture determines the building's character. Its form appears, in equal degrees, to be stable and unstable. Especially in its distinct and striking qualities, the form of the building was created by inherent conditions, not by the designer, as if the building were forming its own path. It radiates the traces of time and use. From the first day the building already appeared as if it had long been defending its location.

South facade

Opposite:
West corner of the building, looking down Hochstrasse

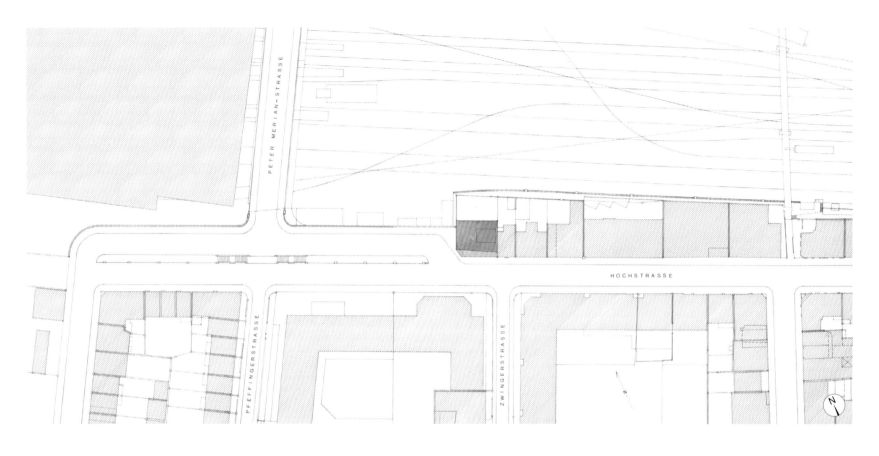

From top:
Site plan
Ground-floor plan

Opposite, from top:
West elevation
Cross-section

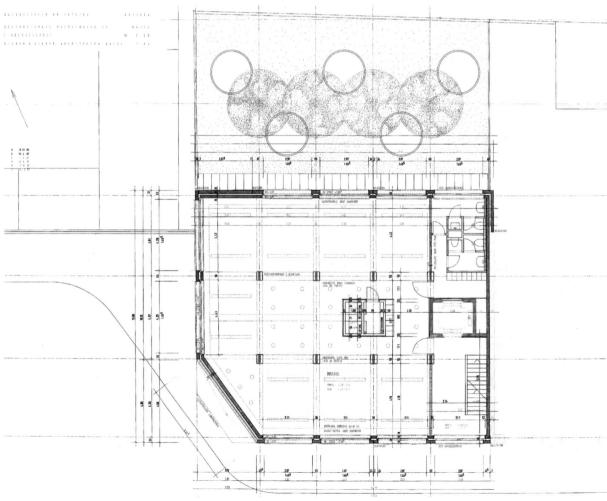

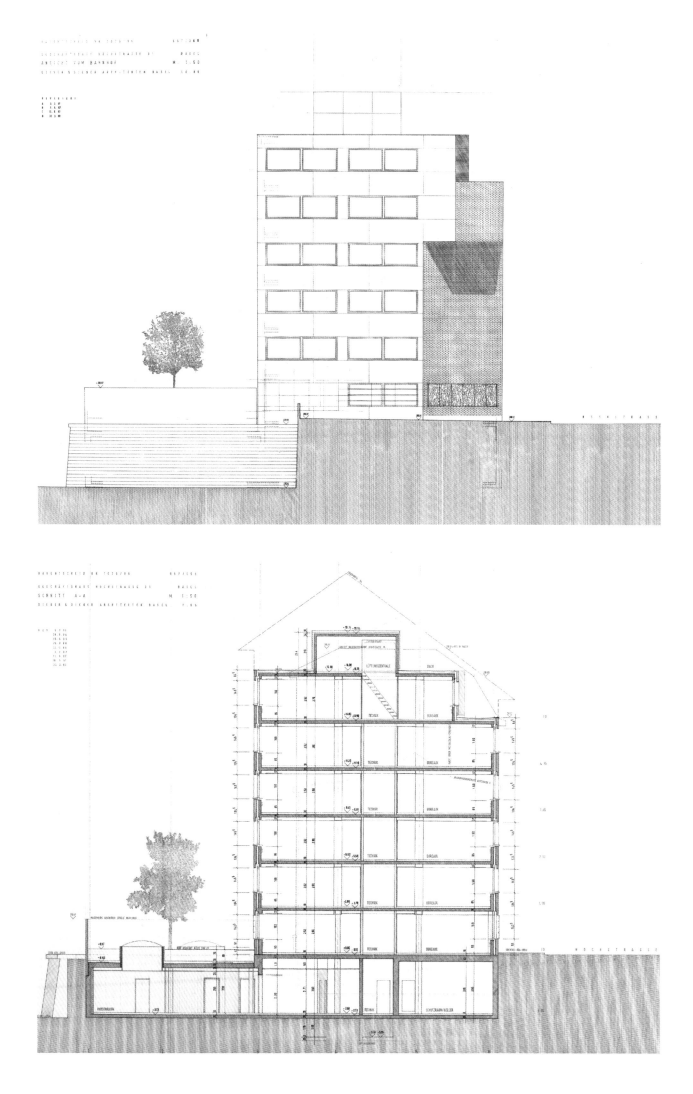

Training and Conference Centre
Viaduktstrasse, Basel 1985 – 1994

Client **Schweizerischer Bankverein Basel** *Structural Engineer* **Cyrill Burger & Partner** *Mechanical Engineer* **Aicher, De Martin, Zweng** *Landscape Architect* **August Künzel Landschaftsarchitekten** *Rearrangement of Hans Rudolf Schiess' Mosaic Window* **Peter Suter**

The irregular topography of the site is defined by a complex set of conditions: to the north lies the heavily trafficked Viaduktstrasse, to the south are the railway yards west of the main station, and a tall retaining wall borders the plateau above the steep Birsig valley that is an incision in the city, bridged by a viaduct from 1903. The Schweizerischer Bankverein commissioned a training and administration centre on this site, where a brewery had formerly been situated.

Next to the building's entrance, on the busy Viaduktstrasse, a fountain and a cashpoint machine have been added to the complex's enclosing wall. A softly curved wall of bricks faces the railway, along which trains bound for France travel at a level below the building and the street. Single bricks that have been fired at a higher temperature appear mosaic-like amid the variegated blue-red colour scheme. Although none of the bricks is identical, the arrangement appears compact and unified. The concrete endwalls facing the street, the railway and the courtyards are plastered with a silvery light grey stucco. The underside of the loggias and the mortar between the bricks are tinted anthracite by the addition of iron oxide. This darker colour binds the materials together, and at the same time references the harsh surroundings.

The building is set into this diverse topography on a continuous base, a few steps below street level. Inside the complex, three long rectangular volumes stretch from north to south; these are intersected by perpendicularly placed volumes that accommodate foyers, staircases, lifts and utility rooms. Seven courtyards, each of a different character, result from this geometry. Unlike the Office Building Steinentorberg, which is close by and set in a typically inner-city site, the Viaduktstrasse project is placed within a site of transit and of transition. Its configuration, however, evokes the building types of monasteries and Renaissance universities, with enclosed outdoor spaces as places of concentration and contemplation.

Opposite:
Detail of the fountain on Viaduktstrasse

The complex, which appears contained from the outside, generates surprising transparencies on the inside: from the rooms into the courtyards, between the courtyards, and through the entire building out to the trees on the Birsig side. Through a combination of brick, exposed concrete, fine wooden panelling and window-frames of wood and aluminium, the interior expresses elegance and discretion.

In the cafeteria courtyard, which is open to the public, the curved outer wall softly counterbalances the strict geometry of the five floors above. Here, the silence that seems to resonate from the staggered, ornamental brick surface is broken only by the sounds of the trees, creating a sense of landscape amid the railway yards.

South facade

Opposite:
View from Viaduktstrasse

RD　　　From the outside, the Training and Conference Centre Viaduktstrasse seems to be contained within itself. There is no specific front facade. Its empty walls abut train tracks and roads. The brick joinery (a mosaic structure with a blueish-red colour scale), the mortar, and the dyed concrete combine in a single, cast form. A silent quality envelops the building. It has the relaxing atmosphere of a park, symbolized in the wall fountain. The water flows like a continuous wave across the moulding on the external wall and falls into a basin that is itself part of the building's structure and which enables the water to be reclaimed.

From top:
Fountain on Viaduktstrasse
The six mosaics of Hans Rudolf Schiess, 1959,
rearranged by Peter Suter, make up the
auditorium window on the south facade

Opposite:
Courtyard facing Viaduktstrasse

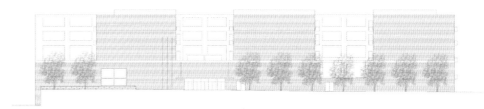

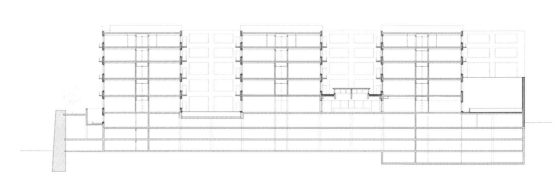

Clockwise from top left:
Site plan
North elevation
Section
West elevation
Model, as seen from the south

Opposite, from top:
Second-floor plan
Ground-floor plan

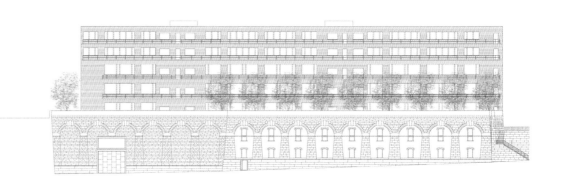

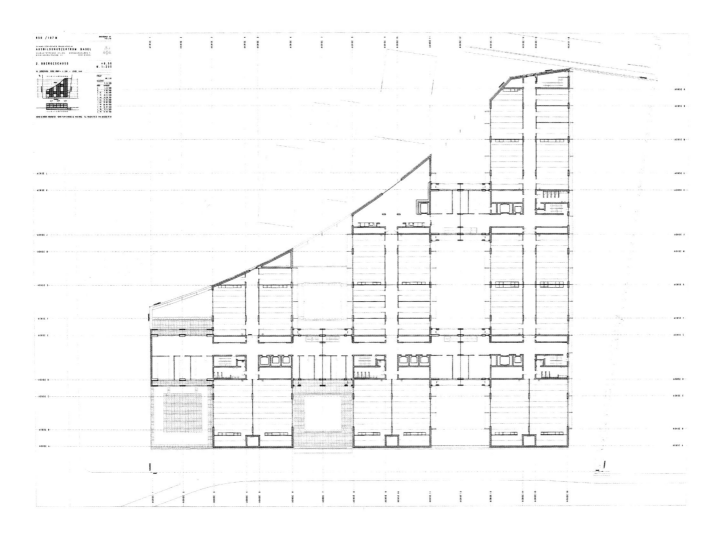

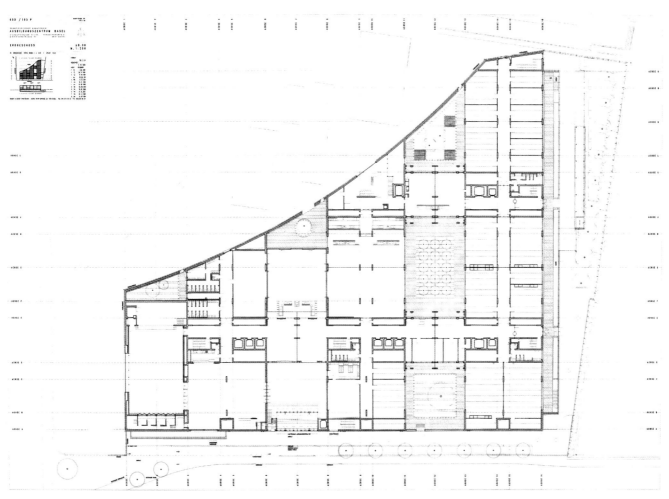

Administration Building Picassoplatz Basel 1987–1993

Competition **1st prize** *Client* **Basler Lebens–Versicherungs–Gesellschaft** *Structural Engineer* **Gruner** *Mechanical Engineer* **Sytek, Müller + Partner, Bogenschütz & Bösch** *Landscape Architect* **August Künzel Landschaftsarchitekten** *Italian Garden* **Luciano Fabro** *Curator* **Martin Schwander**

The administration building for the Bâloise Holding insurance company was built on the site of a villa and its private park. Like most of its neighbouring buildings on Picassoplatz, it does not align with the building line, but is positioned as a solitary object in the centre of the plot. Thus it becomes one of several freestanding monumental structures, all with their main facades facing outwards, which crystallize in the particular geometry of Picassoplatz. Most prominent among these structures is the Kunstmuseum complex by Rudolf Christ and Paul Bonatz, built in 1936, which is aligned with the former medieval moat of St. Alban-Graben. Another is the First Church of Christ Scientist by Otto Rudolf Salvisberg, which is set back from the street. The result of these varied forms is that Picassoplatz is not a contained square; it is animated by these buildings, which radiate into the space.

An urban block composed of several rectangular volumes, the Bâloise building's shape reads differently from every angle; it can be seen as a single volume, as a composite, or even as two separate volumes. The lower block, positioned towards the square, adapts to the relatively low heights around Picassoplatz, while the rear volume adopts the scale of the office buildings around Aeschenplatz. The alignment of those buildings also informs the entire ensemble of the Bâloise building, which thus relates both to the immediate context of Picassoplatz and the larger context of the neighbouring structures.

These surroundings are referenced, not only in the direction and placing of the building, but also in the pattern of the stones on the facades, which envelop the entire building without creating hierarchies. This continuity mirrors the internal organization of the building, which has an area of 16,400 m² (175,000 sq ft), in which the offices are aligned between the facades and an inner corridor. The building is clad with Andeer granite stones with distinctive greenish grey speckles. The pieces are placed so that their vertical joints create a pattern that alternates between lines that are hardly visible and gaps that cast shadows. The result is pairs of stone rectangles that are placed in horizontal bands around the building, and which alternate with bands of double-casement windows. Natural anodized aluminium sashes are set within frames of copper-titanium-zinc sheet

From top:
Stone cladding on the Kunstmuseum Basel
First Church of Christ Scientist

Opposite:
Front entrance of the Administration Building
Picassoplatz

metal such that the middle of each window-pair aligns with the shadow-gap between two pairs of stone. The horizontal format of both the stones and the windows enhances the flow of the facade around the building, as do the continuous sills that project from the facade (which were added to the design after the competition had been won). These horizontal projections, made of artificial stone with a greenish colour similar to the natural stone, are shaped as consoles upon which the natural stone plates are piled, floor by floor. Downstairs, the doors, door handles and windows of the entrance pavilion are framed in bronze.

Where the volume of the Bâloise complex is set back from the building line at varying distances, the grounds become an urban park, directly accessible from the street. The public is encouraged to walk in the park and around the building.

View of Picassoplatz

Opposite:
View of the Administration Building
from the giardino all'italiana

Using rough-edged dark grey slate and light grey granite, laid to form a promenade, artist Luciano Fabro has created a giardino all'italiana (Italian Garden). Over 200 lights fitted flush with the stone glitter like fallen stars from the night sky's Milky Way. At the same time, stones rammed into the earth as rhythmical vertical elements and stone slabs arranged at rough diagonal angles from the surface break the ground open to accommodate existing trees. The oldest elements on the site, the trees were kept as close to the building as the roots allowed. Now they literally touch the building with their leaves and branches.

RD   This building contributes to the urban environment around it, interpreting compositional elements from the existing buildings on the square. The concrete mouldings of the skin, which have not been applied but have been formed as consoles on which natural stone slabs are layered, relate to both the masonry stone walls and cladded stone skin of the neighbouring buildings. The facade of the Administration Building Piccasoplatz does not appear as the traditional image of either a load-bearing stone wall nor a wall clad with plates of stone, but as a play of the interaction between forces created by the interaction of the wall pillars, supports and ceilings.

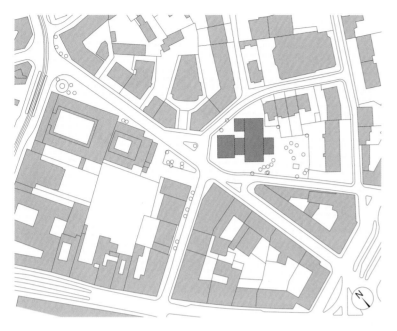

Clockwise from top left:
Site plan
Ground-floor plan
Site plan showing the
giardino all'italiana

Opposite,
clockwise from top left:
(all from the competition
entry)
North elevation
West elevation
South elevation
South-north cross-section
West-east cross-section
East elevation

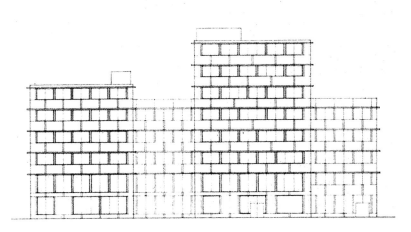

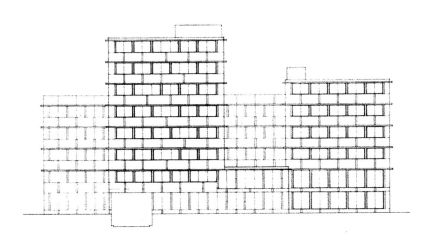

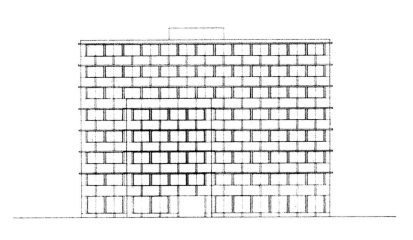

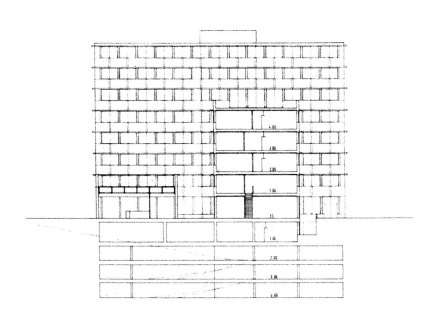

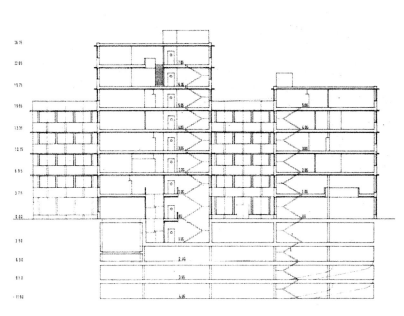

Gmurzynska Gallery, Cologne 1988–1991

Client **Krystyna Gmurzynska** *Structural Engineer* **Pirlet & Partner** *Mechanical Engineer* **D. Studer, Bogenschütz & Bösch**

Marienburg was incorporated into the city of Cologne in 1888, and a few years later a zoning regulation prescribed that only freestanding buildings (offene Bauweise) could be built in the district. Of the large residences of Cologne-Marienburg, most of which originate from the 1920s, some serve today as office spaces and as consulates. The Galerie Gmurzynska had already, in 1980, asked Diener & Diener to design a project for a special exhibition in Basel of female Russian avant-garde artists. In 1988, Gmurzynska commissioned their new gallery, situated on a site along Goethestrasse in Marienburg. The cubic building represents the private nature of the gallery, and counteracts the pretentious decorative elements of the neighbouring villas with a specific presence of material and colour. The facades are a composition of smoothly planed, narrow and wide vertical cedar and redwood boards and panels, all painted red.

From the hall on the ground floor, three steps lead down to an exhibition space that connects to the exterior sculpture courtyard, where a cherry tree complements the building. On the upper floor, a sequence of three salon-type exhibition rooms for viewing smaller works and a hall form a round tour. Workrooms, library and stockroom are located on the ground and basement levels. The spatial organization of the Galerie Gmurzynska, laid out as halls and small exhibition rooms on varying levels, offers a range of different settings. They are typical exhibition spaces and, at the same time, singular parts within the overall building structure.

The abundance of light in the exhibition spaces creates an extraordinary ambience. The entrance hall is lit from the side, through the front and the back doors. The upper spaces are shaped by the frame construction of the sidewalls and the roof. The skylight friezes on both the north and the south sides illuminate the exhibition spaces, complemented by light from the side. Rather than allow artificial light to dominate the spaces, variations in natural light determined by particular times of day enter the gallery space.

Opposite:
Garden facade

Next page:
Front facade, facing Goethestrasse

RD   Unlike Mies van der Rohe's Krefeld Villas, which were also used as exhibition spaces, the rooms of this gallery in Cologne are not open to the neighbourhood. They refer only to themselves.

The southern light that enters the large hall through its large windows changes over the course of the day. Here the spaces and the light provide the actual context in which the exhibited objects are placed. These are elementary, archetypal spaces. Because of their very general form any particular feature will enrich the room to an even greater degree.

Gallery and sculpture courtyard, as seen from the garden

Opposite:
Upper-floor hall, showing the skylight frieze

From left:
Ground-floor plan
First-floor plan

Opposite, clockwise from top:
North elevation
Cross-section
West elevation

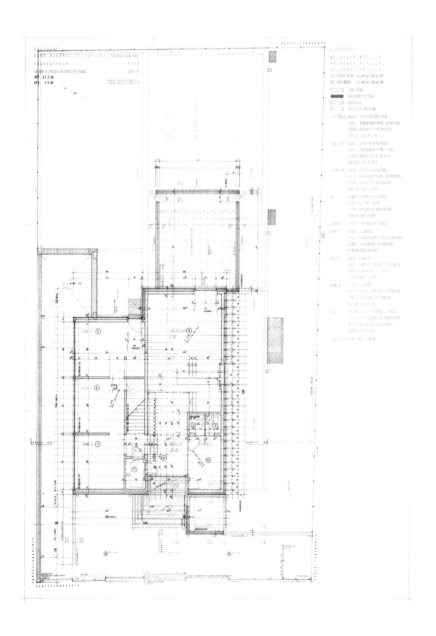

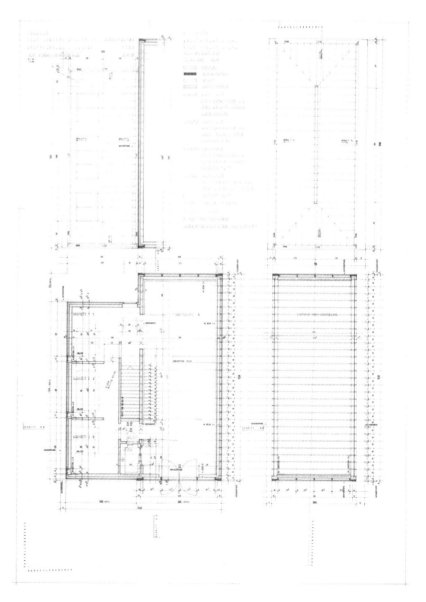

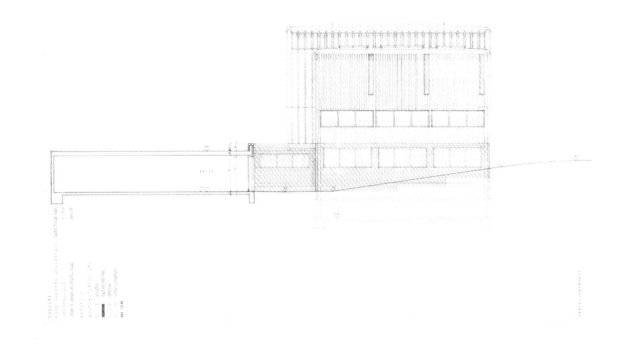

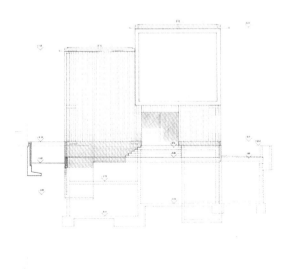

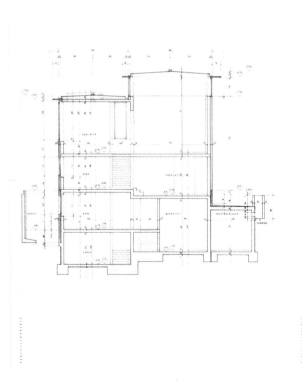

Office Building Kohlenberg, Basel 1992–1995

Client **Marcus Diener** *Structural Engineer* **Cyrill Burger & Partner** *Mechanical Engineer* **Bogenschütz & Bösch, Selmoni, Voirol**

The office building on Kohlenberg, on a street corner facing Barfüsserplatz, the Barfüsser church and the Stadtcasino Basel concert hall, is composed of two facades of 8 metres (26 ft) each, enclosing a 40 m^2 (430 sq ft) space on a site measuring only 65 m^2 (700 sq ft). The six-storey commercial building prominently faces the city between two gable walls of a building from the 1970s, which are adjacent on both sides; its roofline exceeds the neighbouring building by just 51 cm (20 in) and the facade wall is an even, continuous surface from the ground up to the roofline. The thickness of the wall is minimized by insulating from the inside, thus exposing the structural concrete wall.

The building's presence is defined by the large horizontal windows set into the walls of exposed load-bearing concrete, stained with yellow pigment. The resulting ochre of the facades underlines the autonomy of the office building, while the colour relates it to the larger volume of the Gymnasium Leonhard, which dates from the early twentieth century and shows Art Nouveau influences, and which is located higher up the narrow Kohlenberg street. Like a rock that has rolled down the hill, the concrete block with its earthy tint faces the square.

The fact that the building is not actually a volume, but two facades enclosing a space between two perpendicular party walls, focuses the architectural statement on the theme of the windows. The large horizontal windows, with dark enamelled aluminium frames and sills of the same yellowish concrete, shift against one another in a different pattern on each side. As Martin Steinmann said in a 2009 lecture, the facades are 'open systems that engage the spectator's gaze'. However, the two walls with their unaligned large-scale openings make the building not only an object to be contemplated, but a form that addresses the city as scenery, as the movements of the windows start from the corner and appropriate the forces of the complex surroundings.

Opposite:
View from Barfüsserplatz

RD   The Office Building Kohlenberg forces its immediate presence with the material density of the cement of its exterior walls, and the clear-cut perforations defined in those walls by the windows. As Martin Kieren has stated, the house does not emphasize the corner in an urban planning context. Rather, it is the corner.

Barfüsserplatz, seen from the interior

Opposite, clockwise from top left:
Site plan
Fifth-floor plan
Section
East elevation

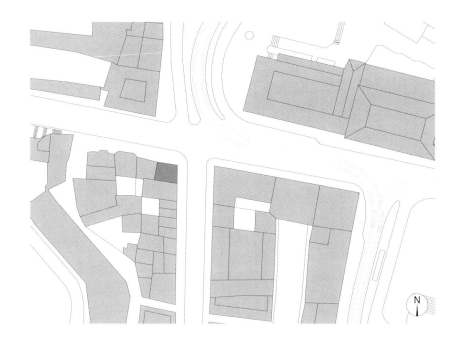

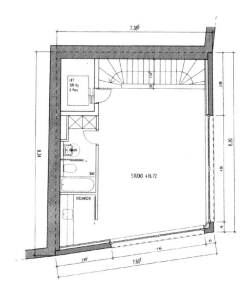

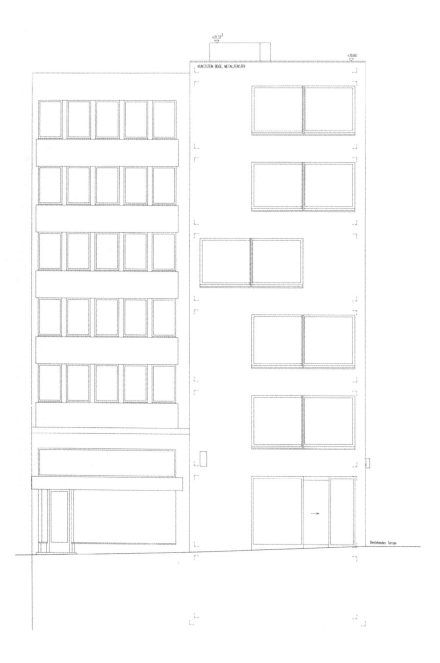

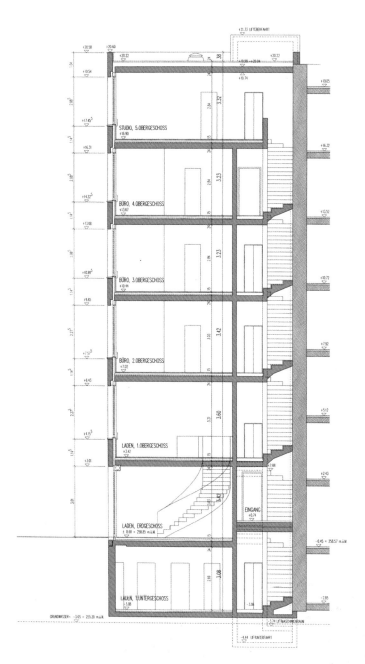

Vogesen School Basel 1992 – 1996

Client **Baudepartement Kanton Basel Stadt, Hochbau- und Planungsamt** *Structural Engineer* **Cyrill Burger & Partner**
Mechanical Engineer **Bogenschütz, Hunziker + Partner** *Colour concept for classrooms* **Peter Suter**

The Vogesen Schulhaus was the first new school building to be constructed in Basel in twenty years, realized as part of a programme to accommodate the spatial needs resulting from education reform. The new school adopts the building lines of its surroundings. It forms a courtyard together with the older, freestanding Pestalozzi and St. Johann schools. In this ensemble, which remains open to the south, the new building is independent and equal in scale to the other two buildings.

At the steps leading up to the entrance, which are parallel to the adjacent St. Johanns-Ring, the two offset volumes create a sense of rotation, which is then continued inside the building. The granite stone of the exterior stair is carried on into the interior circulation, where the corridors branch off from the entrance hall into the two volumes of the figure. The staircase, diagonally across from the entrance, is suffused with light from the large windows and animates both the courtyard outside and the corridors inside. In plan, the staircase is positioned off the corridor's axis, creating a movement through the building that, rather than merely shifting between floors, resembles an undulation.

The composition of two volumes shifted with respect to one another is also the result of a prerequisite that the school be built in two phases. The first part was completed in 1994. Thanks to a composite system of steel and concrete, construction could be finished within a year and allowed for great flexibility in the disposition of the classrooms. In anticipation of the second part, the new building overlooked the adjacent gymnasium hall with a gable wall. In 1996, on the inauguration of the Vogesen School after the completion of the second phase, the building became a composite of two volumes. On the outside, blocks of sandblasted stone, into which green-tinted granite was mixed, wrap the entire ensemble. The sandblasting brings out different tones and textures, which makes the industrially produced blocks appear natural. This single solid skin accentuates the heavy mass and solidity of the building.

Opposite:
Vogoesen School, from the south

The large windows, measuring 5.6 x 2.7 m (18 ft 4 in x 8 ft 8 in), open panoramically towards the outside, communicating the openness of the institution to the public. Between the corridors and the classrooms, interior windows above eye-level allow light into the corridors, where the white-painted wood of the doors and frames stands out from the light grey of the walls, announcing the classroom entrances. Within the classrooms, lightness prevails, deriving from the combination of daylight from the large windows and the two colours used in each room. On two adjacent surfaces on the corridor side of each room, different shades enliven the space and counterbalance the windows, which are animated by the view.

RD   In the Vogesen School, the relationship of the classroom to the city is open and balanced. The classroom appears from the outside as part of the social space and while smaller windows cut in a more traditional manner usually provoke an individual to glance to the outside, here the prevailing impression is that of participating more widely with the city. The arrangement of the large rectangular windows creates the framework for a specific perception. The interior is borne on the light and colour of the city. This colourfulness extends the effect of the rooms developed by Peter Suter.

Peter Suter   As in an image, the tonal wealth of the numerous nineteenth- and twentieth-century buildings in the St. Johann-Quartier form a counterpoint to the Vogesen School. The colours in the classroom walls take their cue from these prevailing colours. Unlike the colours from a paint pot, the walls bear the material character of the plaster.

From left:
East facade
Classroom window

Opposite:
Typical floor plan of the Vogesen School, with the Pestaluzzi and St. Johann schools

ST.JOHANNS-RING

SPITALSTRASSE

1

2

N

Housing and Office Buildings Warteck Brewery, Basel 1992 – 1996

Client **Warteck Invest** *in collaboration with* **Suter & Suter** *Structural Engineer* **Burger & Partner and Suter & Suter**
Mechanical Engineer **Kriegel + Schaffner and Suter & Suter** *Landscape Architect* **August Künzel Landschaftsarchitekten**
Entrance Detail and Fountain **Peter Suter**

The Warteck brewery buildings, constructed between 1890 and 1935, have become a familiar feature of the Basel cityscape. When, in 1991, the factory halted production, the brewery buildings, except for the landmarked corner building (formerly the brewery pub and today the Restaurant Brauerei), were to be demolished and a perimeter block was planned for the site. The local population objected to the redevelopment but the investor did not want to abandon the project. Against this background of conflicting interests, Diener & Diener were commissioned to design an alternative scheme.

The complex's principal buildings – the water tower, brewing house, malt silo and draff (spent grain) storage – were kept and dedicated to non-commercial use. Warteck Invest AG, the property development group that owned the site, came up with a revised scheme that combined new construction with renovation, and accommodated both cultural and commercial activities. In the cost and density calculations, the brewery buildings were not included and were therefore not subject to market conditions. A collective of artists and artisans were offered a permanent lease at an inexpensive rate, and founded Werkraum Warteck pp, 'pp' standing for 'permanent provisional'. Warteck pp is probably best known for hosting the alternative Basel art fair 'Liste' each summer but it is also a vibrant site of cultural production throughout the year.

The new development complements the landmark brewery buildings and maximizes the allowable surface areas on the plot by forming two volumes of five storeys each; the high density makes this solution economically feasible. The development is still topped by the water tower and the malt silo, which are visible across the nearby Rhine. Along the main street, a greenish-grey block accommodates retail services on the ground floor, offices around the light-well above, and housing for elderly people on the two top floors. A facade of horizontal concrete elements marks the deep block as a counterpart to the historic buildings, while retaining an industrial and tectonic appearance.

In the residential building, six entrances group the eighty-two apartments around the courtyard; twelve studio units face the square next to the water tower, where a fountain was added. By placing living rooms and kitchens, where daytime activities occur, on the west facades facing the courtyard, the traditional inside-outside organization of block buildings is avoided. The west and south facades, composed of horizontal windows with two, three or four casements forming openings of the same height, also express the interior activity by their rhythmical variation, while on the east and north facades, the bedroom windows with two casements are repeated steadily. Thirty-three separate roof gardens (unlike Diener & Diener's earlier housing projects at Hammerstrasse and Riehenring, where the terraces form a continuous uninterrupted space) are available to individual residents on a rental basis, while the corners of the terrace are common spaces.

By moving the street facade behind the building line, the usual block structure of the quarter was dissolved in favour of generous spaces to both sides of the building. The separation of what is 'inside' the project – the courtyard – and what is 'outside' the

The square and the water tower

Opposite:
Generous spaces have been created between buildings

project – the narrow street – was also overcome by wrapping the building all around with clinker bricks of varying shades of dark red, relating the compact volume firmly to the paved ground.

The block, with an open end to the north side and a passageway to the south, encloses a court without making it private. The urban qualities are drawn from the surroundings into the site. The spacing between the buildings, as well as passages through them, keeps the densely built quarter permeable to the adjacent streets. The distance between the restaurant and the office building, of less than 3 metres (10 feet), feels like an inner city alleyway, and the continuous paving of the wide spaces between the buildings and on the square weaves the ensemble into the space of the city. The entire site is a square, occupied by buildings that relate to each other.

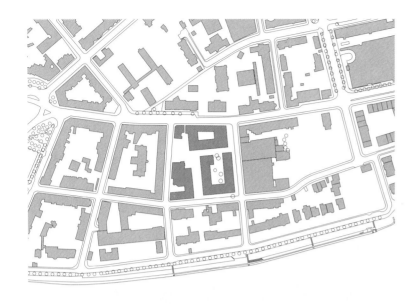

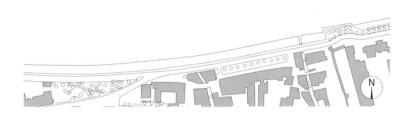

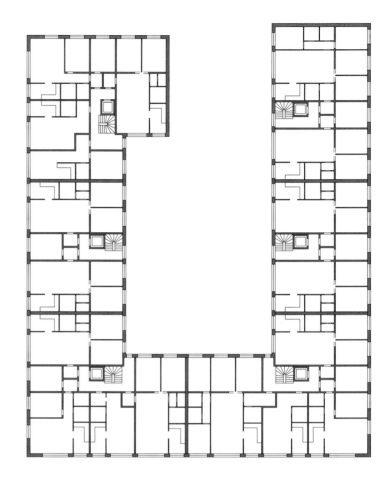

Clockwise from top left:
Site plan
First-floor plan
Cross section

Opposite.
Ground-floor plan

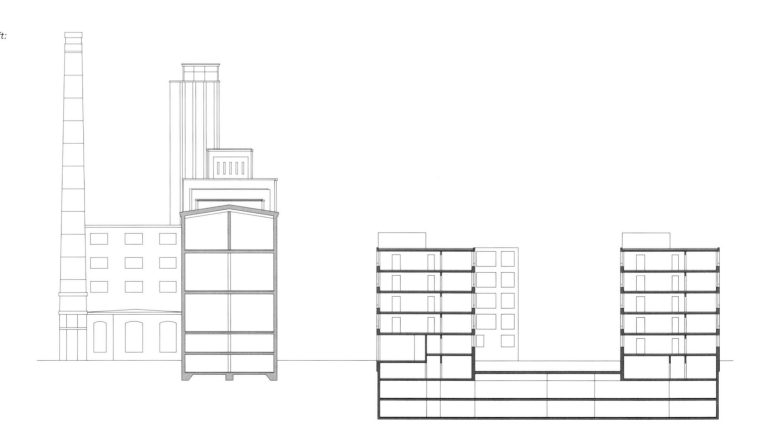

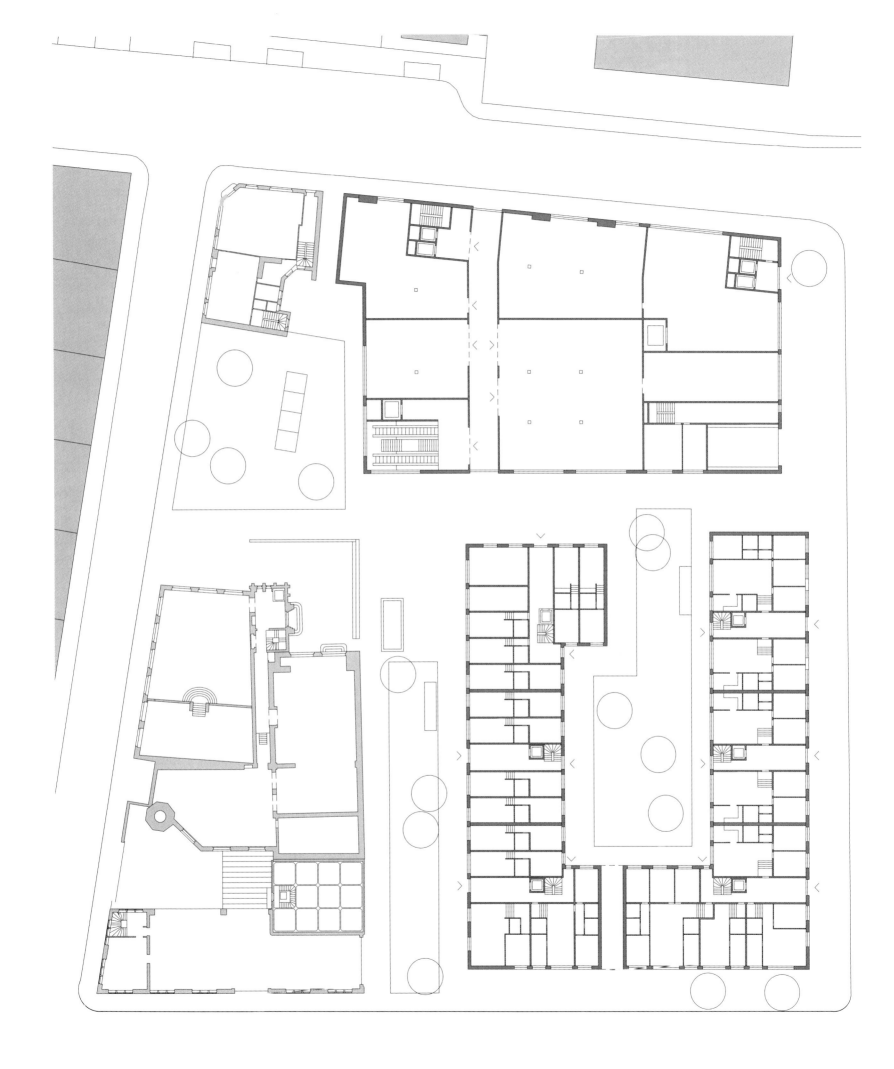

Apartment Buildings Parkkolonnaden Berlin 1994–2000

Client **A+T Projektentwicklungsgesellschaft** *Structural Engineer* **Leonhardt, Andrä & Partner** *Architect of Record* **Hochtief Construction** *Interior Design* **Mahmoudieh Design** *Landscape Architect* **Gustav Lange Landschaftsarchitekt**

The Parkkolonnaden (literally, 'colonnades along a park') result from a masterplan competition held in 1994 by the Asea Brown Boveri (ABB) corporation to redevelop part of the centre of Berlin. Giorgio Grassi's winning proposal unified the varied urban spaces and their relationships to each other via a homogeneous sequence of courtyard blocks along Tilla-Durieux-Park. This linear park follows the tracks of the former Potsdamer Bahnhof, which was destroyed in World War II and subsequently remained vacant as part of the East–West border zone. The area of Grassi's masterplan extends south to the Landwehrkanal and neighbours, to the east, a heterogeneously built quarter on the other side of Köthener Strasse and, to the north, the Daimler-Benz complex at Potsdamer Platz. The density of this new urban fabric increases as one moves north along Köthener Strasse and the park promenade, towards Potsdamer Platz, but voids between the buildings interlock with the surrounding urban spaces.

Diener & Diener's two residential buildings, situated between Köthener Strasse and Gabriele-Tergit-Promenade, have retail spaces on the ground and mezzanine level, and were built within the U-shape of the outline given in Grassi's masterplan. They form the southern end of the building sequence, which contains offices, other residential buildings, a school and a train station, all situated on a deck over an underground railway tunnel running parallel to the park. The L-shapes of the buildings figuratively enclose the volume of the tunnel, which rises towards Landwehrkanal, and forms a topographical mark in the urban fabric.

In their architectural articulation these two L-shaped residential buildings differ from the H-shaped office buildings designed by Grassi within the same masterplan. The facades of both building groups are clad in red clinker brick, but the exterior walls of the Köthener Strasse residences are reduced almost to a framework by large windows and slightly set-back parapets. The expression of these walls rests in a fragile balance between two different construction methods – the frame and the infill masonry wall – but in fact it is the interior, parallel, concrete cross-walls, which form a grid in the plan, that bear much of the load of the building and allow for these structurally dissolved facades.

Opposite:
Narrow passage between buildings

Within the concrete walls, apartments of various layouts and sizes, on one or two levels, can be inscribed and in this way, the construction system satisfies both a complex architectural idea and the property development market's demand for variety.

The apartments are grouped around a courtyard that is open to the south. The colour of the red brick, a common tone in Berlin, together with the Scots pine trees planted in the sandy floor of the courtyard, create a strong presence, reminiscent of the Märkisches Viertel housing estates with their early twentieth-century, red-brick blocks, but here transported to the city's very centre.

Courtyard with Scots pine trees

Opposite:
Entrance hall

RD   The building's form is the result of regular structures that have been super-imposed until an independent form emerges. Buildings created from such processes maintain a balance between concise and casual elements. The design appears neither exorbitant or distorted. Rather, it remains embedded within the framework of the system that produced it. This procedure creates space and time. It provides the viewer or user with the necessary scope to become accustomed to the building.

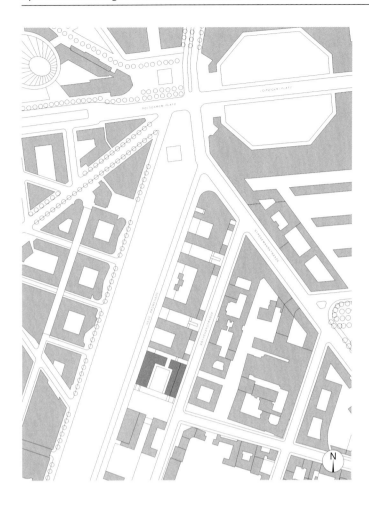

From top:
Site plan
Typical floor plan

Opposite, from top:
West elevation
South elevation
Cross-section

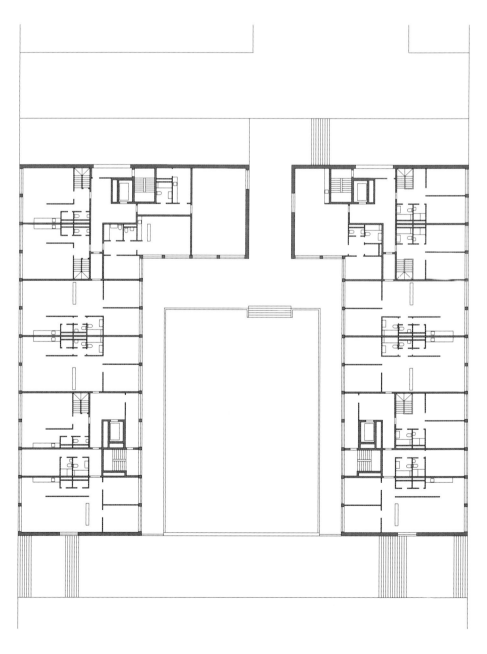

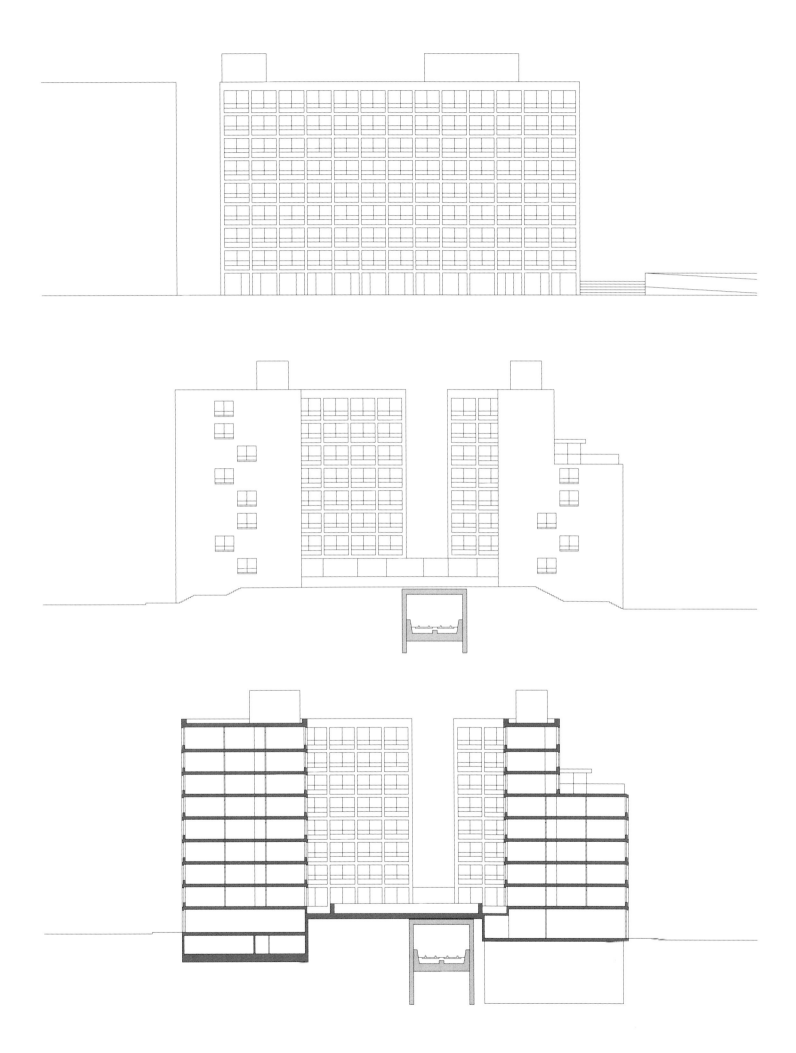

Extension to the Centre Pasqu'Art Biel 1995–1999

Competition: **1st prize** *Client* **Centre Pasqu'Art Foundation** *Structural Engineer* **Dr. Mathys & Wysseier** *Ingenieur & Planer,* *Mechanical Engineer* **tp AG für technische Planungen** *Landscape Architect* **Kienast, Vogt + Partner**

Since 1990 the Centre Pasqu'Art, located in a former hospital, has enriched the cultural life of the city of Biel. When a generous donation made it possible to build the much-needed larger exhibition galleries, a competition was launched. This winning entry proposed a new appearance for the contemporary art centre: on the east side, the extension with its contemporary facade of greenish-grey stone slabs counterbalances the traditional frontages of the hospital building and the former nursing home on the west side. The glazed ground floor, set back beneath the volume as an entrance, draws the ground plane into the building. With this welcoming gesture, the museum's extension makes manifest its openness to the public.

This new volume is not only lifted off the ground, it is also set apart from the former hospital by a gap. The extension is a wing, not only in an architectural or metaphorical sense, but in the word's anatomical meaning: anchored in the existing building, it extends outward and levitates up. This configuration initiates an open composition, where further extensions in the same row of buildings can be imagined.

On entering the building, the feeling is of moving below and not yet being completely within it. The staircase, which was extended to the ground plane by just a single flight of stairs, draws the visitor from the foyer, which is flooded with daylight from both sides, into the building's depths. The new flight of stairs is similar to the old stairway; the old handrail joins seamlessly into the new, which is made from the same wood, but in a lighter tone. A new lift serves all the levels. With split-level circulation, the old and the new parts of the centre unfold from the staircase's central spine.

The Neo-Classical hospital building, with its stone base and steps leading up to the raised ground floor, remains unaltered. It continues to be used for art exhibitions, which are complemented by larger spaces in the new wing. From the central circulation, one moves through the sequence of these older rooms along the facade, where the original windows, as well as the wall-mounted radiators, have been retained. The outer glazing, which was traditionally only installed during the winter months, now serves as climate control throughout the year. This historical sequence of rooms lingers as spatial memory

Opposite:
East facade

Next page:
South facade

in the first upper floor of the extension, where three taller rooms form a cinematic experience. Narrow vertical windows, placed at opposite corners in each room, create a sense of rotation inside the space and a dialogue with the outside. On the top floor, a passage through a compressed vestibule exaggerates the surprising and climactic end to the sequence: one large space lit by six long skylights. Called the Salle Poma, this room was named after the patron of the extension and refurbishment of the museum.

The top floor sequence also shapes the exterior space – an overhang on the back facade, it counters the weight of the hill. While the front facade on the ground floor is set back from the front plane in order to draw in visitors, the back facade projects out above the ground floor, creating an intimate enclosure between the building and the slope. The footbridge and the rear building remain unchanged, and the new stair of cast concrete along the retaining wall of moss-covered rocks is well integrated into the existing site.

From left:
Exhibition spaces in the hospital building
Exhibition spaces on the first floor of the extension

Opposite:
The Salle Poma on the second floor of the extension

The greenish-grey artificial stone of the extension's facade, tinted by fragments of Andeer granite, oscillates between countering the yellowish stucco of the hospital building and assimilating the moss-covered stones of the hillside. The vertical elements are laid out evenly across the facade, without noticeable joins, made possible by making each mortar joint flexible, so that they appear as fine fissures rather than cracks in the solid surface.

RD   What makes this project special is its position between things. Old and new establish a delicate balance in an open composition made up of three unequal parts: the former city hospital, the retirement home and the new extension. However, this feeling of precarious balance is evident to the visitor through the entire building. The city hospital's staircase provides the key for a spatial system that relates the different sections of the Centre Pasqu'Art in an immediate yet suggestive manner. It is like a metaphor for a city through time: the existing structure generates the new and the new is ultimately preserved within this existing structure.

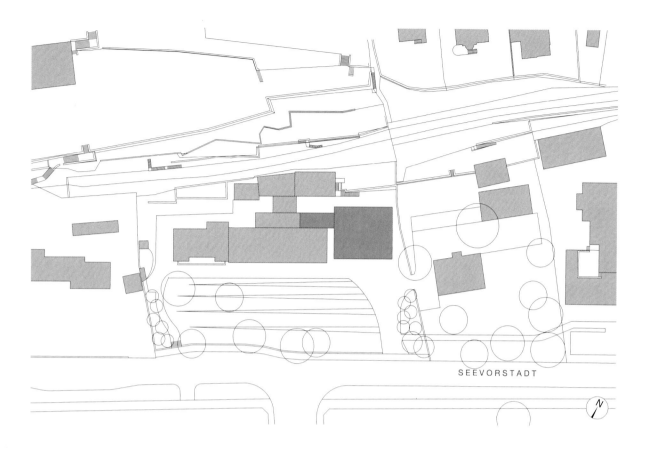

From top:
Site plan
Cross-section

Opposite, from top:
Second-floor plan
First-floor plan
Ground-floor plan

SEEVORSTADT

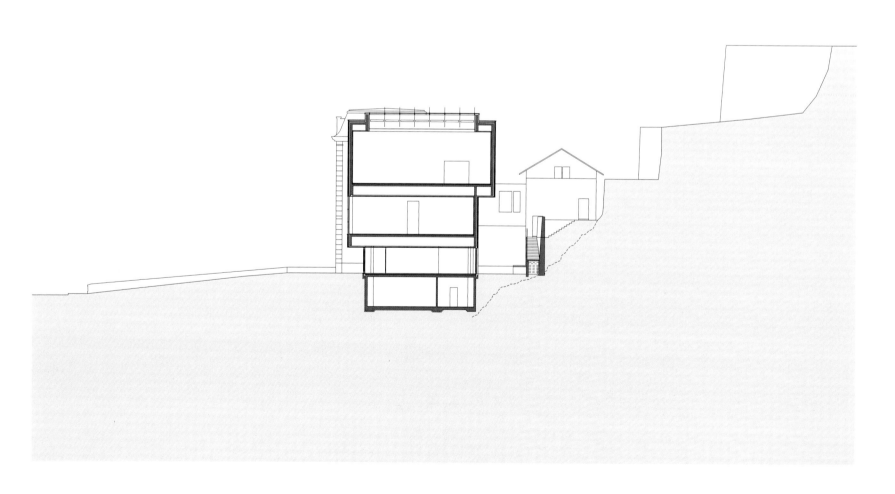

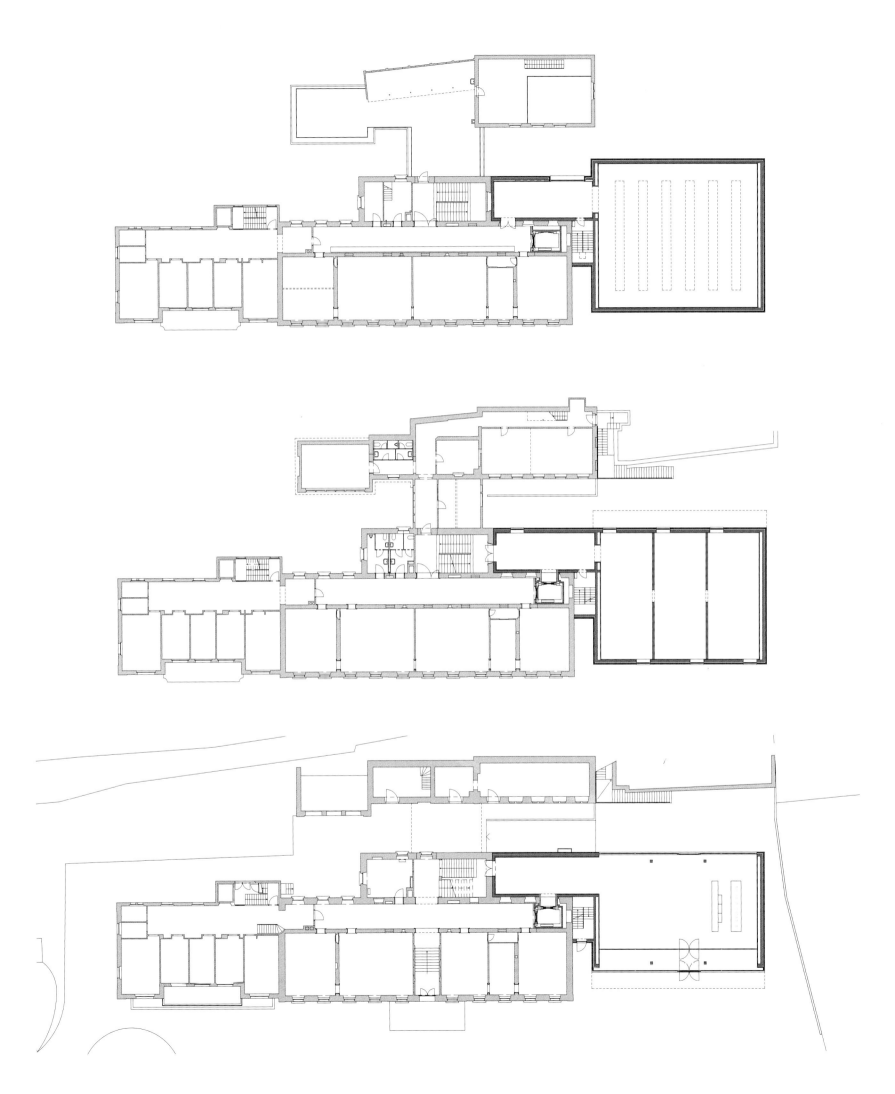

Hotel Schweizerhof, Migros Supermarket, Migros School, Lucerne 1995–2000

Competition **1st prize** *Client* **Migros Genossenschaft, Hotel Schweizerhof** *Structural Engineer* **Bucher Dillier Ingenieurunternehmung, Schubiger Bauingenieure** *Mechanical Engineer* **Aicher, De Martin, Zweng** *Landscape Architect* **Stefan Koepfli** *Colour scheme of Migros school* **Peter Suter**

The Hotel Schweizerhof in Lucerne's city centre was designed by its founders, the Segesser brothers, as a late Classical villa on the edge of Lake Lucerne. In 1845, when it first opened, the building was entered from the hillside. From 1863 to 1865, after the water-front promenade had been completed and the entrance had been moved to the lakeside, the architect Leonhard Zeugheer attached a festive Great Hall, a kitchen and a laundry, all in neo-Renaissance style, to the side that is now considered the back. The Great Hall is positioned asymmetrically to the hotel's axis.

In 1995, a competition was launched to replace the now-obsolete kitchen at the rear and to place a large Migros retail store, a Migros Klubschule (offering a range of adult education courses and leisure activities) and public parking on the site. The architects made the rear, hillside facade, which had been partially hidden under additions, once more open to the exterior. A conference room was placed in the restored Hall, as part of a spatial sequence composed of existing salons and meeting rooms. The programme was structured into three independent parts: the freestanding volume of the shopping centre and the hotel together form a courtyard, where the hotel can hold outside events, and from which the underground car park can be accessed. A smaller building for the Klubschule is built onto the hotel complex at its east side, facing Töpferstrasse, the pedestrian street that leads to Schweizerhofquai at the lakefront.

Heavy pieces of irregularly cast glass at the Klubschule building create introverted spaces that are used for movement and dance. From the exterior, the translucent surfaces of the cast glass give the building an appearance of weight and mass, despite its fully glazed facades. Transparent float glass and translucent cast glass alternate at rhythmical intervals, thus exploring different qualities of glass.

The volume of the new supermarket, with its stepped roofline and basilica-style section, forms a distinct volume next to the prominent Matthäuskirche (St. Matthew's church). The lower height of the side facades adapts to the dense fabric of the surrounding old town houses, but the stand-alone position of the building is emphasized by its unusual facade, made of long vertical panels in clear glass, translucent glass and oxidized

The Great Hall,
designed by Leonhard Zeugheer

Opposite:
Supermarket, next to Matthäuskirche

copper sheeting, on which the light reflects softly. The elongated proportions of the elements suggest a contraction that reflects the density of Lucerne's inner city, while at the same time giving the volume autonomy and a strong physical presence.

Contrary to the density and contraction that mark the exterior, the interior is expansive, referencing market halls from the past. The wide, horizontal space contains long travelators that lead upwards and downwards, connecting the three retail levels in a fluid motion and allowing for visual contact between the floors. The upper shopping level extends to a double-height space with views to a mezzanine where, through the fully glazed partition, the movement of people on their way to the classrooms above can be observed. On this level, the rooms look out at the roofs of the church, the Great Hall and the hotel through full-height windows of the same geometry as the facade panels, which tilt outwards from the bottom to emphasize, in a third dimension, the vertical movement on the facade.

The courtyard between the hotel, supermarket and church

Opposite:
Supermarket

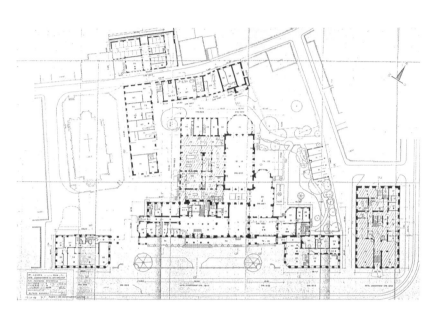

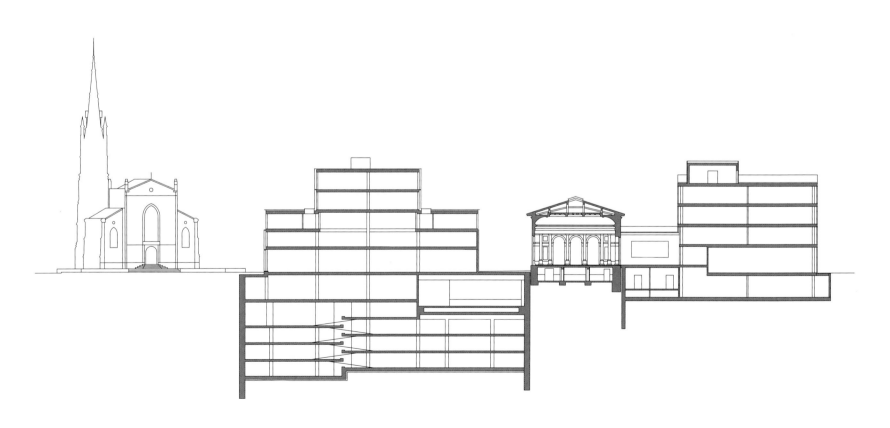

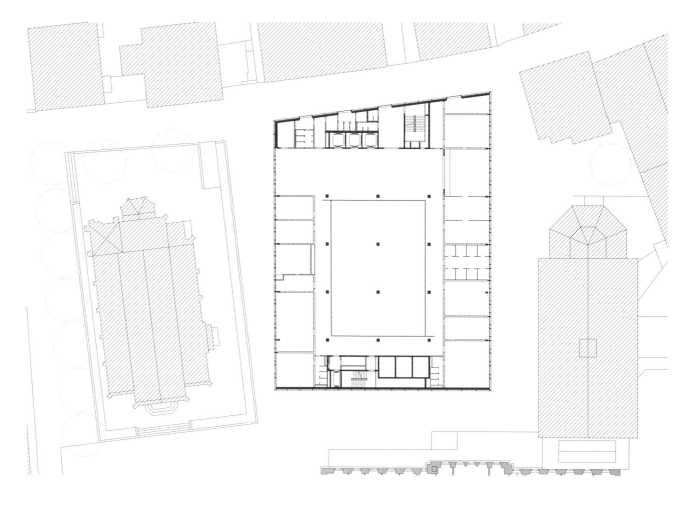

From top:
Second-floor plan
Ground-floor plan

Opposite,
clockwise from top left:
Site plan from 1905
Site plan
Cross-section

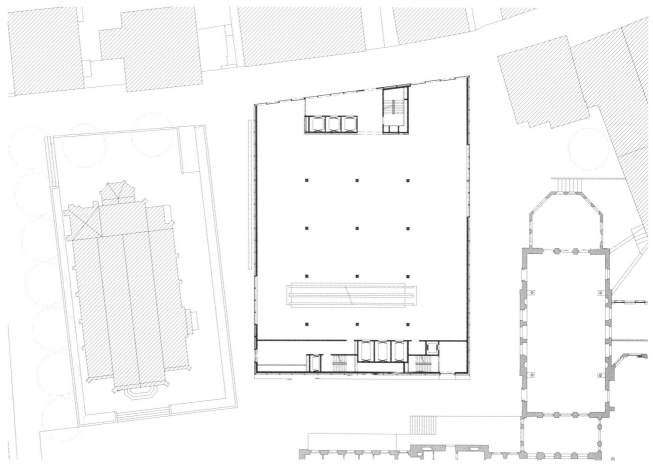

Apartment Buildings KNSM and Java Island, Amsterdam 1995 – 2001

Competition **1st prize** *Client* **Amstelland Vastgoed BV** *Structural Engineer* **Ingenieursgroep van Rossum** *Landscape Architect* **August Künzel Landschaftsarchitekten** *Structural Engineer* **Bureau Amsterdam** *Local Architect* **Bureau voor Bouwkunde** *Colour scheme for courtyard* **Peter Suter**

The landmass of KNSM and Java Island originated as a wave breaker that was built in 1890 and extended in 1900 as the last major expansion of Amsterdam's eastern harbour. It is referred to as the Y-island because of its shape. From its western end, most departing ships headed towards Indonesia, hence 'Java'; the eastern end was used by KNSM (Royal Netherlands Steamship Company), and from one of its piers the Dutch royalty used to board its ships.

Situated at the Verbindingsdam bridge that leads from the city centre to the KNSM and Java Island harbour complex, Diener & Diener's two new buildings mark the transition away from the city proper. They are the third phase of housing built on the island as part of a masterplan devised by Jo Coenen. Two superblocks – large expressive volumes of little relationship to the industrial past – had already been built, designed by the architects Bruno Albert and Hans Kollhoff with Christian Rapp. The masterplan had proposed a Z-shaped superblock for the third phase. As an alternative proposal, Diener & Diener suggested an ensemble of two autonomous buildings that would retain the ambience of the harbour with its remaining warehouses, harbour administration buildings, ships' captains' residential quarters and the Loods 6 storehouse that is now used as a cultural centre.

The two new volumes are set between the existing structures in such a way that each element retains its own presence, yet simultaneously becomes part of this constellation of mutually supporting buildings and surroundings. The two buildings exist in a precarious balance between the industrial genius loci and the urban designs developing within it. A long block and a courtyard building, the two do not resemble each other, yet they are of equal weight, suspended in a balance of two unequal volumes.

The new housing projects retain the power and rawness of the harbour environment. The buildings' function cannot be read from the brick facades, meaning that they could be taken for warehouses or even a hotel. At an earlier stage of the project, the long building and the courtyard building were conceived as counterparts, in different colours. In the built project, they are faced in the same reddish brickwork. Only the walls of the courtyard, with circulating balconies, are clad in two shades of greenish-grey brick.

From top:
Warehouse at the harbour
Aerial view of KNSM and Java Island

Opposite:
South facade on the water

These brick surfaces were given great importance and bricks were specially imported from Ipswich, in England. The windows are shifted half a brick from each other, and although this is almost imperceptible, it does alter the overall impression of the facade. By this subtle window offset, the opening disconnects from the geometric rule of the grid, and becomes an autonomous element. The window opening is no longer a negative inscribed into a geometry of figure and ground, but structures the facade as an active element in its own right.

Without a closer look, it is impossible to tell that 172 apartments of various sizes are accommodated within the long block. On the ground floor, studios with extra high ceilings for artisans and artists give the building a public front.

The east–west orientation of the existing harbour buildings became the reference for the placement of the new buildings. Both were constructed using a tunnel structural system, in which concrete is cast in tube-like units, producing highly directional spaces. This very economical system limits possible penetrations in the sides, but creates fully open ends. In the longer of the two buildings, these tunnels are directed north–south, mediating between the water and the new urban condition; in the courtyard building, the east–west orientation establishes a connection with the existing buildings. The courtyard building cantilevers dramatically. Facilitated by the system of walls above, the first floor extends boldly over the entry doors into the residential street, emphasizing the direction of the building and making contact with the neighbourhood.

From left:
Courtyard building
Courtyard with balconies

Opposite:
South facade of the long building

Within the larger tunnel units of the long building, which have a span of 7.2 m (23 ft 7 in), different types of layouts are realized. The relatively short width of 4.2 m (13 ft 9 in) of those in the courtyard building created a longitudinal type that persists throughout the building. The rooms in this building are not shaped according to function, but instead as segments of an extruded geometry that is constructed as a spatial tube by the tunnel system. All the rooms – whether entry hall, living room or bedroom – measure 26.5 m^2 (285 sq ft); their functions are defined by their position in relation to the circulation, the other rooms and the loggias, and they differ only in the positions of the doors and the placement of windows on either the long or the short sides of the rooms.

RD   Above and beyond the spatial constellation, the relationships between the old structures of port buildings and the new apartment buildings are relationships between similar building organizations and structures and, ultimately, even between the bricks that connect the old and new buildings and distinguish among them.

Living room in the long building

Opposite:
East facade

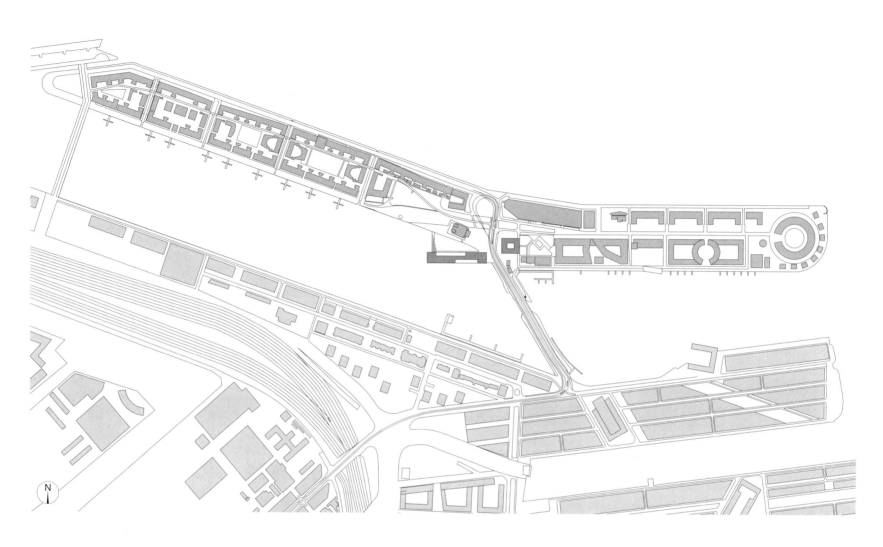

Clockwise from top left:
Site plan
Typical floor plan,
courtyard building
Cross-section,
courtyard building

Opposite, from top:
Typical floor plan,
long building
Ground-floor plan,
long building
Waterfront elevation,
long building

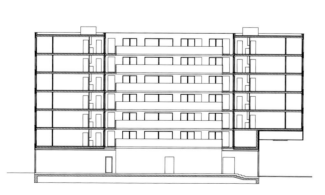

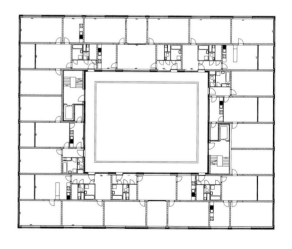

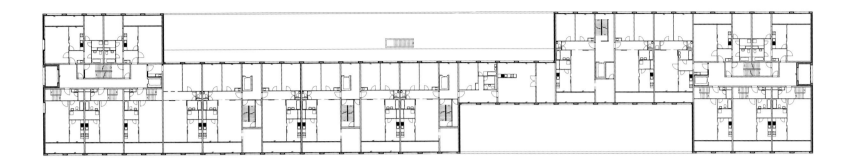

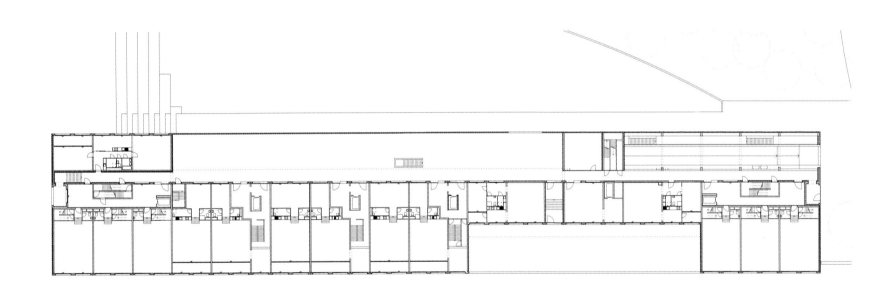

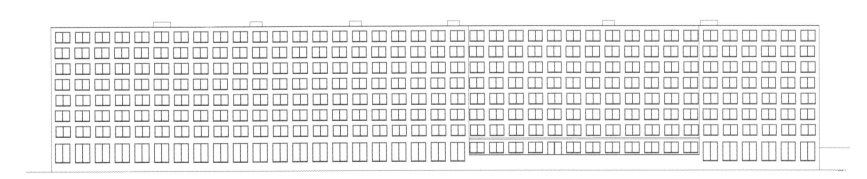

Swiss Embassy, Berlin 1995–2000

Competition **1st prize** *Client* **Eidgenössische Finanzverwaltung, Bundesamt für Bauten und Logistik** *Structural Engineer* **Walther Mory Maier** *Mechanical Engineer* **Waldhauser Haustechnik** *Garden Design* **Kienast Vogt + Partner** *Concrete Facade Consultant* **Jean-Pierre Aury** *Relief, West Wall* **Helmut Federle** *Interior Design* **Peter Suter** *'Kunst am Bau' (Art & Architecture)* **Pipilotti Rist**

Aerial view, 1935

Opposite:
Relief, west wall

At first glance, the contrast between the Neo-Classical palace on Fürst Bismarck-Strasse, in which the Swiss Embassy has resided since 1920, and the 1995–2000 extension on its east side, could not seem greater. Yet these two building parts – together with the former party wall on the western edge of the older building that was expanded into a 60 cm (2 ft) thick relief – are weighed against each other to form a new whole. The interventions on both sides of the palace are references to the past, when it was part of an urban block. Now that it is again contained within ends, it is no longer a single object, but has become an urban fragment on the building line of the former Alsen quarter.

The palace was originally built in 1870–1 as a private home for the Charité university hospital's director by Friedrich Hitzig, a student of Karl Friedrich Schinkel, and extended in 1910. In 1938, many of the surrounding villas were demolished by the National Socialists to make way for their gigantic Volkshalle of the monumental Germania project. A few years later, most of the remaining Alsen buildings were razed by bombings. After World War II, the Swiss outpost in Berlin stood isolated, near the Berlin Wall, and attempts to sell the building found no takers. After 1989, with the reunification of Germany, the situation changed again: now that the palace represented a legacy and occupied a strategic site in the very centre of the city, the Swiss were no longer willing to trade their embassy's location.

In response to the competition brief, in which the Swiss government called for ideas to reuse and expand their former embassy in Berlin, Diener & Diener looked, as a reference, to Gunnar Asplund's 1936 extension to Gotenborg's municipal building, where the asymmetry and lightness of the new facade create a movement away from the existing building. In Diener & Diener's project, however, the visual rotation is directed towards the palace's facade. The heavy volume of the addition is lightened by a large opening in both the elevation and plan. This forms a new entrance that, as well as acting as a focal point for the rotary motion, creates a sense of hospitality. While designing this void, the architects referred to the characteristic wall openings in the front of Adolf Loos's 1926 house for Tristan Tzara in Paris.

The intention was to unsettle the seemingly aimless, lonely autonomy of the historical, monumental facade, and to make it swing and sway, in order to achieve a new whole. This extension is not an autonomous volume that has moved close to the original, but a part developed from the existing building. Unlike the extension to the Centre Pasqu'Art in Biel, where a gap clearly separates the two parts, here the new volume is tightly pushed against the older building. The project extends and transcends the categories of old and new; it establishes physical relationships between the two.

The volumes and the materials speak of the difference in the time at which they were constructed, and they speak to each other: the difference between the old and the new does not create distance. Instead, it triggers a series of spatial dialogues: between inside and outside, between solid and void, between open and closed. The waiting room and the reception to the chancellery on the new ground floor are separated from the ambassador's reception areas. On the second floor, above the new large entrance opening, a top-lit terrace sits between the residence and the new chancellery, which is the only place from which the terrace can be accessed. Offices and meeting rooms in the new volume offer ample working spaces for the chancellery's eight departments. The void above the terrace on the third floor serves as a light-well for the offices on the top floors.

The materials also activate an exchange between old and new: Oberdorlaer shell limestone, already contained in parts of the existing facade, was added into the flooring of the new wing. Subtly tinted with a unique mixture of coloured sands from Thuringia, the exterior concrete of the extension was designed to match the natural stone of the existing facade. In order to eliminate horizontal joints, which result from building up concrete in layers, the walls were cast in a single pour. This unusually exacting method of construction in a continuous process was achieved by gliding scaffolding that moved up the building as the cement mixture started to harden during the course of the 35-hour pour. The concrete was smoothed further, through sanding, to achieve a fine counterpart to the palace's travertine.

From left:
Public entrance to the new chancellery
Garden facade

Opposite, from top:
South facade
View from northwest,
with the Reichstag in the background

The Ionic semi-pilasters of the palace's facade and Neo-Classical interior were restored with outstanding care, sometimes exceeding conservation requirements. As the architects explain, 'the tissue was reinforced, but no make-up was added.' The original box windows were retained but thermal safety glazing was added inside. The wallpaper, however, was replaced by wall linings in strong colours in order to balance the optical weight of the wooden and stucco ceilings and yet remain within the language of nineteenth-century interiors.

The relief on the west wall was conceived by the artist Helmut Federle, as an integral part of the competition entry, and was cast on site in rough industrial concrete. Federle's relief invokes memories of vanished buildings, so that it is not only a sculpture but remains a wall integral to the building – a wall that is blank and represents what is absent. In all the facets of this project, the past remains present: as volume and as void, as material, texture and colour.

Helmut Federle   The relief has no function, it has no openings, and I gave the surface a corporality through the horizontal and vertical structuring. The grid gives body to the surface. This corporality implies a heaviness, or durability.

From left:
View to the garden from the waiting room
Ambassador's reception area

Opposite:
Light-well on the third floor

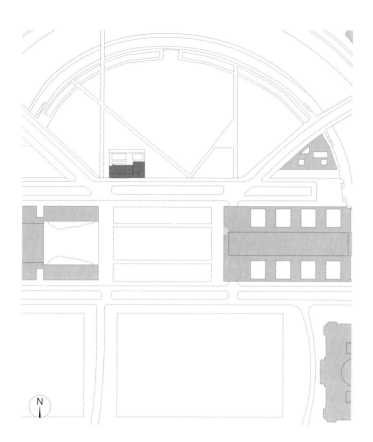

From top:
Site plan
Ground-floor plan

Opposite, from top:
Third-floor plan
South elevation
Longitudinal section

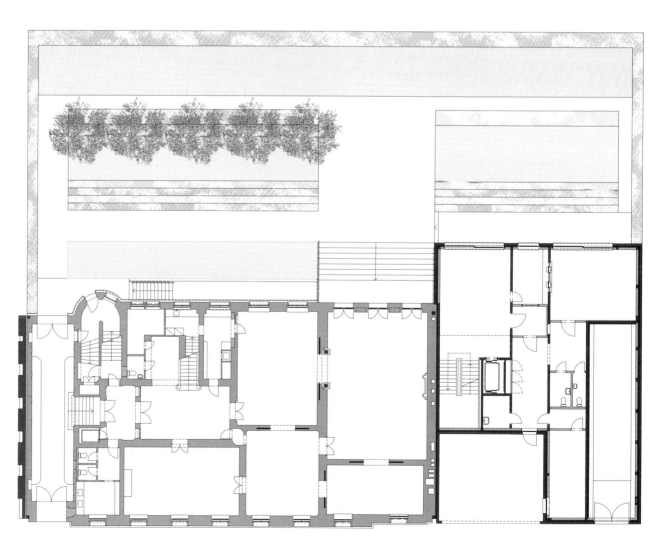

Architecture beyond design

Adam Szymczyk in conversation with Roger Diener

Roger Diener joined the company established by his father, Marcus Diener, in 1976 and then, in 1980, founded his own architectural office, Diener & Diener. His works, his public developments, his residential and commercial buildings as well as his urban plans are an important contribution to Rationalism and the other strands of Modernism in Switzerland. The following conversation with Adam Szymczyk took place on 13 December 2009 in the office of Diener & Diener in Basel.

AS: Did you always know you would become an architect?

RD: As my father was an architect, architecture was an option from early on. However, because he only worked in his office, I rarely saw him at work. Hence, I had an image of an architect but no idea of the architectural practice. It was only later when I was in my final years of grammar school that I took a look around his office. Architects, draughtsmen and the construction managers were strictly separated. I did not really like the atmosphere. Working as an architect did not, therefore, appear desirable, even though I was fascinated by the idea of designing houses.

But in the end I wanted to become a sculptor. Following the recommendation of a friend of my parents, himself a sculptor, I decided to study architecture. He too had gone down this path when training as an artist in Italy. When I arrived at ETH Zürich in 1969–70 I suddenly stepped into the ongoing debate over university politics. I spontaneously enrolled in an unconventional introductory course. That is, I did not enrol with Bernhard Hoesli, the undisputed leading figure among architectural professors. Rather, I signed up for the course with the sociologist Hermann Zinn. From the very first class we dismissed as irrelevant all formal or even compositional aspects

of art and architecture in light of the pressing societal questions raised by architectural construction. It was there that I made the decision to become an architect.

The profound changes in society after 1968 had an impact on architecture. Architects initiated discussions about the role of public space and function of architecture and urbanism. Architecture was to become the means that enabled people to meet in public spaces as subjects actively engaged in society. It provided them with a stage, a platform for communication and participation, a playground and a shelter. Do you see a connection between your work today and the radical concepts of architecture's social function as it was formulated at the time?

At the time, the ETH distanced itself from all such ideas. Bernhard Hoesli based his classes on the foundations of Modernism as laid down by Le Corbusier or Mies van der Rohe, while making the concept of transparency available to architecture in analogy to art. To those of us who sought to draw an immediate connection to social conditions, these radical concepts appeared too formalist. As students in Zurich at the time, there were other radical concepts that occupied us and that have continued to exert an influence on me to this day. This included the Italian Rationalism as introduced to us by Aldo Rossi as well as the attitude taken by Luigi Snozzi, who would become one of my most influential teachers at the ETH. Both Luigi Snozzi's teaching and practice contained a singularly utopian aspect. This also concerned the relationship existing between individuals and the public space. This is a concern also central in our work, though it is less pronounced and expressed with greater rhetorical restraint.

Residential unit in the Gallaratese quarter, Milan, Aldo Rossi, 1969–70

The bombarded city as a monument to the World War II, project for Braunschweig, Luigi Snozzi, 1974

When you were starting out, figures such as Cedric Price, Gianni Pettena, Ettore Sottsass and Yona Friedman were questioning the object-oriented work of the architect. They were emphasizing architecture's utopian dimension. Were their ideas of importance to your development as an architect?

A concern with design and a drive to be creative seemed to overly determine their projects. For this reason it seemed of little relevance if this structuralist production process were to alter the architectural practice. Buckminster Fuller's work held a far greater interest for us – a truly utopian dreamer. Or indeed, Christopher Alexander, who made the individualistic claim to influencing the house's form and its iconic quality part of the architectural production process. I think the greatest difference derives from the concept of utopia. For us this idea remains closely linked to that of the city. It gauges the quality of the public space and the extent to which the individual can avail of it against the yardstick of the city's basic elements and its experience over a great period of time. Our more radical projects make this most apparent – those that are aimed at transforming the city substantially. These are themselves aimed at the city and are concerned with the fundamental distinction that exists between the buildings and public space as well as with the presence of the monuments in this space. The surprise is that our continued attempt at returning to the basic elements of the house and at assembling these to once again form a whole has repeatedly enabled us to create a very special situation within an existing city, whether this be quietly subversive or evidently polemical.

If I understand you correctly, yours was not an attempt to introduce the Modernist renaissance as a neo-style. Rather, your aim was to have at your disposal an architectural ABC. In your

attitude, a structuralist component and an inspiration derived at the time from the linguistic context appear to converge. Now, if typology itself were a merely supra-political category containing a multiplicity of both reactionary as well as progressive types, we could make the false assumption that architecture were a neutral language of forms. How do you respond to this passive, apolitical attitude that considers architecture as the history of merely changing forms?

Yes. There does initially seem to be a contradiction. We have learned to read and to understand architecture, to consider the conditions from which it emerged and how to interpret these, to describe them as conservative, even reactionary, or progressive. When we then describe our designs as having been constructed devoid of any values, this does appear contradictory.

However, a window is quite undeniably a window, as a door is a door. Taken on its face, architecture can hardly be said to speak. To give an example: Julius Posener noted that we are generally too hasty in defining 'fascist' architecture. More often this is simply the case of a pronounced classicism. This is always the case. Nevertheless, it is equally the case that every window expresses those technical, economic and cultural conditions under which it was made and these conditions define the window. I remember an interview, with a journalist, that included Mario Botta and Jacques Herzog. If I remember correctly, Botta said at the time that he was haunted by the idea of not being able to complete all the designs in his head. When we start designing a house, I do not have anything in my mind. The specific premise for the design can only develop from the given conditions of the building project at the given location.

Apartment Buildings Hammerstrasse, Basel

Appartment Building Novocum, Como,
Giuseppe Terragni, 1927–28

West facade of the Swiss Embassy, Berlin,
Helmut Federle

How do you establish a relationship between the design and the given conditions? You had an empty plot at your disposal when you designed the Hammerstrasse residential area, while the Swiss Embassy in Berlin was located in a no man's land near the Berlin Wall. But mostly you needed to fit your design into a densely built-up area.

As I said: we don't shy away from the given conditions, even restrictions that are connected to a specific building project and site. And if we cannot find these constraints, we will even try and discover them. This confrontation with the constraints is vital to us, whether they are real and understandable or whether they are imposed and even when they are annoying.

Following this critical approach, nearly amounting to an architectural 'Minima Moralia', architecture would emerge dialectically from the confrontation of various external events and influences that would include the economy, technology and social conditions, but also the limitations imposed by the client and restrictions resulting from the administrative regulations, each time specific to a given site and situation. The architect, whose work could be likened to that of a skilled translator and not merely creator of new buildings, would be responsible for giving these dynamically changing conditions a specific formulation and interpretation. I'd like to understand the point at which you decide to introduce specific architectural language in order to modify or change the structure that appears to emerge seemingly naturally, as rational conclusion of the different external conditions – and thus turn into your architecture.

As architects we are looking at our projects from different distances at the same time. We try and introduce the themes and develop the rules that will result in a specific design. Within this process we also try to include options that didn't quite correspond to how we imagined them. So far, we are included as participants within this activity. But then there is always also the view onto the whole, the bird's-eye view, so to speak. From this perspective we initially measure out the themes and then subsequently judge the resulting options. For the design of the Hammerstrasse building in 1976, our emphasis was slightly different. Aside from the Rationalist and typological aspects that determined how we shaped the edges, we made quite literal references to specific sources – in this case, the residential building projects of Italian architect Giuseppe Terragni.

You worked with artists on several of your projects. How do you arrange this collaboration and why do you need artists to collaborate on your buildings?

In every case it was a necessity. From the outset we couldn't have imagined working on either the project for the Embassy in Berlin or for Novartis without Helmut Federle. This was due to his body of work. It was this that first enabled us to recognize the potential open to such a collaboration. But the dialogue with Federle as well as his radical defence of his work's autonomy – a defence he upheld despite his great solidarity with the project – these factors were very important and introduced a clarity that then enveloped the entire project.

Some buildings that you developed as the extension to existing buildings overcome the existing building's language and architectural statement, including their political content and their historical determination. The expansion of the Swiss Embassy in Berlin does not interpret the existing building historically. In place of a boring modern variation that has its roots in the morphology of the existing building, you put forward a building

Administration Building Hochstrasse, Basel

that defiantly resists its historical context. And, furthermore, makes a fairly radical political statement concerning the ruin's significance. In my opinion, Helmut Federle's work of art on the building's west facade not only holds the house together – it is also reminiscent of a healing wound, giving the surviving segment of the Berlin Wall a fitting metaphor.

Yes.

Considering what the building stands for, the project's fusion of architectural and artistic thought is significant.

In its archaic and monumental quality, Federle's relief relates to both Berlin's construction and its destruction. And, indeed, it is impressive how much this autonomous work of art can contribute to the project's architectural synthesis.

For your buildings, the immediate neighbourhood and their placement within the city centre appear to be of great importance. Your buildings offer sensitive, discursive answers to the urban environment.

For us, this is probably the greatest challenge. Superimposing the insights, the innumerable achievements and tendencies of Modernism on the idea of the city. These are attempts at finding structural connections within the city that would drive contemporary design, and vice versa. Such buildings are open in both directions. They engage the location, its history and identity, and at the same time they look out beyond this location, and in doing so, they transform it. This should not be understood as a literal complexity, as a visible overlaying. The buildings internalize this tension. The numerous constraints that are extant in the location and within the plan are not

placed in explicit contrast to one another. Instead, these are sublimated within the building's composition. [Looking at a photograph showing the office building on the Hochstrasse in Basel.] Here, for example, the specific outline of this small plot of land defines this office building constructed in 1996. And in that the shape of the oriel was deduced from the given legal requirements; it gives voice to the existing dialogue between building and city space.

With its 'shaved' corner?

Yes, with its shaved corner and overhanging oriel. When the opportunity arises, as is the case with this office building, we don't shy away from giving sculptural expression to our architecture.

Indeed, and it results in an almost anthropomorphic, suprematist portrait.

Discussing the building's cement walls, Martin Steinmann has noted that the surface colouring appears to contain patterns similar to those found in a Rorschach test, into which the viewer projects his own meaning.

Can you name significant sources or other examples of work from which you took existing elements to use in one of your own houses? Are you open to this, or do you try to avoid it?

We have copied elements that we have discovered and that we have found convincing. For example, the Kunstmuseum Basel's exceedingly slender hand-rail. It is unsurpassable. And so we measured it and copied it out. But our design doesn't really include any examples of a consciously apparent strategy to appropriate such elements.

'Basel' door handle, Glutz, 1981

Do you make allusions?

As mentioned, our early designs were direct allusions to the
architectural style known as Neues Bauen [New Building or
New Objectivity]; respectively to Italian Rationalism of the
inter-war years. Over time these allusions disappeared. When
such repetitions are found in more recent work the intention
is not that of quoting the original.

What does this process look like in the office?
You have frequently stated that design comes last.

Yes. But this is only our attempt at describing that drawing does
not provide an approach to design. We talk about the design
and discuss the references within our own work in order to
outline our specific goals with a given design. This process is
both more precise and richer than that driven by the drawing.

But the question is, how does this discussion get translated
into design, before this design has been realized?

In these discussions we outline the design in terms of the
formal aspects that enable this design to be reflected in the
drawing. These conversations are in preparation for the
visual representation.

I've just seen the door handle in this room. Why is it called
'Basel'?

The door handle was initially called 'Diener'. But then the man-
ufacturer realized that other architects didn't want to order
this door handle because it was named after another architect.
And so they changed its name.

Why did you develop a door knob?

It sounds like an anecdote. There was a sales representative
for this company who wanted to sell us door handles. However,
we were not convinced by these handles and so in the end he
offered us the opportunity to come up with our own design.
Our suggestion was to make cost-effective handles using a
zinc-injection moulding with either a polished or enamelled
stainless-steel handle. We only used them in black and white.
But in the meantime all colours have become available, with
the handle even being adapted for windows. We never received
anything for its design, and there is no contact with the company any more.

I was thinking of the extremely simple and precisely finished
form of the door handles in Wittgenstein's house on the Kund-
manngasse in Vienna. In your work I see a tension between
ideas that are close to pure abstraction and ideas that tend
towards functionality and groundedness. The essence of the
object is strongly present in your work.

We were attracted in equal degrees to the plain functional form
as to its appropriation through use, as what Walter Benjamin
described the emancipative form. This in contrast to the individual, contemplative form, which did not interest as much.

Benjamin aimed rather to foreground the object, the specific
house or habit, and to preserve it from any loss of content and
significance suffered through the process of history. He sought
to foreground it and in doing so to underline the material ob-
ject's emancipatory content. For Benjamin the mass-produced
object encountered on the street elicits associations not unlike
those belonging to a mystical secular experience. This stands

Kunstmuseum Basel Extension, Basel, 2009

in contrast to Heidegger's contemplative penetration into the essence of things, comparable to a cult.

This reminds me of something else: in the proposal we developed jointly for the Kunstmuseum Basel's extension, the wood cladding in the rooms poised over the road reminded me of a musical instrument case, like that of a cello or a double bass. It delineates the instrument's form while protecting it. Seeing a musician carrying such a case always awakens my curiosity. I always wonder what kind of music he or she plays. The wood-clad rooms above the streets could also elicit such curiosity.

In a number of writers and thinkers we encounter the idea that reading is a process that is very similar to writing. I'm wondering whether these observations have any bearing on the effect of your buildings, specifically the manner in which they interact with existing urban structures. How these buildings fit into the environment is not only a form of translating the city's structure – it is also a way of reading it. The house is legible, but it also shows your way of reading. It is an interpretation of the environment. Your houses stand out and they assimilate. Just like something that ceases to exist, only to suddenly emerge again.

I think you are referring to important aspects. These reflect back on our practice and onto our position within the architectural scene. One of the effects the Denkmalpflege [Preservation of Historic Monuments] appreciates in contemporary architecture as you describe it, is that it doesn't threaten to reduce the existing historical architecture. However, those who want buildings to have a greater charisma doubt this approach capable of such buildings. This is not a priori wrong, but it does fall short. The Berlin project showed that a visually powerful facade of monumental architecture can unfold the effect you

describe. Do you think this effect of fading and appearing is due to the non-iconic aspect?

I am not trying to polemicize against the much criticized idea of the 'iconic building'. But we can say: there is an iconic aspect to most buildings, and a moment ago you yourself discussed the jettisoning of a false Modernism, or rather the confrontation with the historic neo-Classicist building of the Swiss Embassy. The existing building can be considered an iconic building because it expresses its political power in its use of the usual formal language, such as colonnades, the colossal order, etc. Your extension does not so much oppose it as a metaphor, but rather as an obstinate material presence, a resistance that remains impermeable. Earlier you noted that your building is nearly primitive, even archaic in its appearance. What I think is interesting is that this appearance is not stylistic, is not the result of a process of archuizing. Rather, it is archaic in that it is the result of a very rudimentary decision on translating its function as a very specific facade.

It may be helpful to again turn to our example of our project for the Kunstmuseum's extension. Of course the connecting walkway across the street develops a strong iconic presence as an object, but it also quite effectively conveys its function. This may be part of the special effect you referred to earlier. While the building derives its form from its internal structure as determined by its mission, the expression of its functional value does not change this form. It does not put itself on offer, does not turn towards the viewer.

These explanations allow us to again turn our attention to architecture's dialectic dimension. I am referring to your project for the Gauforum [a monumental complex only partially com-

Office Building Spreedreieck, with "Palace of Tears", Berlin, 2004

pleted by the Nazis between 1937 and 1945, and intended as a model for buildings in other cities]. Your proposal didn't suggest returning to the structure as was designed by the National Socialists. Instead, you wanted to make the skeletal structure visible as it had been erected by the Nazis and then place the shopping mall in front of it.

In the case of the Gauforum, the Weimar Denkmalpflege asked us to design an appropriate facade for this hall. An investor from southern Germany had purchased it and was planning to turn it into a mall offering the latest in shopping experience. This example shows how important it can sometimes be to set aside the announced programme in order to consider the existing situation. In place of the facade we suggested making the shopping mall an ordinary hall erected on the monumental square in front of the Gauhalle. Our intention was to return the Gauhalle to its incomplete state as it existed at the end of the war in 1945.

That is to say, you wanted to place the shopping centre where, according to the plans, the Nazi Party followers would have congregated for their rallies?

Yes. We would have preferred to leave the mass rally square unobstructed as well. However, the square's temporary occupation by a commercial building lasting for, say, thirty years seemed to be more appropriate than turning the hall into a shopping paradise. As we saw it, the unfinished state of the hall put it in a unique position for recalling the Nazi Party's immeasurable and murderous intent as well as its downfall. Because the incomplete hall was given a pragmatic transformation under East German rule, the architectural monument had been obscured since the 1960s.

Which other projects would you include in this series of interventions in historic building sites?

We worked on a similar case for the Tränenpalast [Palace of Tears] in Berlin next to the Friedrichstrasse railway station. Here too we wanted to preserve the monument in the complexity of its construction and save it from the investor's drive to destroy and gentrify. This great multipurpose hall, an example of cheerful and functional East German architecture, was the dramatic scene of many tearful goodbyes after the erection of the Berlin Wall. This was where the West German visitors had to say goodbye to their families under unspeakable conditions. In front of the building two barracks were erected as protection against the weather while queuing for the mandatory and interminable control procedures. To us, these barracks were indispensable components of the Tränenpalast as an architectural monument and so we made these integral to our restructuring concept. However, our concept stood no chance in Berlin, even though we received a lot of support from the Denkmalpflege.

This interview was first published in German in *Prix Meret Oppenheim* 2009, Bundesamt für Kultur (Bern, 2010).

Firmitas

Roger Diener

Collage of Uffici courtyard and
Le Corbusier's Unités d'habitation,
from *Collage City*

As I speak to you today,[1] I am reminded of my own studies at ETH Zürich. Specifically, the winter term of 1974–5, when Mario Botta, invited by Jean-Claude Steinegger, who was a guest lecturer at that time, gave a truly memorable lecture. The school he had designed for Morbio Inferiore was almost completed, and Mario Botta spoke about it for the first time in the German-speaking part of Switzerland. It was a lecture that threw out a lot of sparks, a true firework of ideas. He presented his great design, referring to Le Corbusier's and Louis Kahn's projects for Venice that ultimately led to his own design for the school. You tend to remember only a very few lectures you attended while studying, and for me, this was surely one of them. Mario Botta spoke, if I remember correctly, in the main hall, which was filled to the brim – the place where, before, we had discussed university politics. The main building nurtured a highly intense atmosphere at that time, which you will be hard put to imagine today in what is now mainly used as a day-time convention centre. Mario Botta, though hardly older than we were, encouraged us with his Morbio Inferiore school project to dedicate ourselves to architecture and its practical applications.

Another long, linear building probably influenced us even more at that time. Much has been written about Aldo Rossi's influence on the ETHZ Department of Architecture – but to us, the students, his Gallaratese housing complex was something of an icon. Although I myself was predominantly influenced by Luigi Snozzi as a student, I could not help but fall under Rossi's spell as well. The housing he designed created an entirely new – both scientific and artistic – demand on architecture.

Some years later, in 1984, the gta Institute (part of ETH Zürich), published a German translation of Colin Rowe and Fred Koetter's influential book, *Collage City*. One collage included in the book illustrates the striking comparison of Colin Rowe between the Uffizi courtyard designed by Giorgio Vasari in the sixteenth century, and the building volumes of Le Corbusier's Unités d'habitation – an illustration of the ideas of figure-ground that *Collage City* made an important part of architectural discourse at the time. Bernhard Hoesli, who was teaching at the ETHZ at that time, lovingly commented on its valiant and contesting theses by making a collage that shows the same space celebrated by Colin Rowe in Florence – this time enclosed not by Vasari's building but by Unités d'habitation on both sides. This tongue-in-cheek homage to Le Corbusier made me want to add another version. It shows the same urban space enclosed by all those buildings that so much affected us as students attending the ETHZ around 1975.

Today, invited to speak about firmitas in relation to our own design practice, I shall define this term as broadly as possible. I shall describe our vision of an urban architecture and discuss firmitas so that we can use this term both freely and associatively. This is, let me add, an attempt to speak rather pointedly about work that tries to avoid becoming all too strikingly expressive.

Apparently, current discussion of firmitas is no longer a debate about the actual strength or permanence of a building. At least, not among architects. If we talk of strength, we speak of expression and meaning within contemporary architecture. This is not something that can be taken for granted, as modern architecture reveals the very core of a building volume, which ultimately forms the static diagram of the edifice. In such an uncovered and unconcealed type of architecture, it may seem that actual strength cannot be separated from its expression and may, thus, very well become the object of such a debate.

Administration Building Hochstrasse, Basel

In fact, contemporary architecture has long gone past that point. As early as 1932, Werner Oechslin recognized a new fragmentation of building volumes occurring in modern architecture, and somewhat ironically stated that the fear of losing the building envelope was ultimately unfounded. Even the new curtain walls, he affirmed, could not protect themselves against an analogy with historical load-bearing and structural systems.[2]

We are rather spontaneously tempted to relate firmitas to how we experience weight and balance, relationships whose value is, as explained by art historian Heinrich Wölfflin, based on our own experience of the body. Vitruvius saw this more simply: in Chapter III of *Book I* of his *Ten Books on Architecture*, where he first defined firmitas, utilitas and venustas as the three essential characteristics of architecture, he wrote: 'Durability will be assured when foundations are carried down to the solid ground and materials wisely and liberally selected.'[3] This concept no longer has much to do with our own work, and thus the term firmitas indicates that an architect has become as much necessary as superfluous to building. A discovery that we are harder put to accept than ever before.

Around the same time that the gta Institute published *Collage City*, we designed a small office building, the Administration Building on Hochstrasse. I shall use it as an example to describe our own treatment of such a building, its structure and envelope, and relate it to the term 'firmitas'.

Let me emphasize something right away: the visible, 18 cm (7 in) thick, concrete wall, stained dark by adding 4 per cent iron oxide, is not part of the load-bearing system, which consists of supports, shear walls and floor slabs. And it does not seem

crucial to us whether such a wall is integrated into the load-bearing system of the entire building. In other designs, which – seen from outside – are hardly different from this one, this proved possible and of course, such a simplification is to be preferred. But for the Administration Building on Hochstrasse, the particular geometry of the building site and the subsequent consequences for the building volume and the organization of the load-bearing structure were much more important to us. A solid, regular skeleton made of reinforced concrete takes up the rectangular ground plan of the building. At its front, it is delimited by a diagonal flush with the boundary of the plot. In its structure, the house is subject to the strict rules integrated into it and it is simultaneously, immediately and compactly fitted into the surrounding urban space. None of its parts is extraordinary, with the sole exception of a projection that was positioned in order to moderate the three-dimensional effect of the building volume created by the diagonally positioned wall. For the same reason, we had the shear wall made of black clinker bricks – something we probably would refrain from today. The window openings are cut according to simple numerical ratios, with each window spanning an entire load-bearing field. The openings are very large. But in spite of their unusual dimensions, they are still windows.

One of the properties of such projects – those that might come under the heading 'firmitas' because it cannot possibly be assigned to any of the other categories Vitruvius listed – is this: they are visibly designed as houses. 'House' not in a pictorial sense but as a fabric of various structures that are by tradition related to architecture. Firmitas, thus, is less a matter of strength than of durability, the permanence of an edifice within the history of which it is an integral part. Such a project does not claim to represent a specific type. We do not aim to distil an essence of architectonic space, and it is not our aim to limit the architectonic form to the absolutely essential. Rather, it is a simple, synoptic handling of those parts that have again and again determined architecture, and our appropriation of them in the course of history, that we emphasize in our buildings. Something seemingly reductionist at first glance may thus actually be the result of a construction or a fabric that we wish to be generous and meaningful and to lack nothing. This method of design, however, does not lead to buildings that you feel you know or that seem familiar. This probably also has to do with our practice of discarding any Classical decoration whatsoever, and with the general expression buildings thus constructed tend to assume. No architectonic gesture seems to determine the character of such an edifice. In particular its special, striking parts seem to be governed by rules outside the architect's ken. But even those parts – such as, for example, the diagonal wall in the Administration Building on Hochstrasse – are once again integrated into the overall structure: in this building, by the projection. Here, a reciprocal relationship between the building and the surrounding urban space is established. The house has been cut into the urban space, and the urban space in turn has conferred form to the building. That's why it is not solely the darkly stained concrete that made the small office building seem to be of indefinite age from its very first day. Only the immovable link the house established with the urban space absolves it from the moment of its own production. The already-mentioned general expression, as well as the regularity of the structure and its various constituent parts, add to this impression of permanence. The 'house' seems to hold both older and more recent buildings within its confines. Here, firmitas means a type of permanence integrated into a general idea of architecture on a specific site.

Based on our design approach, we make a building and its structure assume a certain permanence by using traditional and proven elements. These include the space as such, its organization, and the parts it is limited by – that is, the walls, doors and windows. The load-bearing structure only indirectly influences the shape of the building as seen from outside. Mostly, it becomes one with the rhythm of the facade. The load-bearing structure is visible on the facade much like a shadow falling from inside onto the external wall. The most traditional facade structure – closed walls rhythmically structured by windows – remains decisive. The size and proportion of the wall openings, their depth, and the shapes of the windows are our first concern. They are at the same time a constant and a variable aspect within each composition, a repertoire of structures whose concrete elaboration as a facade generates a new but related figure every time. In some projects, the windows expand and the external walls approach the shape of a skeleton; sometimes they remain without windows at all. Contrary to other assumptions, we subject all design elements within the envelope and its structure to this first, systematic expression. We do not strive for specific meanings to be evoked by the material and its application – in fact, quite the contrary. For us, the external wall is there to support the primary building envelope and relate it to the urban space. The wall is not a mirror image, a reconstruction of the construction. Instead, much like a membrane, it enables an exchange between the building and the town. Sometimes, the interior of the building seems to breathe through this wall membrane. And this has nothing to do with whether the wall is made of wood or concrete, nor with the size of the openings or the windows. It is much more a matter touching upon the relationship of the material to the structure of the building and the surrounding town. In the best circumstances, the wall structure will be accepted as a

East facade, Vogesen School, Basel

Classroom window, Vogesen School, Basel

matter of course and is, thus, so matter-of-fact that it seems equally part of the building and part of the town. It remains an integral part of an entire network of relationships generated by the individual elements and their arrangement within the edifice. The substance of the wall does not stand out from the simple iconographic programme of these parts. We do not try to provoke another perception outside the given, conventional meanings. The buildings remain integrated into an architecture whose perception is irrevocably linked to its individual and social appropriation – to a way of life.

Thus we ponder the depth of the window within the wall – the reveal, the place where the interior of the building relates to the town and all of a sudden becomes a space of its own. Where the general and permanent coincide. Once this detail is selected and constructed, the uniqueness of the building is determined. We are not really interested in any attempts to reduce the expression of a building so that its volume alone becomes effective as an object in its particular composition; nor in a rich play of gestures with attached pictorial elements (this is a position outside current tendencies: to some, such buildings seem not clear-cut enough; others consider them suspicious because of their trivial appearance).

The analogy to so-called Concrete Architecture, in the sense of Max Bill's artistic principles, has occasionally been mentioned in relation to our buildings. However, Max Bill's approach was to remove radically the parts that he used from their traditional fabric, in order to combine them into a new, autonomous entity. In our compositional process, we use parts that retain their coherence with architecture and its appropriation. From this point of view, the process recalls Christopher Alexander's pattern language, rather than Max Bill's Concrete Architecture.

When discussing firmitas in relation to our wall construction, the relationship to the load-bearing structure of a building is of minor significance – sometimes only consisting of necessary, geometric and spatial coordination. As mentioned before, we seek a shape for the external wall that is able to render the building legible within the surrounding urban space, while still being anchored to the building itself and its logic, to something not present on the outside. For the Vogesen School in Basel, we went back to the wall construction we first used around 1987. Prefabricated concrete modules are combined into a wall. The individual modules are 160 cm long, 70 cm high, and 12 cm deep (63 x 28 x 5 in). The joints between them are narrow and filled with cement, flush with the surface. Porphyry within the concrete helped create a green tint. Different window sizes for the classrooms, the staircase and the lavatories are arranged to avoid a hierarchy of openings within the facade. The facade seems dense but not heavy. The building is able to assert itself against the two large school buildings with which it forms a courtyard. But it also suggests that its spatial organization is less rigid and institutional than its neighbours. In fact, it is a composite-steel load-bearing structure that we selected in order to enable us to build it in as short a period as possible. The entire composition strives to balance the various forces it is affected by – the urban ones as well as the functional ones. In the final design, they all remain within this envelope, which does not assign priority to any of its individual aspects. The windows are rather large, it is true, but the concrete-module walls are arranged so that their dimensions do not generate an excessively striking effect.

Administration Building Picassoplatz, Basel

Gmurzynska Gallery, Cologne

The interior space is integrated into a similar structure, to allow it to find an appropriate relationship with the town outside. Here, the arrangement of the large, rectangular classroom windows creates a special atmosphere, an effect enhanced by the colourfulness of the rooms. The light and colours of the town, visible through the large windows, equally affect the interior space. The idea of calibration, of establishing a balance between the inside and the outside, becomes quite apparent. The classroom walls are painted in colours that, according to the principles of painter Peter Suter, are based on a variety of stucco colours found on the nineteenth- and twentieth-century buildings in this neighbourhood. The urban atmosphere carried into the building through its large windows is thus captured and restrained.

The envelope regulates the exchange between the building and the town. You might say that here, strength or firmitas is achieved not by the dominance of the edifice but by a balancing of the various forces which, in turn, allow a lighter construction of the envelope.

The external wall of Administration Building on Picassoplatz in Basel, was designed in the same manner. The dominant features are corbels on all sides of the building, between which cast-stone tiles are erected to the height of the entire storey. As at Hochstrasse, we wanted to construct a coherent, closed building and the relief-type corbels, surrounding the whole structure, blend the various building volumes into a whole. This external wall has, however, become something of a small 'fall from grace'. From our point of view, our attempt to combine urban and architectonic aspects in its design has turned out to be somewhat too expressive. It is ironic, then, that this very facade drew special attention; Martin Steinmann has said

that it was a realization of load-bearing both as a construction element and as an image of construction, and that it had been less technical than perceptual and psychological considerations that had determined the design. In this interpretation, the building seems to adopt a Classical theme of architecture and interpret it in another form, separate from the edifice itself. However, the driving motive behind the design was less a novel interpretation of load-bearing and load, or even of 'weight', than an examination of the treatment of a particular form and the way architecture has generated it time and again. Such a form may also include meanings not necessarily or explicitly interpreted in a novel manner. These meanings are part of the forms. Let me add that the external wall design of this office building was generated by the client's demand that the building be clad in natural-stone tiles and thus distinguish itself in a favourable manner from our earlier projects.

The Gmurzynska Gallery, designed in 1988, has sometimes been related to those examples of Soviet avant-garde art that the gallery has systematically collected and promoted for many years. However, it would be wrong to consider it a kind of contemporary reaction to this progressive artistic concept and vision. As already mentioned, for our work, references to traditional aspects of building are equally as valid as those of the twentieth-century avant-garde.

The red colour is, however, not without significance. Set in a park in Cologne, red is particularly vivid against a background of its complementary colour – green – found on the trees and bushes there. Red is a warm colour. It seems to approach the observer. At the same time, the red establishes a certain coherence. The special force of this colour enabled us to design the individual surfaces of the building volume in distinct

Office Building Kohlenberg, Basel

ways without discarding the overall impression of a single entity. Red protects the wooden cladding, which, in turn, shelters the entire structure in a protective layer. In spite of its signal effect, the red remains, we think, rather informal. Its choice lets us suppose that it is a matter-of-fact part of the mental and material world so unique to this gallery.

This example shows clearly that such an architecture is not created as part of a process of reduction. Quite the opposite, in fact: known objects are compacted into a general form comprising many different things. The building is made part of a real relationship that it helped create in the first place. The edifice has found its complex form in a process. In the best scenario, it is an expression of the balance of the manifold forces affecting it. The composition is, thus, a result of a debate. It is neither idealized, nor purified. No strong direction or decisive design vision can be perceived. Somehow, the building appears to be moved by external as well as internal forces. It remains balanced, whether the framing of the upper-floor hall was made a visible element on the gabled facade in order to emphasize the special public purpose of the building, or whether it was done in order to make a particular arrangement with the door on the ground floor of the facade.

None of the functional or structural conditions of the edifice is enhanced or taken as a theme, though they are integrated into the overall design. In 1853, Karl Rosenkranz proposed similar compositional rules for something he called 'das Kunsthässliche' [approximately, ugliness in art]:

Art has to show its secondary nature and then remind us that it originally does not exist by itself but only as part of the beautiful or as opposed to the beautiful, as its negation. If it is shown in this accidental position, everything that affects it as a moment within a harmonious whole has to be taken into account. It may not be pointless but prove to be necessary. It has to group in an appropriate manner and subject itself in its entirety to the laws of symmetry and harmony which it violates with its own design; it may not stand out more than suitable for this context and has to show a force of individual expression which nevertheless allows us to recognize its significance.[4]

Here, we emphasize the importance of the compositional rule that specifies that not only the sublime may be included. However, we should speak only of balance in lieu of symmetry and a harmonic order between the various elements.

If we add the term 'clarity' to that of 'firmitas' as an important quality in the perception and understanding of an edifice, we have to include the social, economic and cultural dimension of building production. A building such as the one in Cologne, situated among bourgeois villas, may only be explained on the basis of the impetus provided by the client specifying that she wanted a house for her art gallery. In order to understand and channel these production processes, which are often trying to satisfy conflicting or confusing forces, it may be necessary for the architect to insist on examining parts of the building process that are not normally thought of as part of their task.

Thus, I stated my opinion at a symposium on the possible sense and purpose of a reconstruction of Schinkel's Bauakademie [Building Academy, 1831–5, destroyed 1961] on the same site it originally occupied – namely, that urban planning or archi-

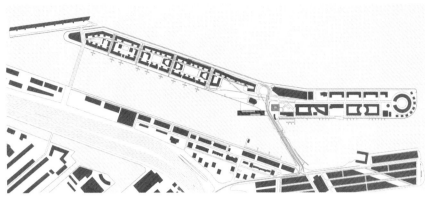

Aerial view of KNSM and Java Island, Amsterdam, 1987

Site plan, Apartment Buildings KNSM and Java Island

tectonic arguments alone would not justify a reconstruction. Another precondition would have to be a meaningful relation between client, building tasks and building type. This requires a production logic resting within the building proper – its *raison d'être*. I proposed Deutschen Ziegelindustrie [the German Brick Industry Association] as builders. Thus, a newly erected Bau-akademie could be made witness to the act of reconstruction and approved as a representation of an industry, demonstrating the tradition and usefulness of the industry's product.

In the Office Building Kohlenberg, on Barfüsserplatz in Basel, we considered the relationship between inside and outside, determined by spatial dimensions and windows: ultimately, a compositional exercise. We were seeking dimensions for the rooms and their openings that would relate the inside to the outside, dimension to be found in the tension between a tradi-tional window-frame and a large glazed surface that seems to dissolve the usual boundaries of a room. As we realized when building the Vogesen School, in the best of cases we experience such rooms as places that open informally towards a town-scape while at the same time forming an integral part of that town. These rooms are not restricted to a specific function, but are for the tenants to use in a general way – equally suitable for work and as dwellings in a stricter sense. They are drawing from the surrounding town and – once they have become part of it – participating in it.

This Office Building Kohlenberg is situated on an inner city square in Basel. It is a corner building, erected according to our plans on a plot of only 66 m² (710 sq ft). The load-bearing construction consists of a one-layer external wall of yellow-stained concrete. Inside, a heat-insulation layer was applied. There is one window per storey on the side facing the street.

The windows are staggered and create a slightly rhythmic play of forms. In spite of this, the facade does not seem restless but rather restful. A first, regular inner arrangement of the facade was modified to integrate the building more precisely into the given urban context. The facade composition was not inciden-tal, but we tried to avoid the impression of thorough regularity. There is no gesture. The building does not emphasize its corner position – it simply forms a corner. The impression of strength is only created by the urban context by which it is surrounded. Alone, the building would appear to disintegrate.

Even in a free urban context, the impression of permanence may be bound to other buildings. In the building complex of Java Island, in Amsterdam's Eastern Docklands, where we are working on apartment buildings, this becomes quite clear. An aerial photograph shows the island in 1987, with the town-scape in the background. Since then, most of the two sides of the island have been built on and urbanized.

Our proposed building project for this transitional area uses for reference the character of the island bestowed by the historic Amsterdam docks. This project creates an understanding of how the island came into being, and puts its entire facility within the context of the neighbouring commercial pier and the exam-ples of old harbour architecture.

In such a context, not only do new buildings have to find their meaning but the old ones need to be integrated as well, and thus be re-created. It is the aim of this approach to create a certain balance or harmony between all existing parts. The long, linear building volume in the west, the 'longhouse', acts as a pendulum keeping the entire composition in balance. All volumes seem to be integral parts in this play of forces.

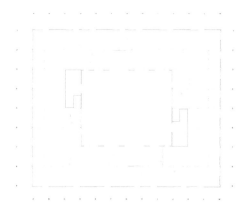

Typical floor plan, courtyard building,
Apartment Buildings KNSM and Java Island,
Amsterdam

'Longhouse', Apartment Buildings KNSM and Java Island,
Amsterdam

Any movement of an individual building volume would make us expect shifts throughout of the entire composition.

The concentric organization of the court type and the orientation of the volume along the island's axis have provided the building with its specific shape. The building volume seems to be held simultaneously within static and dynamic forces. This unstable balance continues right into the flats, which are arranged in a non-hierarchical sequence: long and rectangular, with front or lateral windows and doors, depending on the flat's position, the individual rooms seem at once quiet and restless, much like the entire building.

Different from the large residential buildings with their play of windows, loggias and balconies, this longhouse shows only a single window type, but the openings lose their abstract, geometric character as each is shifted by half a brick and thus turned into actual building blocks within the volume. The expression of a rough, ancient building structure with inserts remains paramount.

The proximity to storage or shipping buildings allows the coherence created by the planned houses and the old harbour buildings to remain part of the island's character. Beyond the spatial arrangement, these relationships between similar building organizations and structures, even between the very bricks, link and distinguish the old and the new buildings. Permanence will have to come in time, though, and if it comes to these apartment buildings, it will be only because they contain both the present and the history of this place within themselves.

Let me conclude with an apparent paradox relating to the 'permanence' of architecture and its basis: a design for prefabricated houses that will be part of the large output of Deutsches Fertighaus [German Prefabricated Houses] next year. The load-bearing wood structures are prefabricated at the factory and assembled on site. The cladding consists of solid wooden planks also assembled on site. Each residence has a surface area of 180 m² (1,940 sq ft) shared between two storeys.

The individual houses consist of two cubes, each of a different size, combined and slightly staggered one against the other. Thus an individual spatial system of relationships is developed within each house, and the various parts are able to create spaces among themselves. This arrangement modulates the necessarily accidental relationship that each building will have to its site in this kind of production and distribution system. The different wall surfaces of the building volumes are partially left in their raw state and partially painted. Individual walls could conceivably be clad with photovoltaic panels. The colour hues may change according to the actual place. Whether the site is suburban or rural, has particular topographic conditions or other aspects, may determine whether the building will be used for, for instance, residential purposes or work. Whatever the case, residents will have the opportunity to customize their house with a particular, individual expression towards the external world.

Here, too, we see another type of strength or permanence. And here, too, it is a matter of arranging the entire range of thoughts and things, of preconditions and consequences within the edifice and combining it into a well balanced whole. The essence of firmitas is not weight, nor an accumulated load, but this balance of each and every part and its meanings within an urban fabric, a space, a time.

This has probably always been felt, or at least this is how we interpret the wonderful words of Heinrich von Kleist, written in 1800:

I entered town, pensively, through the arched gate, pondering it. Why, I thought, does the arch not fall down being without any support? It remains standing, I answered my own question, because all the stones would wish to fall at one and the same time.[5]

1 This is the edited transcript of a lecture given by Roger Diener at ETH Zürich,
   29 October 1996.
2 Werner Oechslin, Lynnette Widder, *Otto Wagner, Adolf Loos and the Road to Modern
   Architecture*, Cambridge University Press, Cambridge, 2002), p.131.
3 Vitruvius, *The Ten Books on Architecture*, trans. by Morris Hicky Morgan (Cambridge:
   Harvard University Press, 1914), p.17.
4 Karl Rosenkranz, *Ästhetik des Hässlichen* [1853] (Leipzig, 1990), p. 42.
5 The original German reads: 'Ich ging an jenem Abend vor dem wichtigsten Tage meines
   Lebens in Würzburg spazieren. Als die Sonne herabsank, war es mir, als ob mein Glück
   unterginge. Mich schauerte, wenn ich dachte, dass ich vielleicht von allem scheiden
   müsste, von allem, was mir teuer ist. Da ging ich, in mich gekehrt, durch das gewölbte Tor
   sinnend zurück in die Stadt. Warum, dachte ich, sinkt wohl das Gewölbe nicht ein, da es
   doch keine Stütze hat? Es steht, antwortete ich, weil alle Steine auf einmal einstürzen
   wollen - und ich zog aus diesem Gedanken einen unbeschreiblich erquickenden Trost, der
   mir bis zu dem entscheidenden Augenblicke immer mit der Hoffnung zur Seite stand,
   dass auch ich mich halten würde, wenn alles mich sinken lässt.' Heinrich von Kleist 'Briefe
   an Wilhelmine von Zenge (Letters to Wilhelmine von Zenge)', *Sämtliche Werke und Briefe
   (Collected Works and Letters)* vol 2, p. 593. (Kleist to Wilhelmine von Zenge,
   16 & 18 November, 1800).

Masterplan for the University Harbour
Malmö 1997

Competition **1st prize** *Client* **City of Malmö, Malmö University**

By 1997, with the rise of development encouraged by the building of the Øresund Bridge connecting the south of Sweden and Denmark, Malmö's harbour and wharf remained only partially an industrial site. Although Sweden was once the world's second largest ship-building nation, many of its associated industries had been relocated. The inner harbour area, just across from the main station and next to the old town, became home to a newly founded public university.

This winning scheme, chosen from an international competition, proposed the university's successive expansion onto several harbour islands. In the first phase, two buildings – institutional and welcome centres – met the immediate needs of the new university. The drawings for phases two and three outlined successive development: new services and businesses would operate alongside the huge cranes that would still load containers onto ships at the north end of the inner harbour. The buildings were modelled on the conglomerate character of the harbour's industrial buildings. Over time, along-side the growth of the North Sea economies, many of the university buildings have been extended. The project appropriates the typology of open-structured clusters, which can grow according to the changing needs of users.

Industrial buildings, Malmö

Opposite:
Aerial view of the harbour, 2005

These buildings, amalgamations of new and old, stand on a continuous public zone, without areas assigned to different modes of traffic; the only rule is that bicycles and cars must yield to pedestrians. The buildings are distributed on the ground plan as nuclei, objects that can trigger further development. This concept of urban tissue as a capillary structure, already a part of the Warteck project in Basel half a decade earlier, was expanded at a much larger scale in Malmö's inner harbour. The surrounding sea lays out a landscape of vast scale that forms the reference for the new urban fabric.

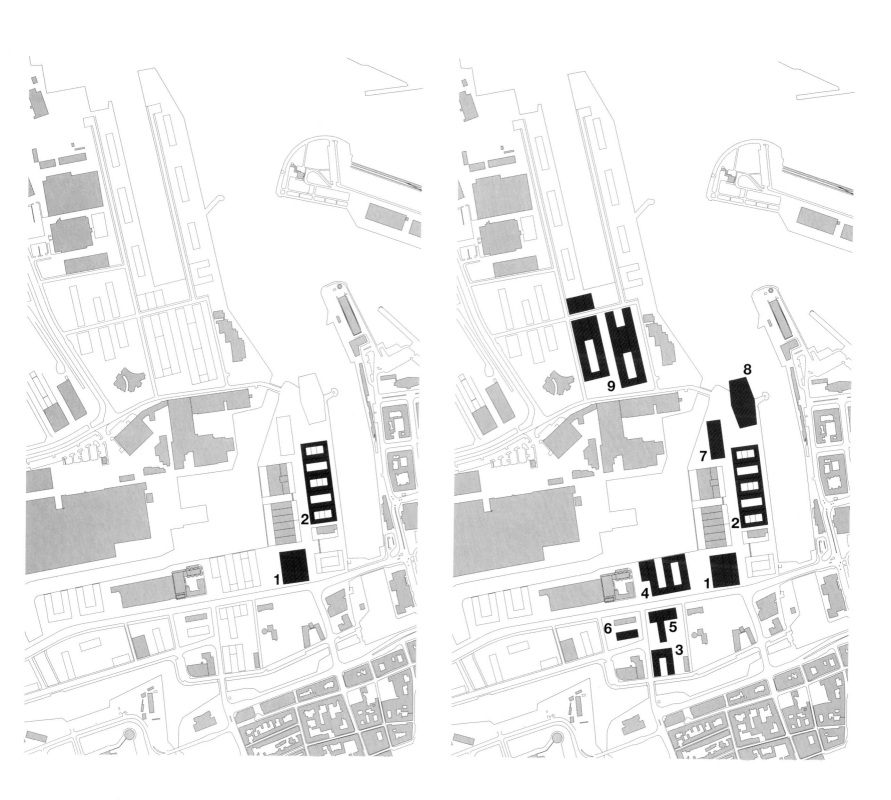

RD   The design for the master plan derived its orientation from the industrial structures of the harbour and the dockyard. The spatial and functional complexity on the
site has an exceedingly urban character. The masterplan is based on the idea of clusters.
This results in an image that offers the possibility for the growth of new structures, and
the initital University Building along the waterfront is itself designed as a cluster.

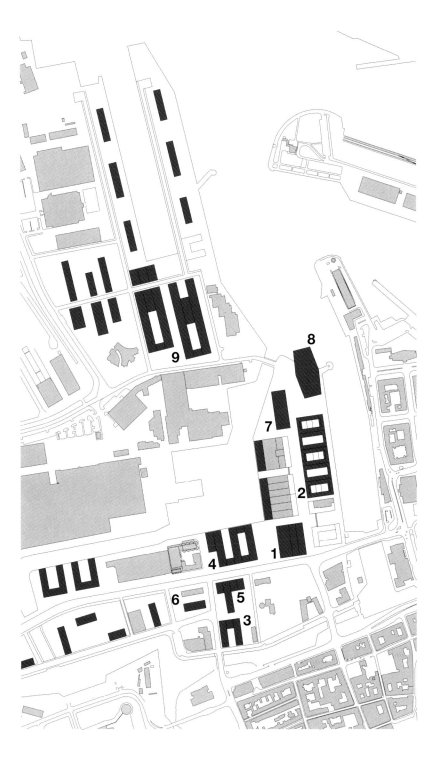

Masterplan, Stage 1–3 (from left to right)

1. Library
2. University Centre
3. School of Fine Arts
4. School of Music and Dramatic Art
5. School of Art and Communication
6. Space for external services
7. Experience Centre
8. Concert Hall
9. School of Education and the Centre for Competence Development

University Building, Malmö 2003–2005

Client **DIL Nordic AB and Deutsche Bank** *Structural Engineer* **Centerlöf & Holmberg** *Mechanical Engineer* **Sycon Teknikkoinsult**
Local Architect **Fojab arkiteter** *Interior Design* **Fojab arkitetker** *Landscape Architect* **Per Friberg**

As a result of planning changes, two distinct programmes for a library and a teachers'
training centre at Malmö University's harbour site were merged into one building. Within
a continuous public ground zone, which is shared by cars, cyclists and pedestrians alike,
and with a main axis called The Mall, the Orkanen building stands as a solitary volume
facing the university building on Skeppsbron Pier. The name 'Orkanen' (Swedish for
'hurricane') was given to the pier and the building by the university. The building mediates
between the harbour and the city centre, which due to the new cultural and educational
programmes, seem to have moved closer since the university was established.

The building – which retained the form of the competition project as a series of
five courtyard units, with the library occupying an additional, taller floor topping the
whole structure – serves both prospective teachers and the public. Its organization creates no hierarchy of access: five passages slice the ground floor into six separate volumes
between which the stairs are located. It is a space that is highly permeable, both to the
street on the west side, and the waterfront to the east. The overhang of the volume draws
the public space into the building and, from there, into the courtyards.

The ground floor houses the main hall, auditorium, cafeteria, gym and administration. Only the main hall, in the third of the five courtyards, is roofed over, creating a
spatial focus. On the upper floors, lecture rooms are placed along the exterior walls and
diverse types of work areas occupy the inside, on the courtyard sides. The different zones
are arranged along continuous corridors, which run through the entire length of the building. The plan's informal arrangement provides the flexibility required by the investor:
at the end of the university's twenty-year lease it would be possible to turn the teachers'
training centre into an office building.

Opposite:
Facade on the waterfront,
showing passages through the building

Next page:
View from northeast

The movement of the facade traces the organization of the plan: the location of each of the courtyards is marked by an inward and an outward bend. Ripple glass, 12 mm (½ in) thick, an industrial material with a standard green tint, is used for the building's front. The facade's substructure and its fasteners are chosen to blend in with the glass. Particular effects activated by the angled geometry of the glass surfaces are multiplied through the layered construction, in which a second reflective surface, made of aluminium sheets covering the insulation, is set 3.5 cm (1 ½ in) back from the glass. In between the two layers a permanent installation by the university's first artists-in-residence displays chrome letters.

The glass reflects the Nordic light, the sky with its clouds, and the sea, creating patterns and shades in green, silver and blue, that continually change according to the time of day and the season.

RD   Architecture aligns itself towards a universal form, irrespective of the many circumstances influencing its specific formation in each individual case. Such an alignment is the necessary precondition for architecture to be inserted into the context of the city.

View from the library on the top floor

Opposite:
Glass facade

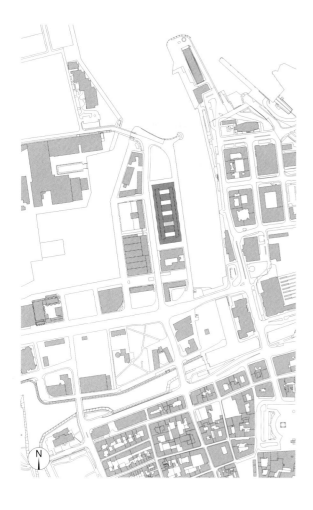

Clockwise from top left:
Site plan
Facade detail, elevation and section
Longitudinal section

Opposite, from top:
Fourth-floor plan, showing the library
First-floor plan
Ground-floor plan

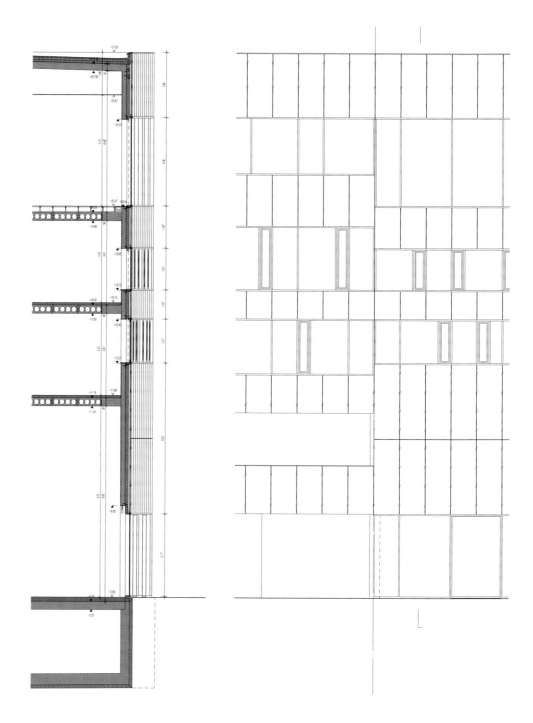

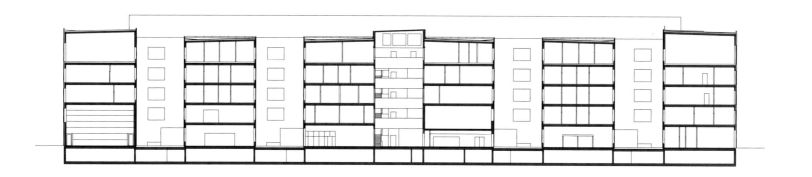

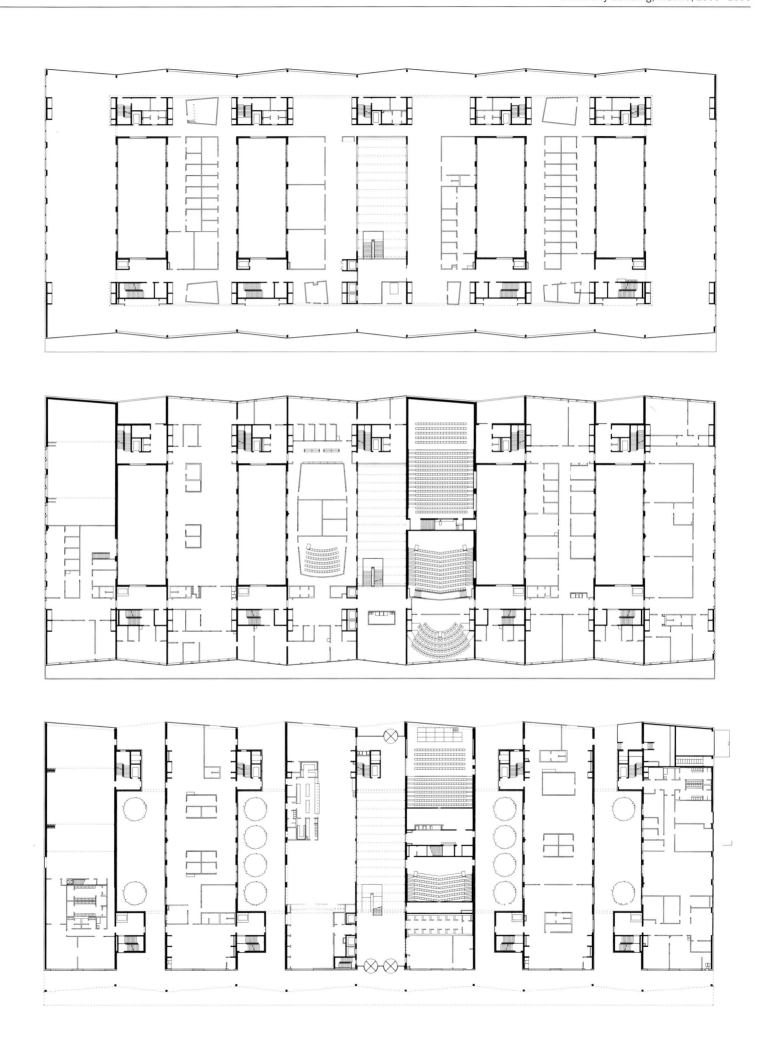

Presentation of the '1998 Guest of Honour, Switzerland' at the Frankfurt Book Fair, Frankfurt am Main 1998

in collaboration with **Peter Suter** *Client* **Bundesamt für Kultur and Christoph Vitali, Haus der Kunst, Munich** *Steel Construction and Textile Fashioning* **Stahl &Traumfabrik**

In 1998, Switzerland was the Guest of Honour at the 50th Frankfurt Book Fair. Usually, the Guest of Honour's literature, culture and history are presented in a specially designed temporary pavilion on Obeliskenhof. In 1998, however, a banner above Obeliskenhof proclaimed 'Switzerland is just next door' and directed the visitors towards an adjacent warehouse. The Swiss Pavilion was not designed as a special edifice, but installed in Hall No. 7, a 2,300 m² (25,000 sq ft) space normally used for storage, which provided an unusually large area. Furthermore, the national presence represented less a promotional statement and more a space for reflection.

The 6.5 m (21 ft) height of Hall No. 7 was visually and acoustically left open, the space divided into sequential units by cotton curtains and felt panels in different colours, with linings to improve the room's acoustics. The curtains were hung from a framework of untreated steel profiles, suspended 40 cm (16 in) below the ceiling. They demarcated seven zones for the different programmes, with a library in the central space forming the main feature. From the foyer, where general information was laid out on tables, a cloakroom was placed to the left, and a café to the right. The TV studio, located behind the cloakroom, was equipped with eight screens suspended from a steel grid, showing different films from Swiss cultural history. The simultaneity of the visitors in the studio, live images and recordings created multiple dialogues. These juxtapositions were further heightened by the concurrent events in the two small auditoriums, which were connected to the TV studio by a second access. At the rear was an exhibition area featuring an installation by artist Hans-Peter Litscher, which presented the history of the Swiss bibliophile Henry van der Weid and the literary culture of his time. At the centre of the large hall, the library's tables of books evoked the atmosphere of a monastic collection, inspired by the one at St. Gallen's cloister. The preciousness of the books and display was deliberately contrasted with the rough and vast architecture of the hall.

'Switzerland is just next door' directed the visitors towards an adjacent warehouse

Opposite:
Curtains are used to divide the hall

In the library installation, 1,400 books were laid out on two rows of long tables, 10, 12 and 14 m (33, 39.5 and 46 ft) in length. The books were wrapped in bindings indicating only each book's author, title and publisher. The colour of each jacket, manufactured specially for the installation, indicated the language of each book: one for each of Switzerland's four national languages – German, French, Italian and Romansch. A fifth colour was used for all other languages. The books in their original covers could be viewed and read beyond the line of desks, alongside the curtains. In this atmosphere, away from hectic publishing business, the pavilion offered a tranquil alternative to the promotional props characteristic of the rest of the fair: just as in a library, nothing here should dispute the primary importance of words.

Peter Suter The decision not to house the Swiss contribution to the Frankfurt Book Fair in a specifically erected pavilion indicates the process of identity formation that Switzerland was engaged in at the fair. Moving the 'Swiss Pavilion' out from the centre of fair underlines this reflective attitude. The mobile and provisional character of the textile spatial dividers also maintains the warehouse character inside the pavilion. The choice to use the hall proved to be more than a mere displacement on the fair ground; the location emphasized the processional quality of the exhibitions, presentations, and conversations, which don't lay claim to being definitive statements.

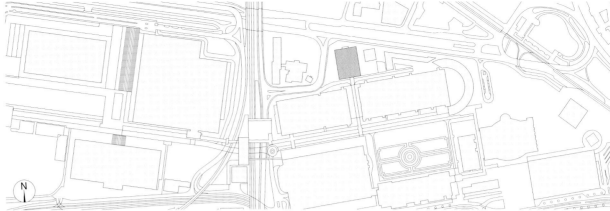

From top:
Site plan
Installation plan

Opposite:
View of the library installation

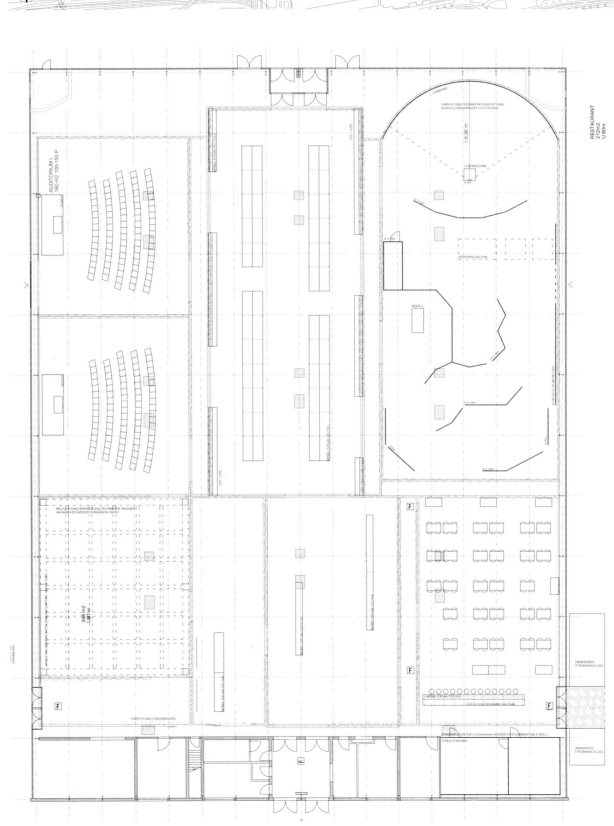

Apartment and Office Building Bäumleingasse, Basel 1999–2005

Client **Edwin Faeh** *Structural Engineer* **Schnetzer Puskas Ingenieure** *Mechanical Engineer* **Rosenmund**

The two-storey pavilion with shop facing Bäumleingasse in 1984

Opposite:
Street facade

Page 184:
Facade on Bäumleingasse

Page 185:
Glazed facade of the rear building

Bäumleingasse, in Basel's old town, connects Freie Strasse and the hill on which the prominent red sandstone Romanesque and Gothic Münster stands. Court and municipal buildings line the small street, and prestigious clothes shops and lawyers keep their addresses there. The plot of 14 Bäumleingasse is narrow and deep. The segment at its centre, historically named Haus Zum Vergnügen [House of Pleasure], dates from the Middle Ages. The earliest documented date is 1327 but most of the existing parts are from the fifteenth century.

A previous project proposed entirely replacing the building, but was thankfully shelved due to the economic downturn of the 1980s. Subsequently, Diener & Diener's proposal was developed in collaboration with the city's landmark department. The facade, the roof and the historical rooms of different periods were renovated using state of the art conservation methods. A two-storey pavilion that was added in 1874 and which had projected from the building was taken down. The restored facade, which is now listed, stands 5.7 m (19 ft) back from today's building line. In front of it is a fully glazed, filigreed four-storey building layer.

In Diener & Diener's scheme, the structure of the medieval building is veiled by elements made of concrete, which are tinted red and sandblasted to blend in with the neighbouring facades, partially built of sandstone. A slender, off-centre middle post, horizontal beams and large glass panes, held in copper-clad aluminium frames, incorporate the geometry of the street into the building front, forming a composition of the many layers of the building's history and use.

The extension allowed additional rooms to be created on all the floors between the medieval facade and the current building line. The ground floor, which extends to the back end of the plot, is rented out for retail use. A first-level courtyard allows light into the office spaces on the upper floors, both in the restored building and in the new building at the back. The top floor houses an apartment that extends onto a generous terrace on the roof of the rear building.

The concrete of the staircase, which serves both the front and rear buildings, is stained light ochre, creating an earthy context for the historic parts. The small courtyard on the first floor combines the facades from different periods into a new ensemble. The inner courtyard is laid with wooden planking, with a skylight to illuminate the ground-floor space. Like the street facade elements, the fully glazed facade of the rear building – with deep, horizontal concrete beams tinted red and sandblasted – establishes a dialogue with the restored historical facade.

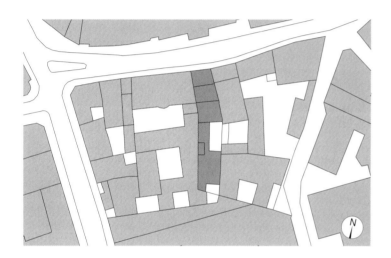

From top:
Site plan
Longitudinal section

Opposite, from left:
Ground-floor plan
Third-floor plan
Fourth-floor plan

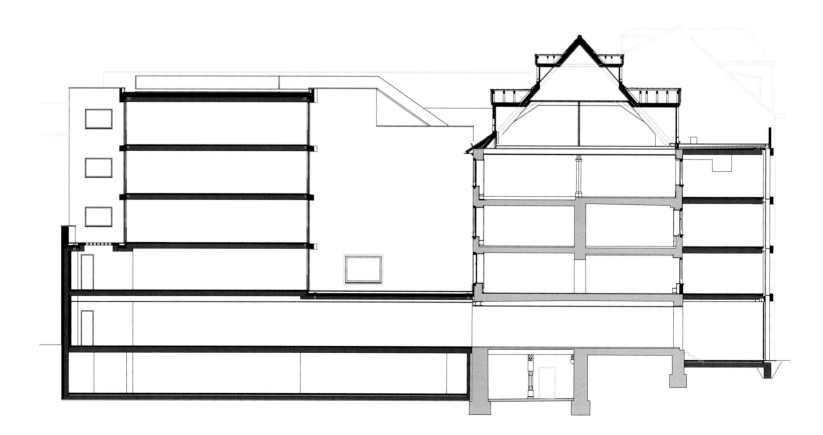

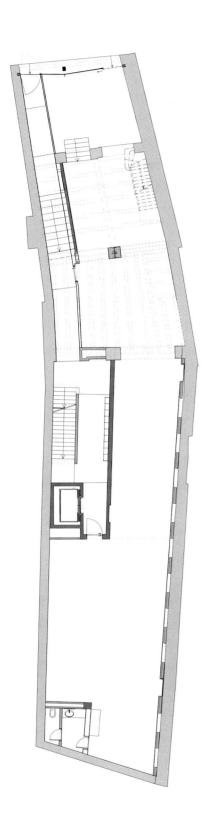
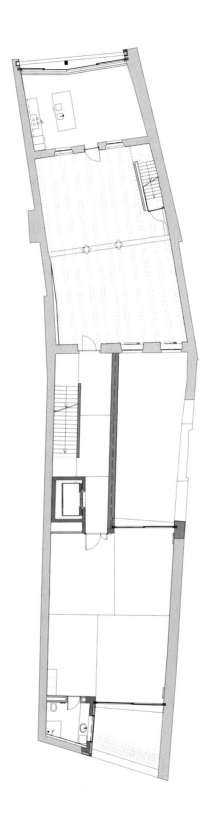
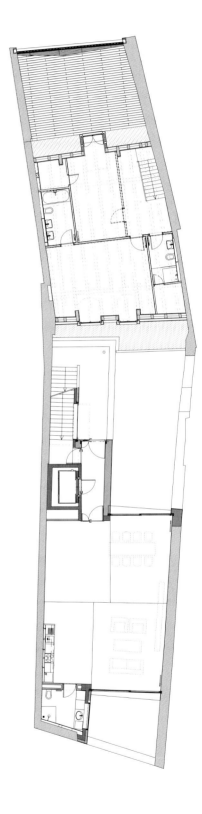

Collection Rosengart, Lucerne 1999 – 2002

Client **Rosengart Foundation** *Lighting Designer* **Ove Arup & Partners** *Frieze* **Peter Suter**

The client for this project was Angela Rosengart, founder of the Rosengart Foundation, who wished to convert the National Bank building prominently located on Pilatusstrasse in Lucerne's city centre, to house her collection of modern art. Built in 1924 by Zurich's Stadtbaumeister (city architect) Hermann Herter, the building was used as a bank until 2000. Its distinguishing traits are a confident and serious appearance, and interior designs specific to each floor. Rosengart asked Diener & Diener for advice, and together they found the former bank feasible for her purposes. The building opened on 26 March 2002 as Sammlung und Picasso Donation Rosengart. Gold lettering on the blank frieze above the stone plinth, naming both the artists whose work is included in the collection and the collectors who donated it, marks the building's new role as a repository for twentieth-century art. The ornamented frieze below the roofline, high above the street, is repeated in another version closer to eye level. This visual and artistic intervention discreetly invites the public into the building.

Visitors enter a hall lined with dark ochre marble. Only a closer look reveals that new views have been added to the interior sequence and that transparency is accentuated. The original glazed doors in their wooden frames allow glimpses of the Picasso collection ahead. To the right, the reception desk welcomes the visitors. To the left, a former doorway in the marble wall, which once led up to the offices on the second floor, has been filled with marble that was previously used in the bank's service counters. The upper third of the arched frame remains open, and allows views to and from the reconfigured stairway. What was previously a single flight has been turned into a double flight, which is now part of an enclosed circulation system. The tone of the entry hall's marble is repeated in the yellowish walls of the museum's reception area.

The three floors, each different in plan and in expression, house three different sections of the collection. A sequence of rooms on the ground floor is dedicated to Pablo Picasso's paintings and some sculptures. The upper floor shows French artists from Pierre-Auguste Renoir to Georges Braque. Also on the upper floor, the former conference room is preserved for study, maintaining an atmosphere of sophisticated silence.

Opposite:
Reception desk

On the ground floor, where the visit to the collection begins, new partition walls form a sequence of rooms along the facade. These spaces circle around and ultimately end in the central hall, which is the former banking hall. The museum walls, classically white, are twice sliced open by vertical voids, symmetrically cut out from the walls between the central space and the layer of rooms enveloping it. This creates a visual connection where there is no physical one, and so establishes new relationships between the rooms. The voids balance the heavy marble pilasters of the Neo-Classical architecture, each negative space moderating the projecting dark ochre stone. Each space also frames a view to another Picasso painting, visually placing it next to another painting hung in an adjacent room.

On the lower floor, in the rooms of the former bank safe, Paul Klee's drawings are protected from daylight. The hand-rail leading downstairs from the ground floor is a free-form shape formed by the combination of two circles, cast in aluminium and anthracite-stained. The wooden floor in the basement, reclaimed from a factory in England, absorbs the weight of the thick walls of the vault.

On the stairway between the ground and the second floor, the reuse of the marble and the perfect reconstruction of the form allow neither the steps nor the hand-rail to reveal the intervention. The reconfigured stair sustains the solemn calm of the Empire-style building.

Peter Suter **The names of the artists included in the collection follow, or precede, the collection's name in the same typeface. This equivalent juxtaposition of the names of the patrons and the artists underlines the personal character of the collection. The frieze of golden letters reinforces the severity of the facade's neoclassical structure while also maintaining the appearance of a contemporary scrolling text. This text does not merely form a girdle around the house but detaches itself, as it were, from the building and has an impact on the city.**

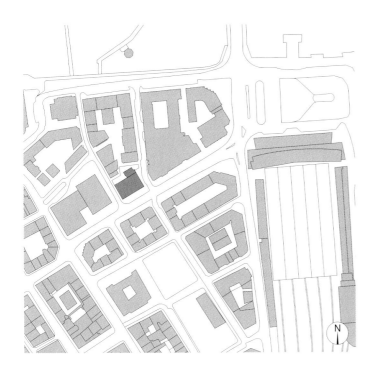

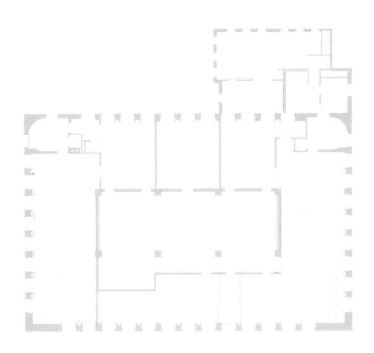

Clockwise from top left:
Site plan
First-floor plan
Ground-floor plan
Basement plan

Opposite, from left:
Facade on Pilatusstrasse,
showing the gold lettering of the frieze
Exhibition space, showing walls sliced
open by vertical voids

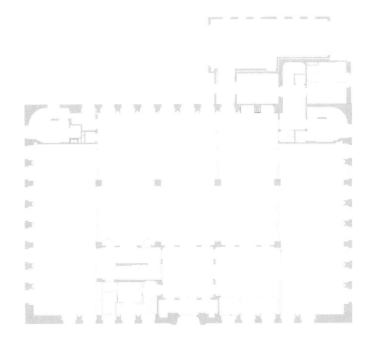

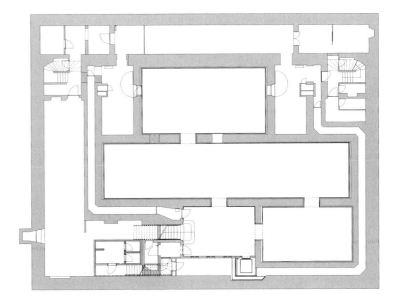

Ruhr Museum at Zeche Zollverein
Essen 1999

Competition **1st prize** *Client* **Internationale Bauausstellung Emscher Park (International Building Exhibition Emscher Park), Entwicklungsgesellschaft Zollverein** *Structural Engineer* **Conzett, Bronzini, Gartmann** *Facade Consultant* **Emmer Pfenninger Partner**

Aerial view, 1932

Opposite:
Zeche Zollverein, with a rendering of the
Ruhr Museum to the right

Next page:
Emscher Park, at night, with a rendering of the
Ruhr Museum to the right

The Zeche Zollverein, when it opened in 1932, was the colliery with the largest extraction capacity in the world. The mining of coal entails a vast underground system of shafts and tunnels. The buildings above are just the tip of the iceberg – nonetheless they are enormous structures. In their design, architects Schupp and Kremmer emphasized the dynamic of the industrial process; in the language of Neue Sachlichkeit, the architecture visualizes the sequence of mining – lifting, sorting, cleaning and freighting off the coal – in a complete ensemble. The buildings are placed along the production and the supply axes, which intersect at ninety degrees. Conveyor bridges connect towers and cubes. The production ensemble staged the continuous flow of the coal, the 'black gold'. Working day and night shifts, most of the region's population was employed in coal mining. When, in 1986, the Zeche Zollverein closed, it left both an underground void and a landmark visible at a large distance.

In 1999 an architectural competition invited plans for a reuse of the coal wash building, to accommodate the Ruhr Museum, formerly located in Essen's city centre, and its attendant visitor facilities. The coal wash was to be one of the attractions of Emscher Park, which today is a popular recreation and tourist destination. Diener & Diener submitted a winning, but ultimately unrealized, proposal that left the industrial legacy untouched. The interior of the coal wash, with its tanks, basins, funnels and conveyor belts, was not to be adapted for other uses; the spaces for the new programmes would be added on top.

Key to this concept was the engineer's realization that the existing steel structure would be relieved from its tendency to bend by adding several floors and, therefore, weight from above, and thus be strengthened. Heightening the coal wash was thus possible without having to change the frames below; only selected steel and concrete corner pillars would need to be reinforced. In a tectonic sense, the project aimed to preserve the history of the vast industrial complex from within. The added floors would accommodate permanent and temporary exhibitions, the visitors' centre, restaurants, an auditorium, a library, offices and storage, forming the end of a sequence that began below,

in the coal wash. In this way, the visitor would view the explanations in the exhibition rooms after having experienced the reality of the raw industrial environment with its original machinery. The stepped-up volume at the peak of the complex would be wrapped in glass, signalling the presence of the Zeche Zollverein into the distance. Like lighted beacons, the new added volumes would glow in the night, alongside the 55 m (180 ft) tall twin pithead gear tower and the smoke stacks of the former coking plant.

RD   In the museum interior, inside the coal washing plant's cold halls, time appears to have come to a sudden stop. For the visitor, the experience of the building, the coal, and the machine is one of great immediacy – without any intervening didactic or interpretative layer. We must not do with less. An extension to a monument only makes sense where it enriches the monument as an architectural, urban or topographical element.

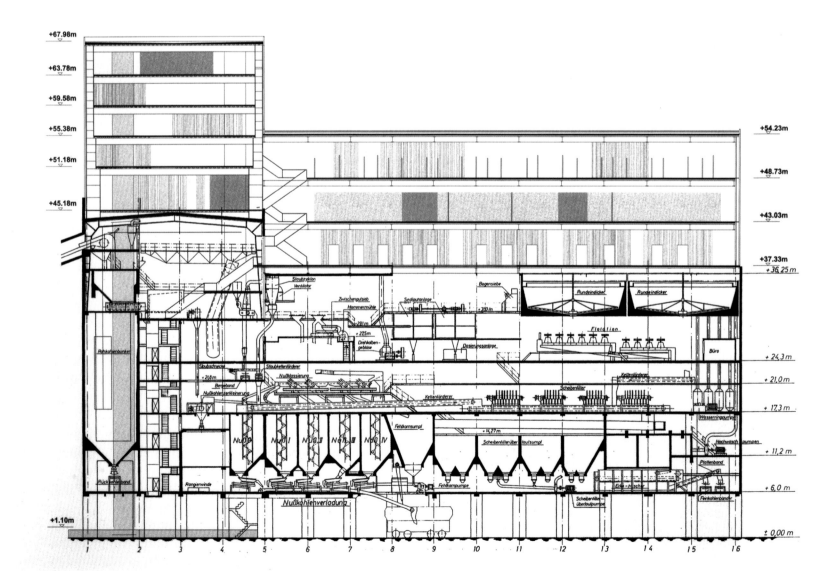

From left:
Structural concept
Cross-section

Opposite:
Longitudinal section

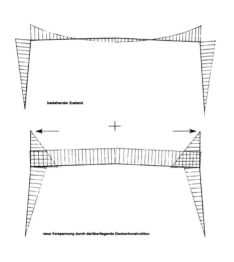

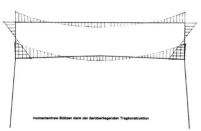

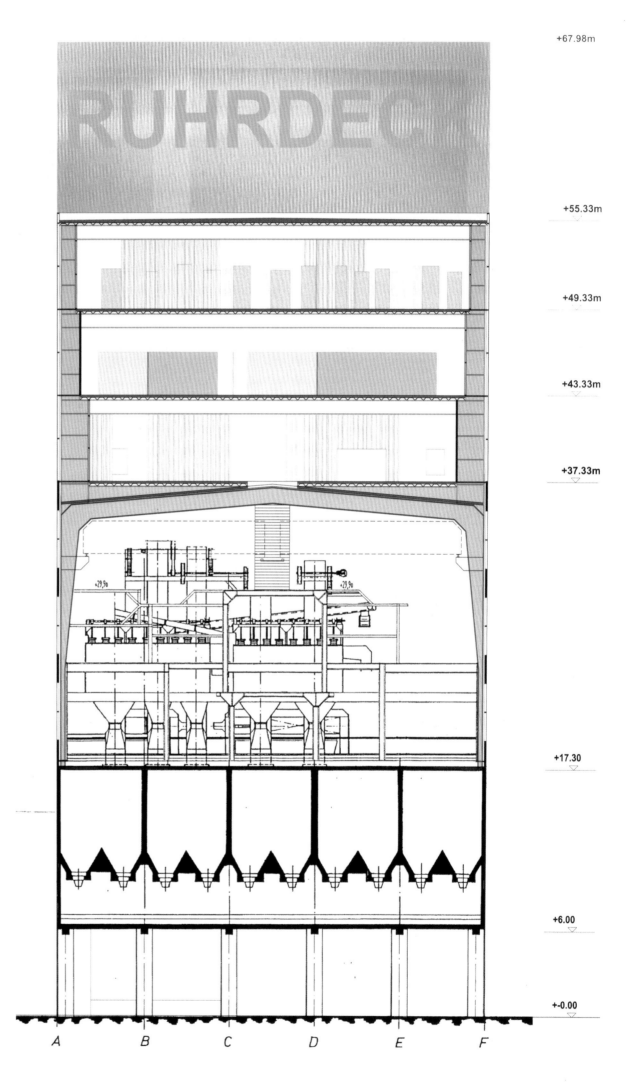

Extension to the National Gallery of Modern Art, Rome 2000–

Competition **1st prize** *in collaboration with* **Peter Suter** *Client* **Ministero delle Infrastrutture e dei Trasporti** *Structural Engineer*
Proger SpA Engineering *Mechanical Engineer* **Waldhauser Haustechnik** *Landscape Architect* **Vogt Landschaftsarchitekten**
Lighting Designer **Institut für Tageslichttechnik**

In 1911, Rome's National Gallery of Modern Art moved into a building designed by Cesare Bazzani, in a park across from the Villa Borghese. The building was extended in 1933 by Bazzani, making a second layer within the existing symmetry of the Neo-Classical structure; and again in 1966, by Luigi Cosenza, with a separate volume. Diener & Diener's winning competition entry of 2000, still awaiting execution, partially replaces the detached addition from 1966 and adds a third layer to the ensemble. This further extension provides space for temporary exhibitions and places an additional entrance on the west side.

The extension can be understood as part of a sequence from three different time periods. On the western facade, large glass surfaces between pilasters of refined stone form vitrines for sculptures, which develop new meaning from their proximity to the ornamentation on the older parts of the facade. Diener & Diener have taken the symmetry and proportions of Bazzani's plans and the Classical canons as both context and reality. At the museum's front, current exhibitions are announced in temporary paint on the wide steps of Bazzani's building.

The extension's main level is dedicated to temporary exhibitions. The spatial promenade set out by Bazzani is continued by in the extension, which connects with the 1911 and 1933 spaces across an interior courtyard. From this point, or via the new west entrance, the new building adds variation to the historical spaces, combining moments of symmetry with spaces in flow. Skylight ribbons mirror the direction of the sequence.

On the lower floor of the extension's interior, special collections are stored in cabinet-like rooms of elongated proportions, which can be accessed only by appointment. The wide staircase serves as seating when the downstairs foyer is used as a small lecture hall. This concept of flexible usage has informed the new spaces many ways, for instance, the roomy entrance hall can be turned into an auditorium by a soft giant spiral of movable curtains.

Opposite:
Rendering of the museum's front, with the announcements for current exhibitions painted on the steps

RD   There is no such thing as a site and its history as such. These first need to be invented, within their context and using as little imagination as possible. The analysis of a site is a project. A site does not exist as an unchanging factor, as a constant, while the project is a variable. Both the site and the project gain their contours in the working process. This is the interest design has in history.

Clockwise, from top left:
Site plan
Museum entrance
Northwest elevation
Longitudinal section

Opposite, from top:
Ground-floor plan
Basement plan

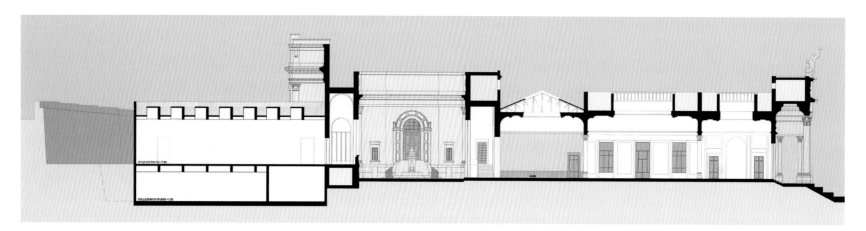

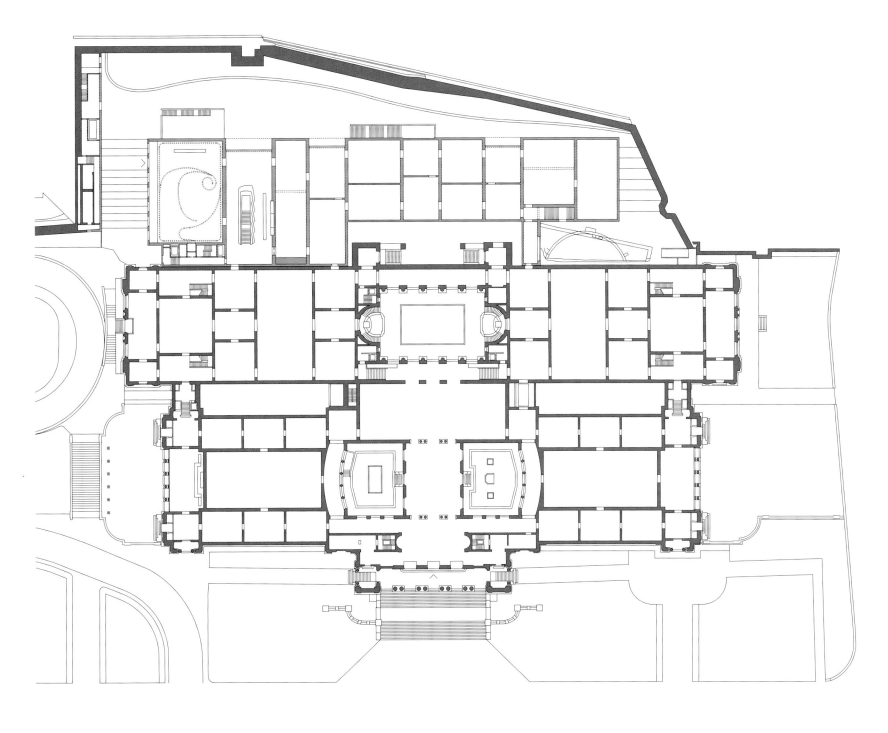
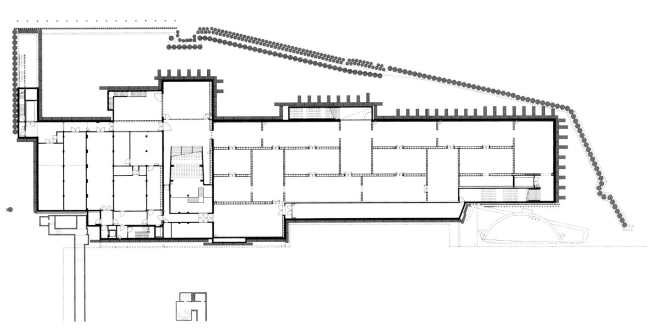

Extension to the Pergamon Museum Berlin 2000

Competition **2nd prize** *in collaboration with* **Peter Suter** *Client* **Stiftung Preussischer Kulturbesitz** *Structural Engineer* **Conzett, Bronzini, Gartmann**

The Pergamon Museum, the largest of the buildings on Berlin's Museum Island, actually houses three different museums: a collection of Classical antiquities, a Middle East museum and a museum of Islamic art. The building was conceived as a Dreiflügelanlage, a Baroque layout in the form of a large U-shaped plan, where the Kupfergraben canal bridge continues as a path through the Ehrenhof (formal courtyard) in the middle of the U-shape, then becomes a symmetrical set of stairs that leads up to the main level of the building. This tall exhibition floor, a piano nobile, displays actual size reconstructions of monumental building elements such as the Pergamon Altar, the Market Gate of Miletus and the Ishtar Gate of Babylon. An upper level contains the Islamic collection as well as temporary exhibitions.

The original museum, which opened in 1901, was designed to accommodate important excavation finds – in particular, fragments from the Pergamon Altar. A new, larger Pergamon Museum was built between 1910 and 1930 under the supervision of Ludwig Hoffmann, according to the design by Alfred Messel. In the 1980s, under the guardianship of the German Democratic Republic, several alterations were made, including the addition of a glass volume for the main entrance.

The 2000 competition required the extension and restoration of the museum, and the improvement of its overall organization and function. The brief specified that the courtyard should be used as additional outdoor exhibition space to house the fragments of the Egyptian Sahure's Temple.

Diener & Diener's competition project proposed that the courtyard be kept as a *cour d'honneur* (a formal reception court), as a mark of respect to the building's history, and that the entrance be relocated to a new two-storey volume of striated glass. This new volume would act as a connecting piece, linking the museum's two symmetrical wings. On the main upper level, it creates a continuous sequence through the antique architectural reconstructions. On the basement level, a narrow platform is inserted between the parts, which thus are experienced by visitors as pieces of an exhibition.

Aerial view of Berlin's Museum Island

Opposite:
Rendering of extension on Kupfergraben canal

The fragments of Sahure's Temple, which are located in the new glass volume and encountered as part of the visitor's sequence through the museum, would also be visible from the exterior, from both the courtyard and across the canal, had this concept been realized. The glass is only partially transparent, and its undulating geometry has a predominantly vertical rhythm, which enters into a dialogue with the fluting of the Classical columns of the original structure – creating a new facade, both solid and fluid at the same time. The original building, the new glass wing and the exhibited fragments of the temple overlap and interact; depending on one's viewpoint and the time of day, the light reflects off the glass's curved surface or penetrates it.

The competition jury report honoured the innovative relationship created between the Egyptian temple and the Pergamon Altar at the opposite end of the courtyard by awarding it the second prize, and appreciated the sequence on the main floor and the continuous promenade on the lower level as being in harmony with the architectural elements of the existing building.

RD   The extension stands immediately adjacent to the existing building – it is useful as a bracket that combines the two wings of the Pergamon Museum to enable a continuous prominade through the building. However, it is not just a building extention; instead it is a surreal box in which gravity and tectonics seem to be inverted.

Rendering of the Ehrenhof (formal courtyard)

Opposite, from top:
Elevation facing the Kupfergraben canal
First-floor plan

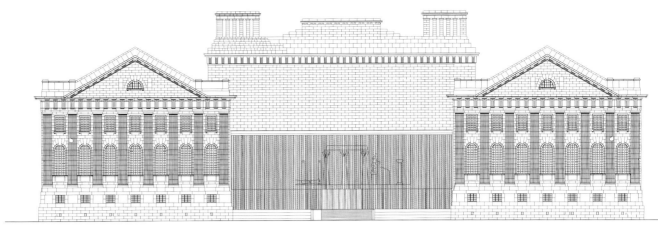

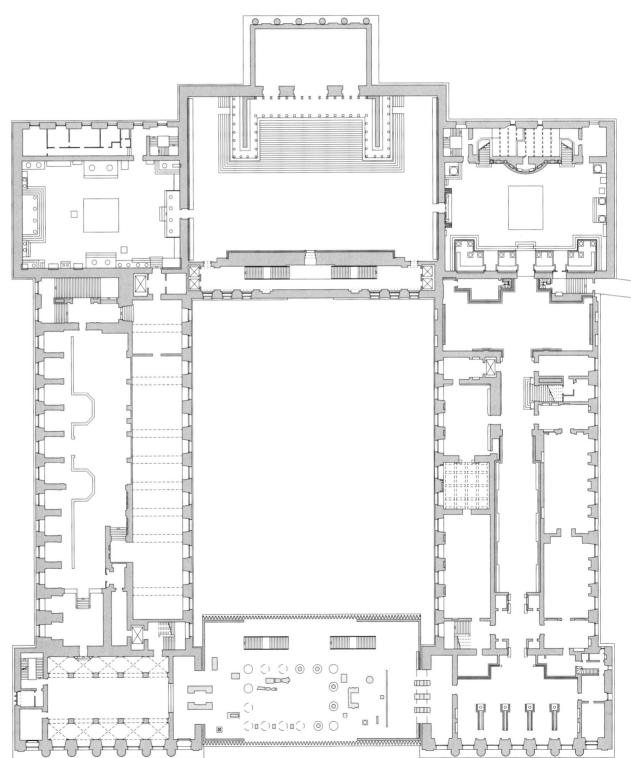

Residential Buildings Ypenburg
The Hague 2000–2003

Client **Bouwcollectief d'Artagnan** *Masterplan and Local Architect* **West 8**

The site for this project is Sub-Plan 6, a residential suburb on a former military airfield, only fifteen minutes from the centre of the Dutch capital via a new transport network. Structured by a system of long avenues and broad boulevards, Sub-Plan 6 contains 497 low-rise dwellings and 155 apartments in various price categories, as well as a school and a sports centre. The buildings were designed by three architecture firms from the Netherlands, along with Diener & Diener. The masterplan for Sub-Plan 6 was created by the Rotterdam office West 8, who aimed to avoid the monotony of the uniform street-scapes that often come with instant cities. At the beginning of the project, the inherent diversity when a city grows over time was simulated in plan by a computer program. The discussions between planners and architects led them to the realization that simply scattering the building types in the most diffuse pattern would again create monotony. Thus the distribution parameters were calculated in such a way that each street front is characterized by a predominant architectural language that is interrupted by facades conceived by other architects.

Diener & Diener's contribution is a house type with an emphasis on horizontal flow, created by layers both on the facades and in plan. Dark grey concrete roof cornices, prescribed by the masterplan, became a key facade motif and are repeated as horizontal bands on each floor. While each of the seven types of the house – with or without garden or ground floor studio, and of varying heights – feature these same horizontal elements, their individuality is accentuated by vertical shifts between units.

The larger height of the top floor can be read as a consequence of the master plan, which determined a roof angle of ten degrees. In the tradition of the piano nobile of Classical residences, this elongated floor gives the buildings elegance and generosity, despite their relatively modest size: even the two-storey buildings do not look small next to the three-storey ones.

Opposite:
Two types of row houses,
showing concrete cornices

The 145 row houses of this type, and all the high-rises, are stacks of brick facades in which window and door elements appear as inserts, each floor separated by the grey concrete bands. The high-rises follow the organizational principle of the row houses, in that they are individual buildings arranged in rows and not tower blocks. But they stand as special expressive forms, and each apartment in the residential buildings is horizontal – located on a single floor – unlike the row houses where the living situation is more vertical, being divided over several floors. The towers are organized in pairs, with one staircase per two high-rises, serving two apartments per floor.

The buildings address the street with a door element consisting of three full-height casements. The doors sometimes serve as the entrance to the entire house, and sometimes as a separate access to the ground-floor office or studio. Three colours of brick – red, white and black – are used in floor-height elements that are flush with the windows and doors, creating a recurring facade pattern that relates to the different types of houses. The concrete cornices project from the rest of this facade, accentuating the vertical shifts between the different units at the same time as the strong visual element of the horizontal bands, creating a score of subtle rhythms.

RD **The towers in the Residential Buildings Ypenburg resemble mutated row houses that have grown tall, a mark of identity that makes the system of the whole development visible from afar.**

From left:
Row houses and high-rises,
seen from the canal row houses

Opposite:
High-rises, seen from the street

From top:
Site plan
Floor plans and sections of three types
of row houses

Opposite, clockwise from top left:
First-floor plan of high-rises
Upper-floor plan of high-rises
Southeast elevation of high-rises
Cross-section of high-rises

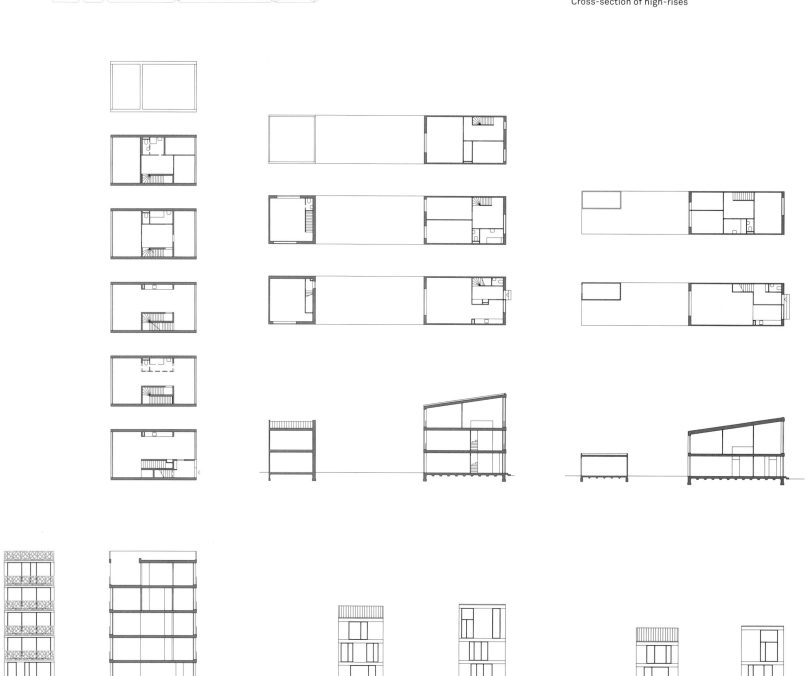

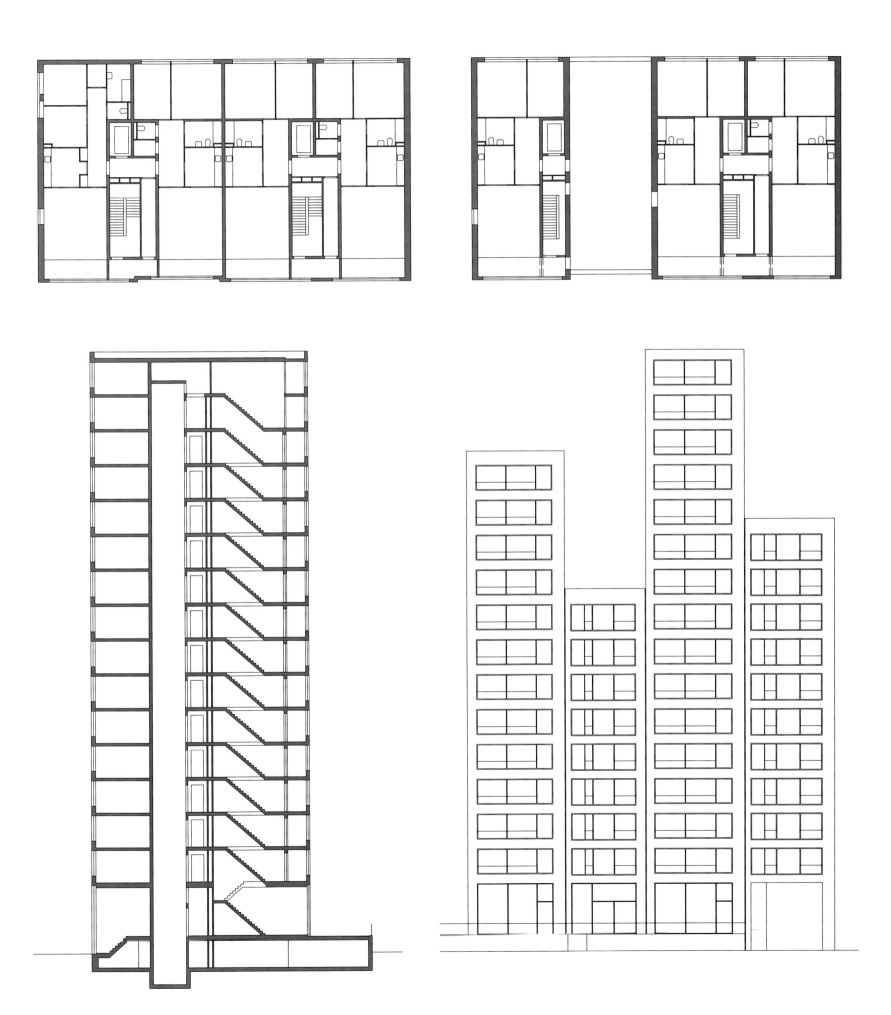

Masterplan for the Maag Areal Plus Zurich 2000

Competition **1st prize** *in collaboration with* **M. & E. Boesch Architekten** *Client* **Maag Holding, Coop, Welti-Furrer, Amt für Hochbauten Zurich**

Between 1913 and 1991, precision cogwheels and pumps were produced at the Maag plant, on the west side of Zurich. Over the last decade of the twentieth century, industrial activity continued to disappear from this area, allowing the city centre to expand towards the west. Diener & Diener's masterplan for this area, now called Maag Areal Plus, encompasses the former sites of the Maag factories, the Coop warehouses to the west, and the storage halls of the Welti-Furrer transportation enterprise to the north. The new buildings are a modern interpretation of the industrial typology and form an elegant assemblage reminiscent of the site's past, while maintaining the cohesive and self-contained quality of the area.

The competition project foresaw that some buildings should be renovated and put to new use, while the new builds should share physical or structural qualities with the pre-existing buildings, preserving the genius loci. The strategy relies on retaining the large volumes that are the basic building block of this piece of urban fabric – maintaining its inherent quality – but allowing for the volumes to be complemented, added to, restructured, extended or replaced by new structures of related character. The masterplan also aims to increase the density of the site without upsetting the subtle balance in the scale and the proportion of the buildings.

An inner street with railway tracks, part of the former Maag factory, was kept as the primary open space on the site, and the new complex was essentially shaped by the curve of the tracks. Instead of an orthogonal structure on a rectangular or square lot, building ensembles have been formed on both sides of the tracks, which branch off westwards from Hardstrasse at an oblique angle. The unique floor plans result from the angle of these tracks, producing fascinating spatial sequences.

Opposite:
Aerial view from above the railyard

A courtyard has been formed between the taller Maag and the lower Coop buildings, taking the spatial conditions that formerly existed between the storage halls – simple open space in a dense quarter – and making it into a large green space that reads in plan as an interruption between the angled geometry of the Maag and the more rectangular layouts of the Coop and Welti-Furrer sites.

None of the facades is conceived as being the front or back of the buildings; public space flows all around the volumes. Where possible, the ground-floor levels are porous, allowing visitors and users of the new development to easily filter through the urban fabric; pedestrians, cars and cyclists share this permeable public ground.

The 25 m (82 ft) roofline is maintained in the competition project and in the specific planning regulations subsequently developed for this site, with the exception of a small number of distinctly taller buildings in special positions. These high-rise buildings are conceived as asymmetrical dynamic centres, a concept perhaps most clearly manifested in a tall tower on the southeast edge of the site, which asserts its presence across the city. Other tall volumes, such as the large U-shaped volume and the tower-like roof constructions on the long volumes parallel to the railway yard, are conceived as integral parts of building groups, which do not demarcate the corners or edges of the site, but instead are placed as centrifugal forces within the post-industrial fabric.

RD   The composition of courtyard and building is of almost geographical size. During the entire rebuilding process, the courtyard persisted as the decentred focal point, with the changes occurring in the periphery or, in reference to Paul Klee's painting, the 'spokes' of the 'wheel mechanism.'

Radiation and Rotation, Paul Klee, 1924

Opposite, from top:
Site model, as seen from south masterplan
Site plan

Mobimo Tower, Zurich 2002–2011

Client **Marazzi Generalunternehmung** *Structural Engineer* **Basler & Hofmann** *Mechanical Engineer* **Amstein + Walthert**
Interior Designer **Studio Carbone Interior Design** *Landscape Architect* **Rotzler, Krebs, Partner**

The Mobimo Tower, part of the development of the Maag Areal Plus masterplan, replaces a supermarket chain's distribution centre. The state of suspension that exists between the grouped buildings and the freestanding buildings is the characteristic feature of the Maag Area. In contrast to the adjacent solitary high-rise building by the Hardbrücke, the Mobimo Tower is a 'tall building' integrated into the existing relationship of grouped buildings.

Standing on a prism-shaped plan, the tower rises up twenty-four floors to a summit of 81 m (266 ft). It accommodates a luxury hotel with high-end residences stacked above. In the tradition of the formerly industrial fabric, the building has no front or back, so that the urban space flows around all five sides.

A terrace to the south and a prospective park to the west set the volume in attractive surroundings. Set firmly onto the ground, the volume is expressed as a building block with proportions of 4:3 for each of the two south-facing facade segments, 2:1 for the northfacing facade, and 3:1 and 4:1 for the side facades. Clad in travertine, the Mobimo Tower follows the architectural tradition of a tripartite structure of base, shaft and capital. The base consists of three over-height levels with windows of up to 3 x 4 m (10 x 13 ft).

At the entrance level, the lobby connects to a restaurant facing the terrace and to two ballrooms on the next floor. A series of conference rooms and administrative offices are located on the third level. In the middle section, from the fourth to the fourteenth floor, 300 hotel rooms and small suites look out onto the new urban quarter, with master suites, a gym and wellness facilities on the fourteenth, over-height floor. The change in window size also marks the transition to the apartments from the fifteenth floor upwards with even larger windows than the hotel floors below, featuring stunning views from Lake Zurich in the southeast to the Limmat Valley in the west. The stacking of the programme is manifest in the shifts of proportion between the stone segments and the openings. Anodized aluminium casings frame the openings in the roughly sandblasted travertine facade. The frames, with their differentiated widths, accentuate the different window sizes and draw subtle lines on the prism-shaped tower.

Opposite:
View to Maag Areal Plus area,
with the Mobimo tower in the centre

Page 218:
Tower, seen from the south

Page 219:
Tower, seen from the west

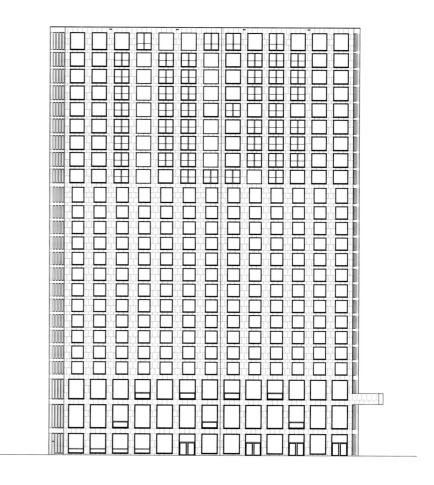

Clockwise from top left:
Site plan
South elevation
North elevation
East elevation

Opposite, clockwise from top left:
Plan, floors 16–18
Plan, floor 23
Plan, floor 15
First-floor plan
Ground-floor plan
Plan, floors 3–13

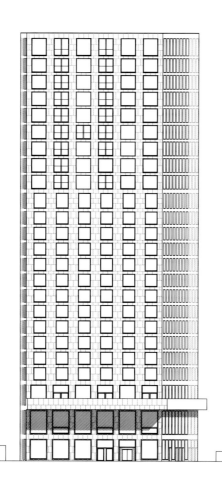

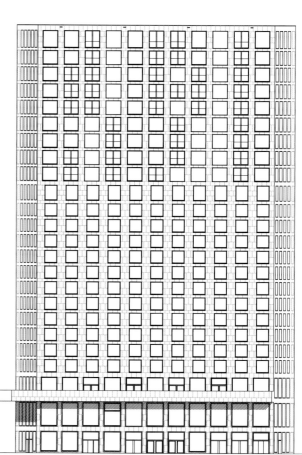

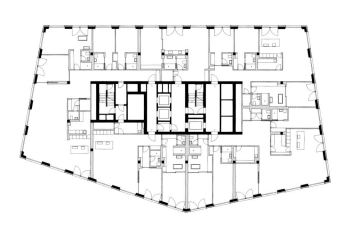

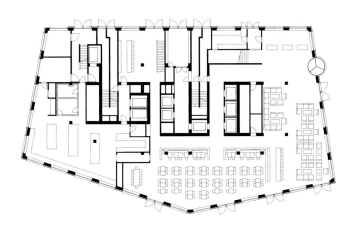
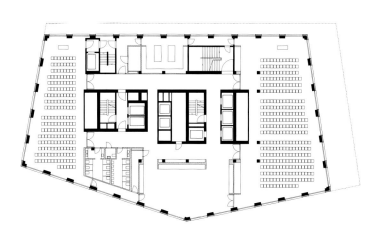

Stücki Shopping Centre, Basel 2001–2009

Client **Tivona Eta** *Structural Engineer* **Burger & Partner Ingenieure** *Mechanical Engineer* **Waldhauser Haustechnik,**
Troxler & Partner, Lippuner EMT *Landscape Architect* **Vogt Landschaftsarchitekten and Fahrni and Breitenfeld**
Landschaftsarchitekten *Lighting and Media Designer* **iart interactive with ZMIK designers**

The Stücki Shopping Centre is located in the Kleinhüningen district of Basel, which borders both France and Germany and was previously home to an industrial chemical plant. This piece of the city now has a diverse set of neighbours: a residential district to the south and the west, industries and a highway to the east, and a harbour to the north. The location of the centre within the city limits enables the public to arrive on the ground level by tram, bus or bicycle; car parking is underground. Four towers mark the corners of the expansive horizontal volume of the new mall.

To the south, a stepped facade divides the centre's main entrance into differentiated public spaces. Here, the large volume is broken down into smaller sections that open onto a square, where food courts and restaurants are accessible both from the interior passages of the mall and from the outside, helping the building to maintain an active relationship with the neighbourhood. The eastern and northern sides of the complex are clad in white stucco, as are the towers, which, in daytime, remain abstract and restrained in their formal expression. At night, they are illuminated by vertical lines of LED lights. Vines, roses, jasmine, old man's beard and lavender enliven the southern frontage, while more subtle green plants cover the long west side that faces the residential neighbourhood. These vertical gardens are grown on an exterior layer of steel rods. A hotel complements the programme on the southeast end of the site, along a busy street. Along the back street, the administration and offices are housed and the rhythm of the facade changes to a narrower spacing between the windows.

Inside, the shopping mall is laid out along a wide, central main street, beneath large window domes, andthe side, where large windows have open views to the neighbourhood to the west. The circulation areas are paved in granite, and diagonal alleyways create shortcuts between the main streets. Details such as the rounded corners of the travelator rails, light-wells, shop-fronts and even the furnishings accentuate fluid movement through the space.

Aerial view

Opposite:
Main ontrancc, ocen from the square

Next page:
Facade of the hotel, administration
and offices

At 35,000 m² (377,000 sq ft), the Stücki Shopping Centre is the largest such facility in the region. The asymmetry of the shop layout, along two streets of different characters, maintains a sense of direction. From every point in the building – whether on one of the 210 m (690 ft) long streets or in the 5,000 m² (55,000 sq ft) retail spaces – there is abundant daylight and views outside or to the sky, which helps provide orientation. The atmosphere inside the centre is created through different applications of light. In addition to natural side light, chrome cylinders with LED-lights and warmer-toned downlights are mounted on the ornamental ceiling canopy. Glass balustrades, interior mirror facings and slender black hand-rails all contribute to the lightness of the architecture. The metal tubes create an endless movement and manifold reflections. The building is at once a long hall lined with columns, and a basilica under a canopy of chrome cylinders that reaches upwards to the light.

Clockwise from top left:
Hotel entrance, seen from the square
Shopping centre delivery area
Night view of the shopping centre window
on the west facade
Shopping centre window on the west facade

Opposite:
A side street in the shopping centre

From top:
Model, as seen from southeast
South elevation
North elevation
East elevation
West elevation

Opposite, from top:
First-floor plan
Ground-floor plan
Lower level plan with parking

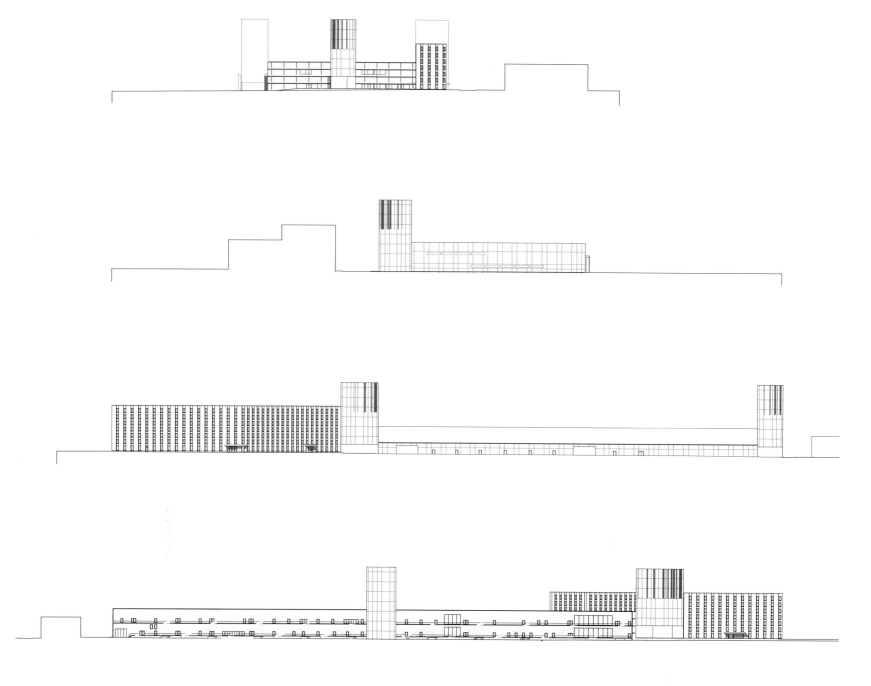

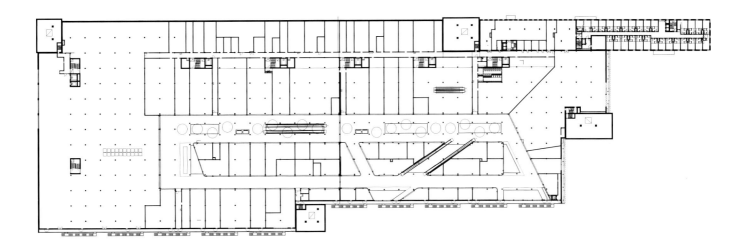

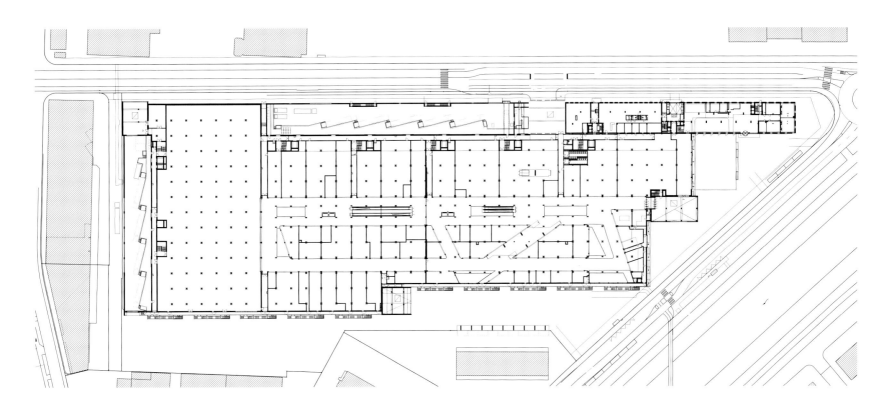

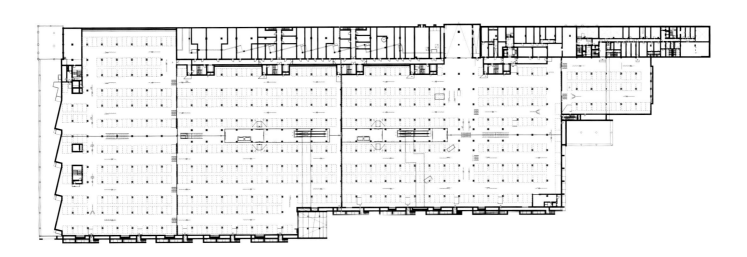

Novartis Campus Forum 3, Basel 2002–2005

Competition **1st prize** *in collaboration with* **Helmut Federle and Gerold Wiederin** *Client* **Novartis Pharma** *Structural Engineer* **Ernst Basler + Partner** *Mechanical Engineer* **Aicher, De Martin, Zweng, Sytek** *Landscape Architect* **Vogt Landschaftsarchitekten** *Facade Consultant* **Emmer Pfenninger Partner** *Workspace Designer* **Sevil Peach Gence Associates**

Forum 3 was the first of many new buildings on the Novartis Campus, built on what was previously the Novartis pharmaceutical company's factory site, which stands at the northern edge of Basel. Forum 3 welcomes visitors to the campus and also represents the rebirth of both the urban quarter and the corporation. The new buildings, designed by internationally renowned architects according to a masterplan by Vittorio Magnano Lampugnani, give Novartis a sophisticated and cosmopolitan appearance. Next to the strictly controlled campus entrance, Forum 3's articulated, longitudinal volume demarcates both the frontage of the campus and the edge of a park. The pictorial facade references the 1952 UNAM university library in Mexico City, where murals by Juan O'Gorman give a notable visual expression to the exterior of the building.

Despite the fact that the building acts as a boundary, its facade is ambiguous, blurred by the many layers of glass that constitute it. As an alternative to the ubiquitous curtain wall, a unique, three-dimensional veil of glass wraps the office building's full-height, double-glazed facade on all four sides. Around the loggias, which are 2 m (6 ft 6 in) wide, the glass panes are kept in position by pairs of vertical rods, each 27 mm (1 in) in diameter, on three planes. The layers of glass are set 20 cm (8 in) apart from each other, creating an effect of spatial depth and blurring of the building's edge.

The pieces are made from compound safety glass of different sizes. The facade uses fifteen different hues: six bright hues of Parsol glass and nine intensive hues of Schott glass. Additional colour variations are created by mounting coloured glass on white carrier glass, as well as coloured-on-coloured glass for even more tones, while white-on-white glass is used for the railings of the loggias. This is a facade of voids as much as of multiple layers. The outer facade varies between bright colours and tones of grey, at times with silver reflections, depending on the light that is cast on it. The glass veil's three-dimensional composition allows multiple readings: from close up it fractures into panels of solid glass with clearly discernible edges (the panels vary in thickness, with an average of 12 mm (½ in)), while from afar, the three, partially superposed layers appear out of focus.

Opposite:
Detail of the facade facing the main square of the campus

Inside, the variation of facade is leveraged to create specific zones of light. Intense hues of glass are concentrated where social activity occurs, around the staircases and in the meeting rooms; in-between, the space is immersed in the full spectrum of light. The atmosphere encourages communication but is calm; the spaces are reduced to the essential and yet are rich in interrelationships. Like a city landscape, the interior spaces form a continuous sequence; at the same time, the many required functions of the programme are given specific locations. The open office floors, defined as 'multi-space areas', are differentiated into zones for the various activities undertaken by the staff: these include both open and dedicated, social and secluded zones.

The ground-floor arcade, created by the first-floor cantilever towards the square

Opposite:
Northeastern corner of the building

Next page:
Building in winter, from the campus's main square

The masterplan specified the overall design approach and dimensions of the building, including the arcades along the boulevard. However, around the campus's main square (called the Forum), the facades are not regulated and the arcades here – unlike those of most of the other buildings on the campus– are column-free; this move expands the interior space into the square, making the building lighter and its spaces more fluid.

      To the north, large sliding windows open the tall ground floor to the Forum. As an expression of continuity and openness within the campus, the foyer, a restaurant, a lounge and seminar rooms are linked to this central space. The upper floors cantilever towards the square. By this shift, the outside is drawn into the building and the structural grid is offset. Both axes of this simple, long volume are asymmetrical. On the short axis, the loggias, which provide an additional working place for Novartis's managers, have

North loggia

columns on the south side but are free on the north. The asymmetry of the long axis is created from the location of a conservatory on the west end of the building. This four-storey space, where tropical trees wind around each other, introduces an entirely different world into the building, referencing the city park outside and creating a contemplative setting for the small conference rooms that overlook the exotic vegetation.

Based on a steel construction around cores of concrete, the architectural language is characterized by refined lightness. Elements such as hand-rails, the casements of the meeting room windows and the lounge seating are covered in light synthetic leather to give the interior a sense of softness. A staircase of dark walnut wood sweeps elegantly between the floors, articulating a vertical continuity.

Artist Helmut Federle and architect Gerold Wiederin collaborated with Diener & Diener on this project, which was truly a shared effort rather than a collection of individual statements. Federle and Wiederin lent their skill and phenomenological approach to the architectural project so that, as the whole group of authors of the project has commented, 'a structure has been generated in which individual and joint contributions have fused into an indissoluble whole.' Their collective achievement has been the synthesis of the monumental and the modern in the Forum 3 project.

Helmut Federle   **This geometry is neither subject to compositional considerations nor does it seek to be spectacular. Its decorative quality, of which I am quite conscious, expresses an existential visionary grandeur. The aim is to add beauty as meaning to the form's rationality.**

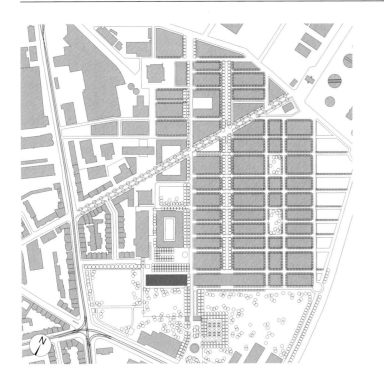

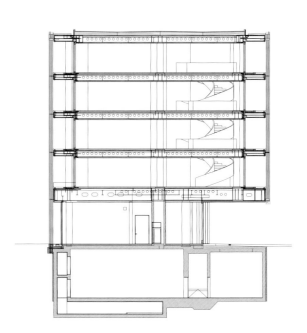

Clockwise from top left:
Site plan
Cross section
Ground-floor plan of the buildings
and the main square of the campus

Opposite, from top:
Longitudinal section
Second-floor plan
Ground-floor plan

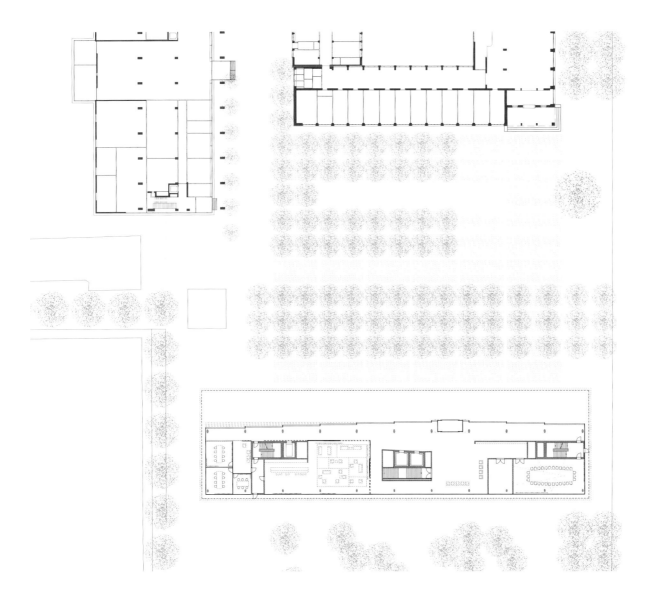

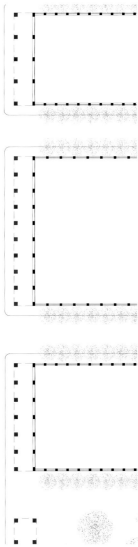

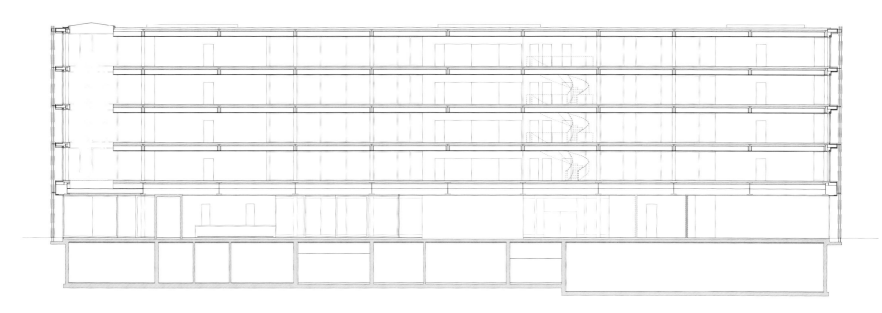

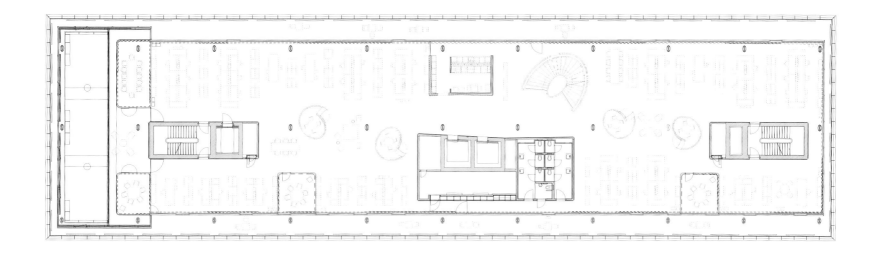

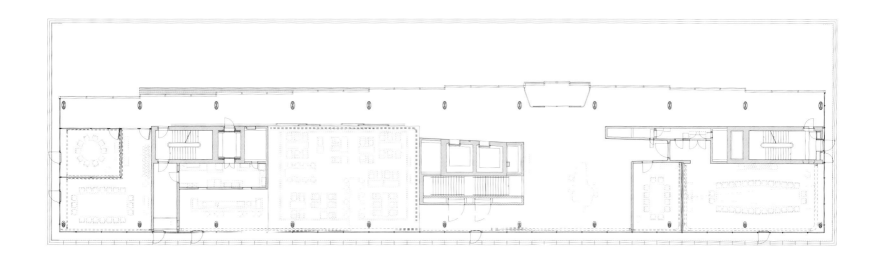

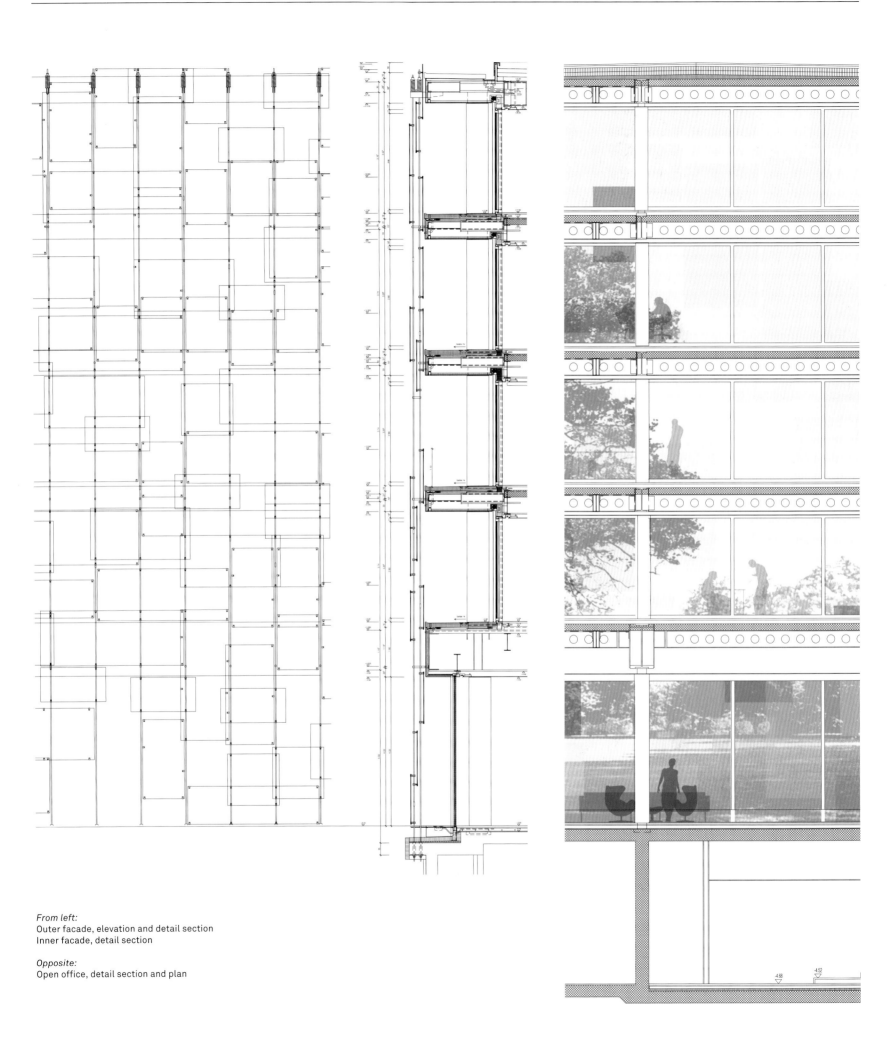

From left:
Outer facade, elevation and detail section
Inner facade, detail section

Opposite:
Open office, detail section and plan

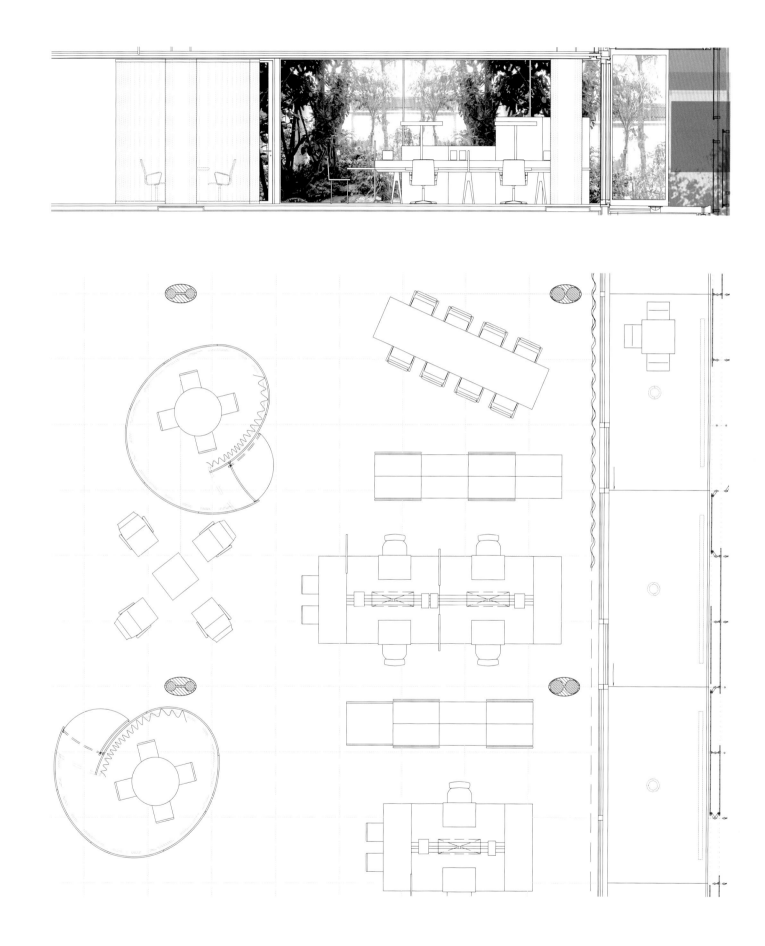

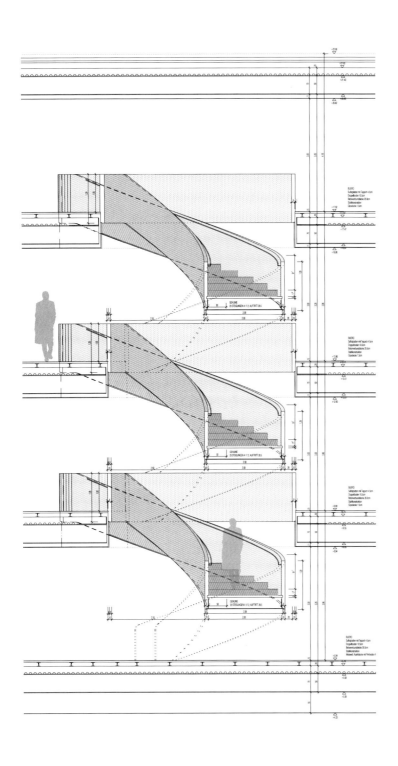

Wooden staircase, section and plan

Opposite:
Wooden staircase

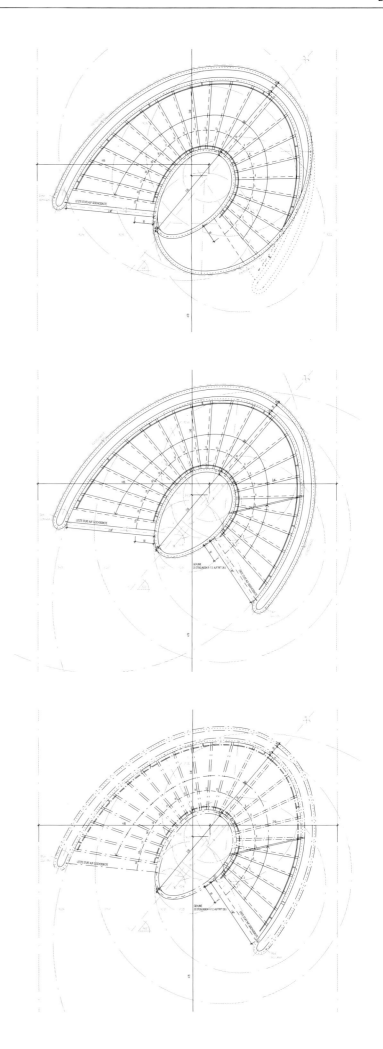

RD   The building produces views that are reminiscent of a city. With each movement through the building, the scene changes. It is as if we were walking down the streets and across the squares of a city. New vistas are always coming into view as an infinite series of distinct and yet related images. As we come to a standstill, the composition rests.

Conservatory, detail section

Opposite, from top:
Open office space next to the conservatory
Tropical trees in the conservatory

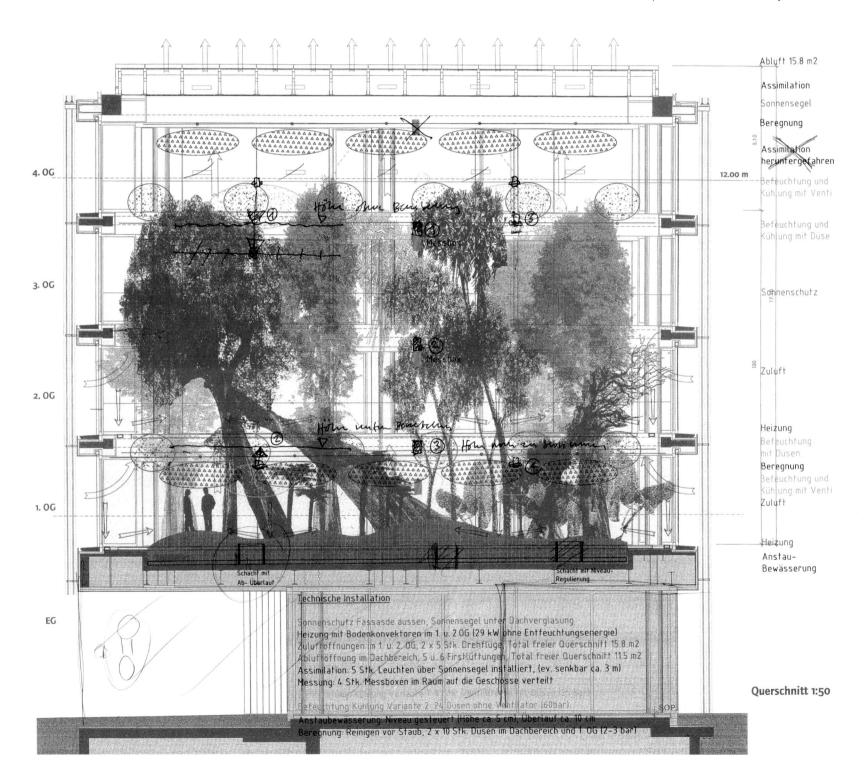

Querschnitt 1:50

Casa A1 at the Olympic Village
Turin 2003–2005

Client **Agenzia Olimpico Torino 2006** *Structural Engineer* **AIA Architectes Ingénieurs Associés** *Local Architect* **Studio Camerana and Studio Rosenthal** *with* **Steidle + Partner** *Landscape Architect* **Andra Lichtenstein**

The masterplan for the 2006 Olympic Village, by Otto Steidle and partners, envisaged a series of buildings that would serve as accommodation for the athletes of the Winter Games and could later be used as housing. As one of the many individual buildings planned for the overall urban design on plots 3 and 4, Casa A1 stands on the north-eastern edge of the site much like a figure on a chessboard. The buildings, designed by a number of internationally acclaimed architects, were spread over the site in a regular pattern and each building was made distinctive by the use of different colours.

The Casa A1 building block is coloured two shades of grey – a darker tone to the south and west, and a lighter grey to the north and east – which emphasize the plasticity of the volume. Acknowledging the Mercati Hall, situated opposite, the 20.2 x 13.8 m (66 x 45 ft) footprint extends to a depth of 15.3 m (50 ft) after four floors. The deeper top three floors accommodate interior courtyards that bring additional light into the apartments. Casa A1, raw stone on the outside, is revealed in the interior to be all about light and air. All apartments have one, two or even three loggias as outdoor spaces, those on the top three storeys face one of the interior courtyards, and the bathrooms are naturally lit and ventilated. These residences were designed to accommodate athletes from all over the world, who lived here for only a short time and were expected to produce top performances during their stay. As such, the apartments also served as meeting places for a diverse set of people.

The plan is divided into five segments, each 4 m (13 ft) wide. Rather than an unambiguous, conventional arrangement of functions within each apartment, this layout allows a flexible exchange of all spatial units. No matter whether the areas are designated for living or sleeping, or a loggia or a kitchen to be installed later, they are all interchangeable. This creates a novel interior structure, a spatial chain of chambers deepening until they reach the limits of the cubic external shell. This syntax is expressed in the composition of the openings: high and low windows staggered vertically and horizontally dissolve the simple division of the storeys, while the building as a whole remains part of the game played between the neighbouring chess pieces on the board.

Opposite:
South facade

From top:
North facade
View from inside the
entrance hall

Opposite,
clockwise from left:
Site plan
Sixth-floor plan
Third-floor plan
Ground-floor plan
Cross-section

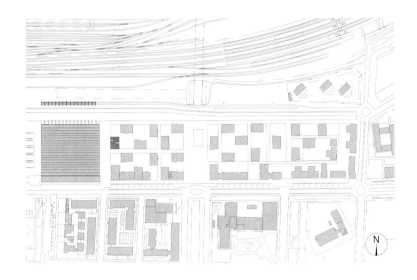

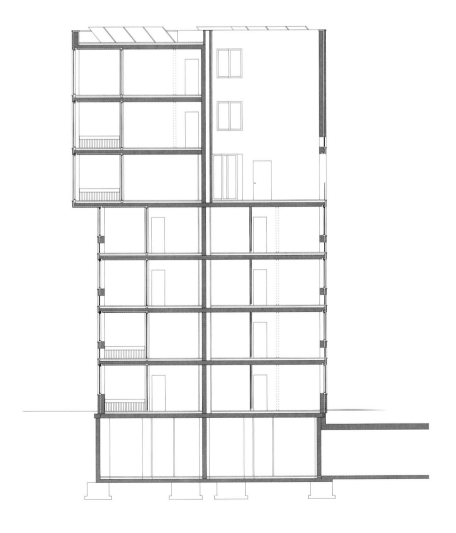

Westkaai 1 + 2 Apartment Buildings Antwerp 2005–2009

Client **NV Kattendijkdok, Project²** *Structural Engineer* **Stedec NV** *Mechanical Engineer* **Arcadis Gedas** *Landscape Architect* **Michel Desvigne Paysagistes**

The development of the Kattendijkdok, consisting of new residential buildings, business, culture and leisure centres in the midst of old dock buildings and the harbour basin, is a recent urban extension project instigated by the city of Antwerp. The two areas comprising the harbour are connected along the Falconplein–Nassaustraat axis, and the outlines of the multi-storey buildings are visible from the city centre. A total of three pairs of towers are planned for the Westkaai. Diener & Diener were commissioned for the first pair along the southern section of the harbour basin, close by Amsterdamstraat. The guidelines stated that the towers should be similar but not identical.

The two towers are each 56 metres tall but in their fifteen upper floors, one contains forty and the other forty-four flats, with retail and commercial spaces on the ground floor of both buildings. They are not aligned but slightly displaced. Windows of different sizes are grouped together and inserted into the outer layer, to dissolve and lighten the volumes of the towers. The 4.2 cm (1.65 in) thick anodized aluminium frames outline five different types of windows, which are fixed glazing or pivot-mounted windows that can be slid open and tilted. The external sunscreen slides along guide rails that have been integrated into the embrasure.

The facade of both towers is composed of complex elements – rippled glass laid over aluminium sheet metal, covering the thermal insulation. The use of rippled glass and adjacent layers had been tested by Diener & Diener in a project in Baden and in the University Building in Malmö. It is further developed in these two towers, where a warmer and a colder tone are achieved by lining the insulation of the facades with two different metallic colors. The gold color of the southern tower sometimes tends toward amber, while the silver color of the northern tower tends toward green at times when the proper tint of the glass mixes with the reflected surroundings. When it is bright with sunshine, the light in the atmosphere is refracted in the glass. At these times, the different colours of the two towers almost balance out and the multi-layered constructions of the towers shimmer iridescently with slightly varying tones. On a cloudy day the sheet metal becomes apparent and the two towers are once again estranged from one another.

Opposite:
Tower 2, on Westkaai

In some spots, the windows are placed at the outermost edge of the building's volume, while in others the windows form part of the inner surface. The visual appearance of the two buildings is primarily shaped by the irregular grid of windows, which appears random but is in fact the result of the systematic combination of eleven different types of flats, with the windows placement signifying the location of the rooms. The internal heights of the rooms within the various apartment types vary between 2.7 m (8 ft 10 in) and 3.5 m (11 ft 5 in), while the floor areas vary between 69 m^2 (743 sq ft) and 359 m^2 (3,864 sq ft). Identically arranged floors are repeated between two and four times and are located vertically adjacent. Larger flats are generally found higher up while smaller flats are more often placed on the lower floors.

RD   A central aspect to the design of the Westkaai 1 + 2 Apartment Buildings was the mirroring of the neighbouring row of small fisherman's houses in the two new apartment buildings. The grouped apartments form a sequence that reflects the rhythmic order of the small houses.

Opposite from left:
Aerial view
Old buildings on the Kattendijkdok

Interior view of an apartment with loggia

Next page:
View to the towers from across the Kattendijkdok

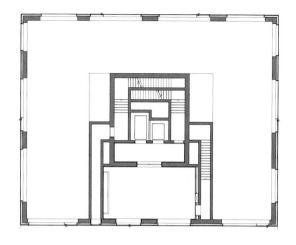
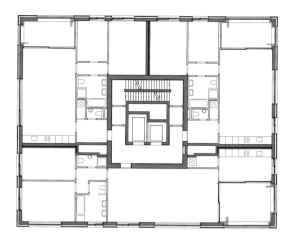
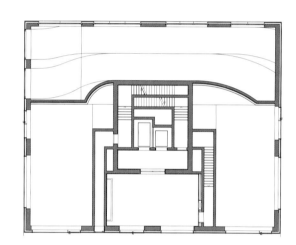
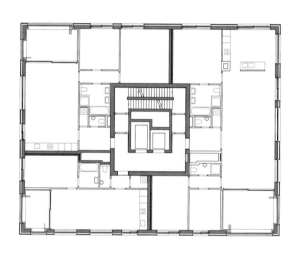
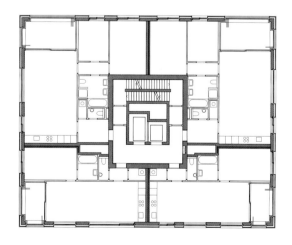
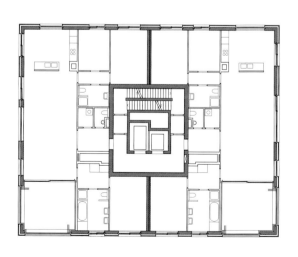

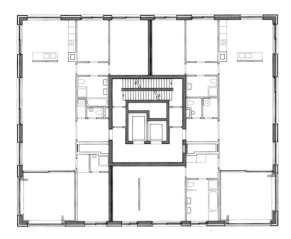

Opposite, clockwise from top left:
Ground-floor plan of Tower 1
Floor plan, type B
Floor plan, type C
Floor plan, type D
Floor plan, type A
Ground-floor plan of Tower 2

Clockwise from top left:
Floor plan, type E
Section, Tower 2
Floor plan, type G
Floor plan, type F

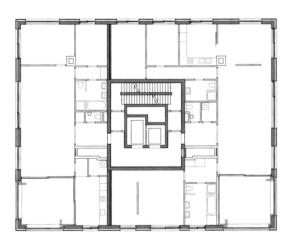

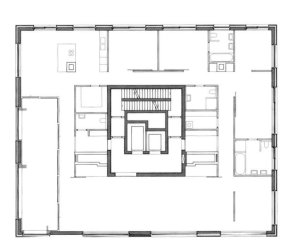

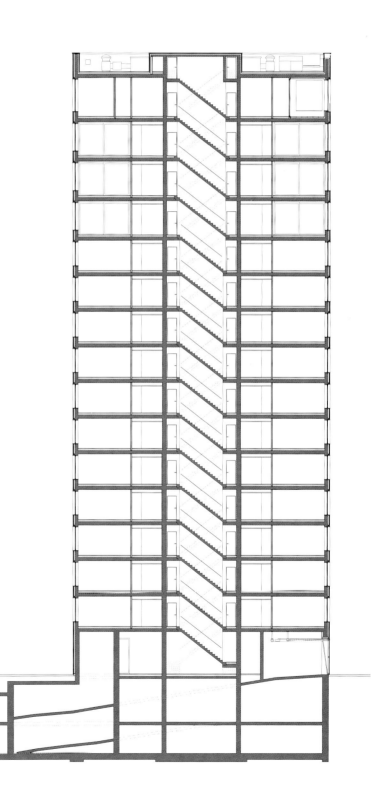

Convention Centre 'ZürichForum' Zurich 2005

Competition, in collaboration with **Peter Suter, Elisabeth Märkli** *Client* **Amt für Hochbauten Zurich** *Structural Engineer* **Conzett, Bronzini, Gartmann** *Mechanical Engineer* **PGMM Schweiz** *Landscape Architect* **Vogt Landschaftsarchitekten**

The proposed site for a new convention centre overlooks Lake Zurich and neighbours the famous 1895 Tonhalle concert hall. Controversially, it is also the site of the Kongresshaus completed in 1939 by the legendary architectural office of Haefeli Moser Steiger. The competition brief outlined a vast programme and complex requirements on a difficult site. The jury's decision to award the prizes to projects that require demolishing the existing Kongresshaus caused heated debates across the entire city.

Diener & Diener's contribution received a special commendation: it was the only entry that included both the Tonhalle and the Kongresshaus landmark buildings as part of a new intricate conglomerate. The complex, like the Kongresshaus before it, creates a sequence of different experiences and merges the detailed functional programme with a richness of materials. The existing Kongresshaus is renovated and integrated into a new ensemble, and used as an extra space for the Tonhalle. Next to the Kongresshaus and the Tonhalle, a hotel tower acts as a spatial anchor. Names of composers are engraved into the stone facade of the hotel.

The move to maintain the Kongresshaus is achieved by positioning the new convention hall to the east side of the site's perimeter, on a plot scattered with trees along the Schanzengraben canal. The lakefront promenade and its parks are used as a landscape motif for the entire building, which emphasizes views from inside to outside, and uses metaphors from nature in the design of the interior. A facade of undulating glass, composed of curved pieces 5 m (16 ft 5 in) tall and 2.3 m (7 ft 6 in) wide, wraps the new convention centre.

Opposite:
Model of the town of Zurich, showing the project on the lakefront

RD   Even though the Kongresshaus was often underestimated, its qualities showed an architectural strength, which became more evident throughout the design process. Finally it was unimaginable to destroy it.

From top:
Site plan
Cross-section

Opposite, from top:
Ground-floor plan
Elevation facing the lakefront

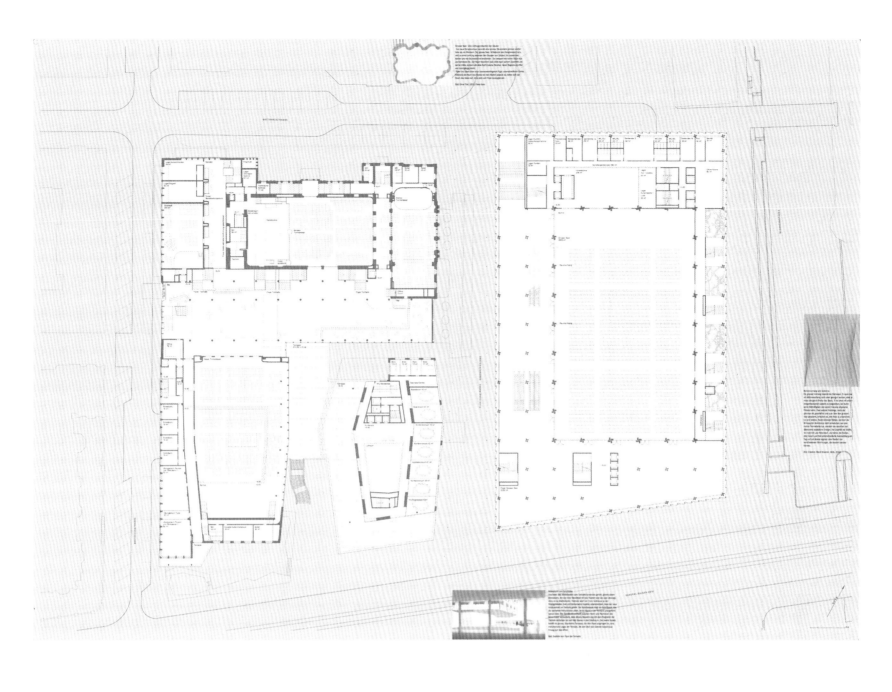

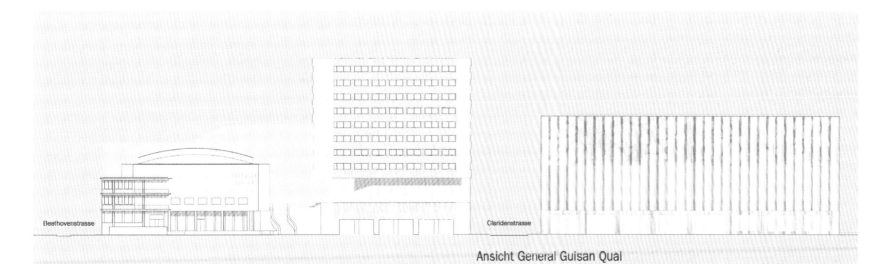

Beethovenstrasse   Claridenstrasse

Ansicht General Guisan Quai

Shoah Memorial Drancy, Drancy 2006–

Competition **1st prize** *Client* **Mémorial de la Shoah** *Structural Engineer* **Setec Bâtiment** *Mechanical Engineer* **Alto-Ingénierie**
Local Architect **Eric Lapierre** *Museography* **Heller Enterprises; Martin Heller, Gesa Schneider with iart interactive**

Under the Vichy regime, 70,000 French Jews and 130,000 foreign Jews were deported to extermination camps, where close to 76,000 were sent to their death. (In France, this calculation is possible due to the deportation lists left behind by the Nazis.) The central internment camp was set up in the Paris suburb of Drancy, in the Cité de la Muette housing complex, which had been built in 1932–4. Designed by Eugène Beaudouin and Marcel Lods, with Jean Prouvé, the prefabricated steel and concrete construction was one of the most advanced of its time.

From 1941 to 1944 the trains to Auschwitz left from here. The Cité de la Muette, a U-shaped block of five-storey housing with a courtyard measuring 200 x 200 m (660 x 660 ft), was occupied by the Germans and used as an imprisonment camp for war captives. Mainly French collaborators operated the internment and deportation camp. Although one block remains and is rented as social housing once again, today La Muette is principally a memorial to the genocide of the Jewish people in France. In 2006 the Mémorial de la Shoah foundation launched a competition for a building to be located near to the former detention camp.

The competition entry for the Shoah Memorial is a compact volume occupying a small plot on Avenue Jean Jaurès opposite the Cité de la Muette. The building will be used for exhibiting information and educational material about the history of the internment camp, and for holding lectures and conferences.

The staggered facade is built from reinforced concrete. The ground-floor facade is clad with reflecting glass, angled in such a way that the square of the Cité de la Muette, the historical site of the deportations during the 1940s, which is diagonally across the street, is presented as a mirror image. The two underground levels house conference rooms. Above ground, floor by floor, a visitor can successively apprehend the events of the past. The ground-floor gallery is dedicated to an introduction to the Shoah. The first floor accommodates archives and offices and the second floor serves educational activities. The top floor is dedicated to the view: the fully glazed front directs the visitor's eye towards the square and the actual site on which the events that shall never be forgotten took place.

Cité de la Muette housing complex

Opposite:
Model showing the top floor space

RD   The floors in the Mémorial de la Shoah in Drancy are a form of remembering,
a 'composite memory'. Remembering is understood as an ever-recurring effort or activity.
The building's elevation arranges and displays the different ways of remembering.
This is the building's monumentality.

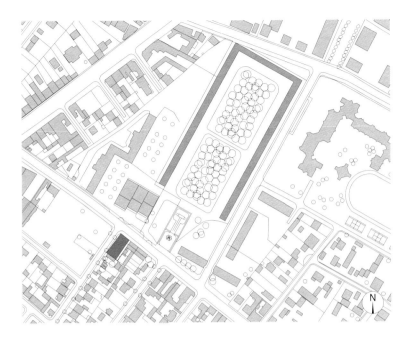

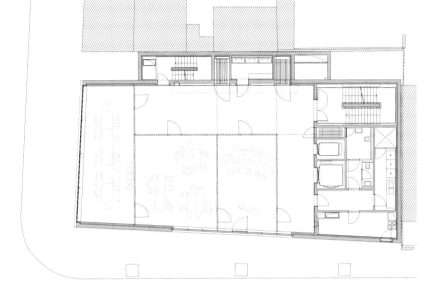

Clockwise from top left:
Site plan
First-floor plan
Second-floor plan
Ground-floor plan
Longitudinal section

Opposite:
Rendering of the angled entrance facade,
clad with reflective glass

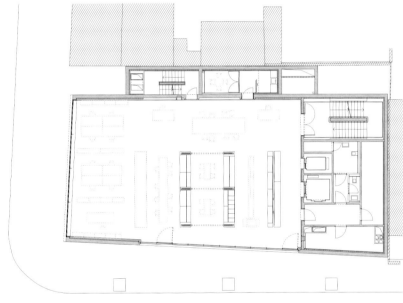

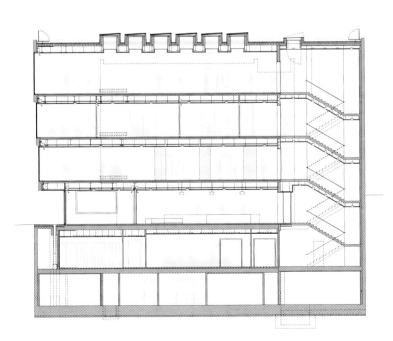

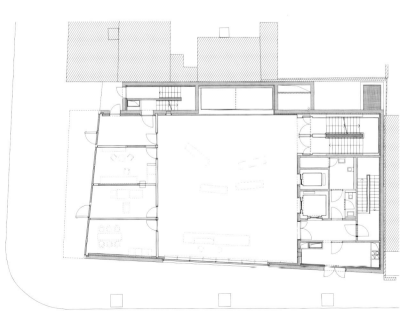

Music House for Instrumental Practice and Choral Rehearsal, Einsiedeln 2006–2010

Client **Benedictine Einsiedeln Abbey** *Structural Engineer* **Conzett, Bronzini, Gartmann** *Mechanical Engineer* **Waldhauser Haustechnik, Bogenschütz** *Local Architect* **Ruedi Birchler** *Acoustics* **Martin Lienhard**

The Benedictine Abbey of Einsiedeln, originally founded in 934, combines medieval structures and imposing Baroque elements. The building complex dominates the hilly landscape and the small town, and manifests a great clarity of form despite its history as a conglomerate from different periods. Adjacent to the abbey's main building, with the school building to the north, the Music House is built on the site of a 1930s music building; its layout is informed by the spatial flow of the impressive Baroque ensemble. The length of the new music school exceeds that of its predecessor, anticipating an extension of the schoolrooms on the east wing.

A garden hall on the ground floor, adjacent to the large courtyard of the school, acts as a new foyer for the school, and as a passage to the classrooms in the east wing. It is a place for encounters, exhibitions and celebrations, which were hardly possible in the narrow corridor of the previous building. The hall opens by sliding doors to the student courtyard, which in the winter is transformed into an ice rink.

A circulation core, containing a staircase and a lift, is located on the south end of the Music House, adjacent to the abbey's main building. On the north side, where the music school's extension is anticipated, a vestibule leads to rooms for storing musical instruments and sports equipment. The series of rooms upstairs, beneath a roof with a low-angled pitch, is made up of ten practice rooms and a hall for group rehearsals and small performances. This upper floor acts like a bridge across the void of the garden hall. The hall is equipped with a practice organ placed in front of a large window to the north. Through this opening, the hall opens to the landscape and the meadows of Einsiedeln become a part of the backdrop of the rehearsal stage.

Opposite:
Aerial view of the abbey, showing the
Music House in the centre toward the bottom

On the tripartite facade, pale concrete frames the wide garden hall's opening. The frames of larch wood have a weathered, faded look, and the concrete – a mix of white cement and white quartz sand, which has then been stained further white – blends into the tones of the Baroque ensemble, which continually change according to the time of day. The motif of the risalit, a projecting facade element taken from Baroque architectural vocabulary, articulates the middle section and establishes a centre in the facade's composition.

Abbot Martin   **It is of great concern to the monastic community to offer a true alternative to the existing school programmes. Through all the reforms, towards which we have always been open, and into the future, the school shall continue to be modelled after the Benedictine tradition. This becomes apparent in our pursuit of a holistic education, of which the artistic dimension forms an essential component.**

RD   **The building faces backward and forward. Like the corner risalits, the new music building asserts its independent position, but at the same time, like the middle wings of the monastary, it stabilizes the entire complex.**

West facade, seen from the courtyard of the school

Opposite:
Practice room

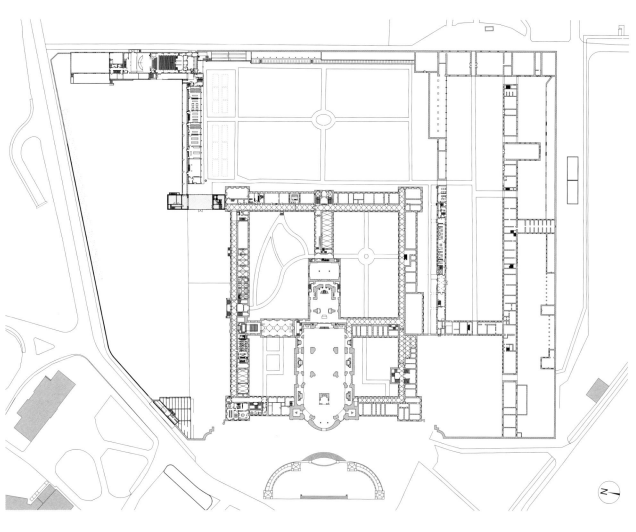

From top:
Ground-floor plan of the abbey
West elevation

Opposite, from top:
First-floor plan
Ground-floor plan
Longitudinal section

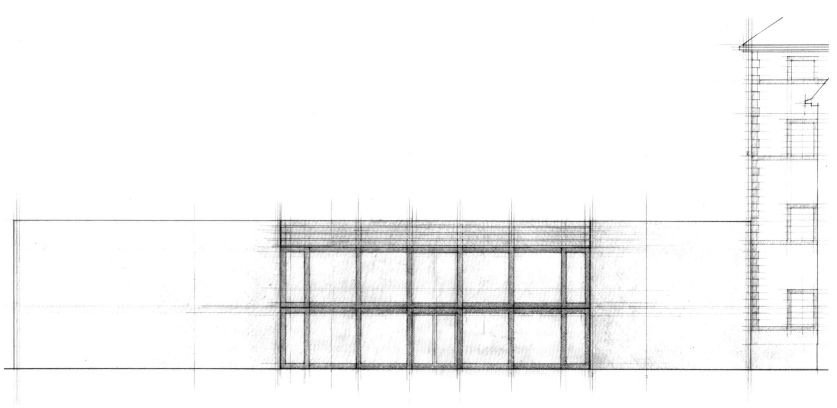

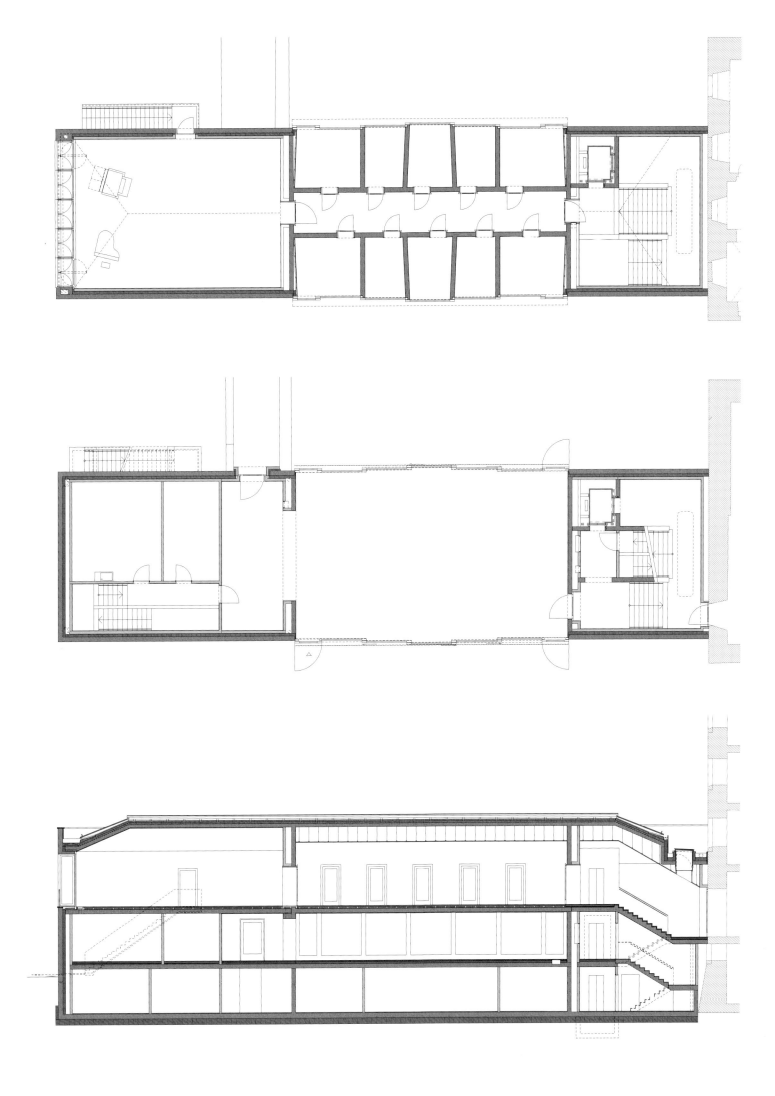

Kunsthaus Zürich Extension, Zurich 2008

Competition **Special commendation** *in collaboration with* **Peter Suter** *Client* **Amt für Hochbauten Zurich** *Structural Engineer* **Ernst Basler + Partner** *Mechanical Engineer* **Ernst Basler + Partner** *Landscape Architect* **Rotzler Krebs Partner**

Kunsthaus Zürich, the city's art museum, situated on the Heimplatz diagonally across from the Schauspielhaus Zürich (the city theatre), was designed by Karl Moser and opened in 1910. The building has undergone several extensions, and after its 2001–5 restoration a competition for an annexe building on the opposite side of Heimplatz was launched.

The requirements for the new building were manifold: flexible exhibition spaces for international art from the 1960s onwards and for new media, graphic art and photography; more traditional galleries to house the nineteenth-century and early modern collection in close proximity to the private collection of E.G. Bührle; new spaces for special exhibitions; a new entrance area with a display space facing the Heimplatz; and an underground connection to the Moser building. Although the competition brief suggested a building facing the Heimplatz and 'art gardens' at the rear, this entry responds to the spatial setting by rotating the building and garden, thus creating an open figure with multiple relationships to the existing building and the square.

The building addresses the square with its narrow side, emphasizing its directionality by a projection of the upper floor. Next to this, steps spanning the entire width of the terrace lead up to the garden level above Heimplatz, which faces the longer side facade. Thus, the building adopts the type of the Classical villa, accommodating the large programme in a long volume above a base. The upper floors create a long facade that fronts the garden, emphasizes the slope of this site, and references the rampart earthworks that, until the nineteenth century, marked the city limits. The terrace is at the same time a garden, a site for events and a space for exhibitions.

The entrance to the new building, level with the square and facing the art museum's main portal, leads to the sequence of spaces for international art and special exhibitions. These tall spaces are lit via a planar glass ceiling, above which eleven skylights project onto the garden terrace. On the first floor, the spaces facing the terrace contain the event and festival room, a foyer and a public café. The top floor, illuminated by north light through a skylight roof, houses the new galleries of the Foundation E.G. Bührle Collection and of the Kunsthaus's nineteenth-century and early modern art collection.

Villa Emo, near Fanzolo di Vedelago, Andrea Palladio, designed in 1564, was an important reference for this project. Its long front opens towards gardens and a walk made of large square paving-stones

Opposite:
View of the model showing, in the centre, the Kunsthaus below the Heimplatz and the extension above

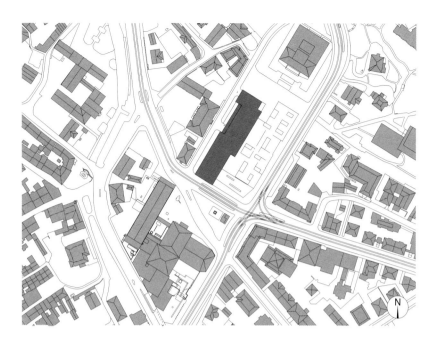

Clockwise from top left:
Site plan
Third-floor plan
First-floor plan
Ground-floor plan

Opposite, from top:
Detail section of the facade
facing Heimplatz
Detail section of the garden
terrace

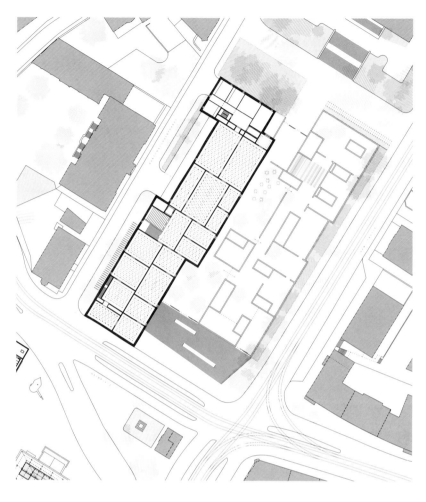

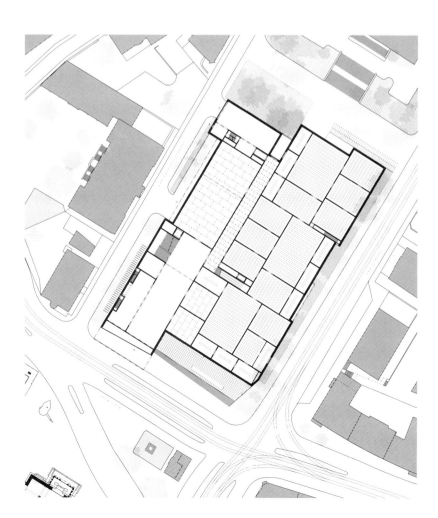

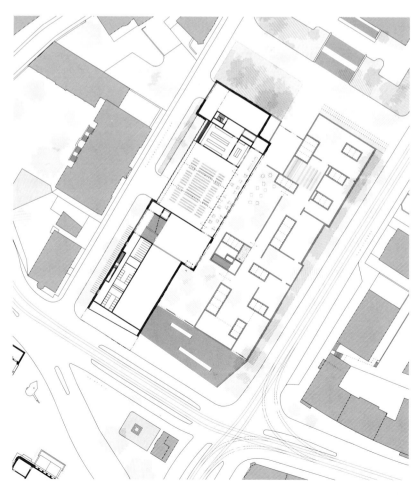

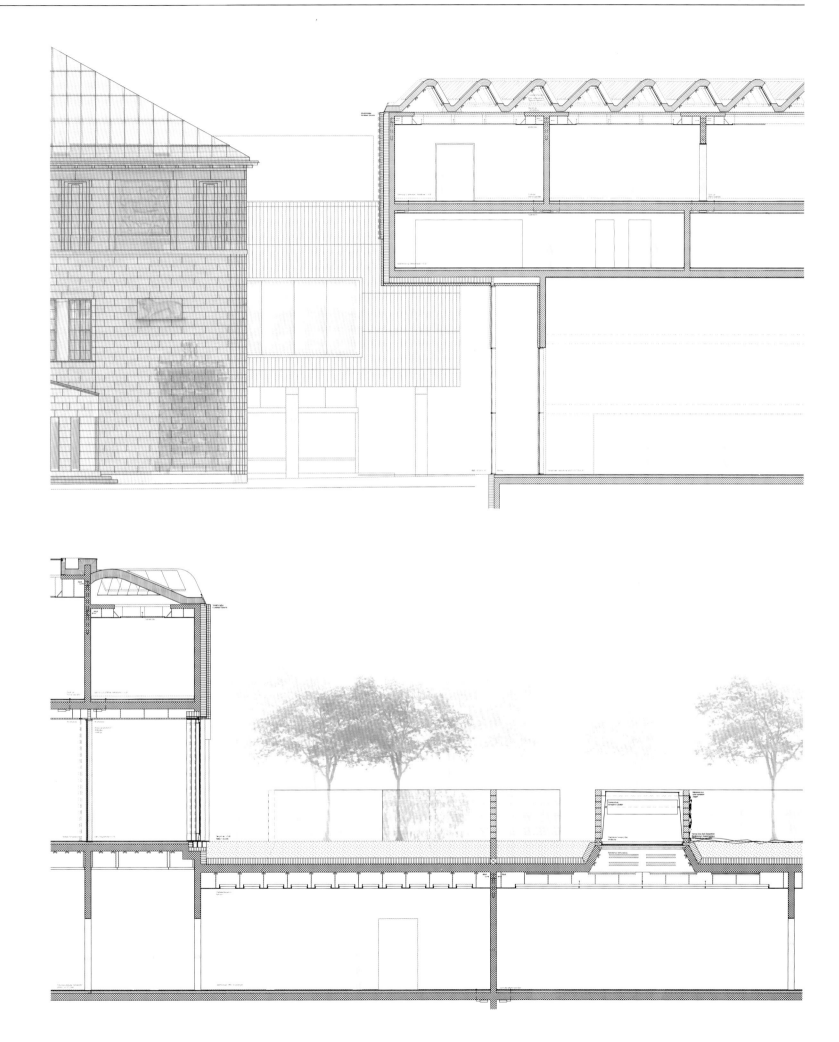

Swiss Re Headquarters, Zurich 2009–

Competition **1st prize** *Client* **Swiss Re** *Structural Engineer* **Ernst Basler + Partner** *Mechanical Engineer* **Dr. Eicher + Pauli**
Landscape Architect **Vogt Landschaftsarchitekten** *Workspace Design* **Sevil Peach Gence Associates**

Since the beginning of the twentieth century, a series of buildings have formed a ribbon along the quays and parks of Zurich's west lakeside. Here on Mythenquai, the headquarters of global insurance company Swiss Re comprise several office buildings, including one from the 1960s that is to be replaced. The new building, home of the executive board and its board of directors, will be the most prominent. Housing up to 800 office and a client area, it will foster a more cooperative approach on the part of the company's management by disclosing the working environment to their key clients, nurturing transparency at various levels. In this radically open structure, unenclosed staircases encourage interaction, and large spans with few columns provide maximum flexibility for the users.

The building's outline is simple: with the first four storeys aligned and subtle setbacks for the two top floors, it relates to the volumes and compositions of its historic neighbours. The undulating glass facade acts as an outer layer to the inner curtain wall and the circumferential balconies, which vary in depth. The surface, animated by a constant interchange of light and shadow, of reflections and transparencies, appears as a volume and enters into dialogue with the pilasters of Swiss Re's 1913 building to the south. The waveform of the glass shell is reminiscent of Classical fluting but in an abstracted form. These generous grooves create vertical movement that is superimposed over the horizontal slabs and brings together the inner and outer volumes as one form.

The three-dimensional layered glass facade ensures plenty of modulated daylight for the floor space, as part of the building's concept for sustainable performance and a high quality workplace. Two full-height courtyards and skylights allow for visual connections and ensure that the inner and lower areas are also filled with daylight. The southern courtyard is part of a spatial sequence, partially under ground, that links the new headquarters to the earlier Swiss Re buildings, forming a continuous inner gallery dedicated to Swiss Re's outstanding collection of art. The northern courtyard, at a lower level, serves as the foyer of the auditorium. All upper floors provide wide, light-flooded decks, guaranteeing an ideal working environment. The office spaces are articulated as open panoramas with only a few glass divisions.

Opposite:
Rendering of the glass facade facing the lake

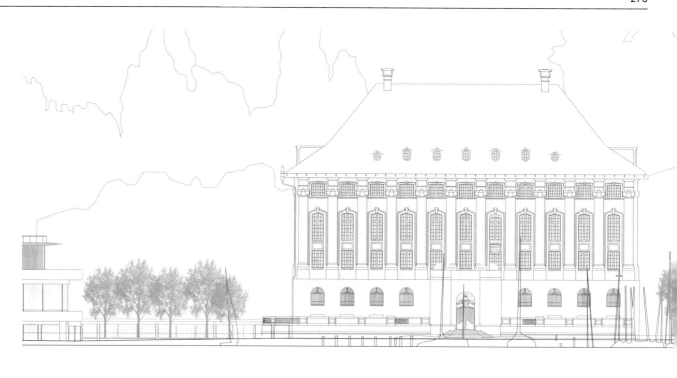

From top:
East elevation
Ground-floor plans of the new building,
Swiss Re buildings from 1913 and the
adjacent 1958 clubhouse

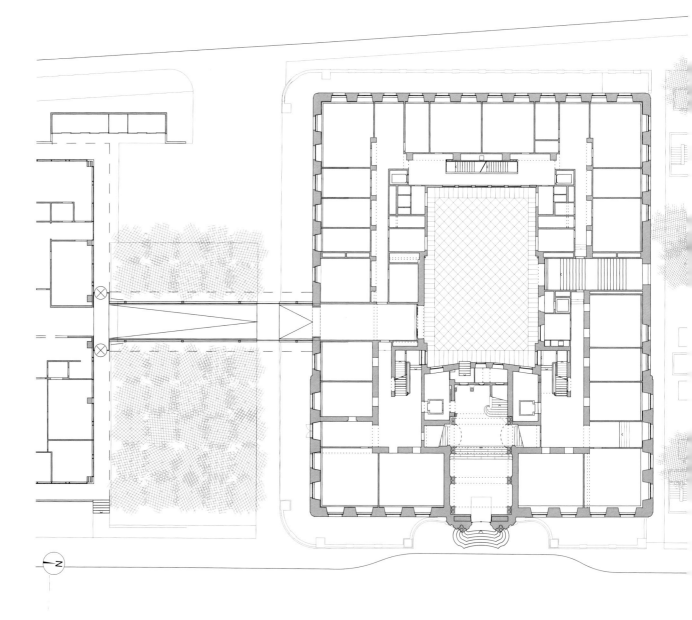

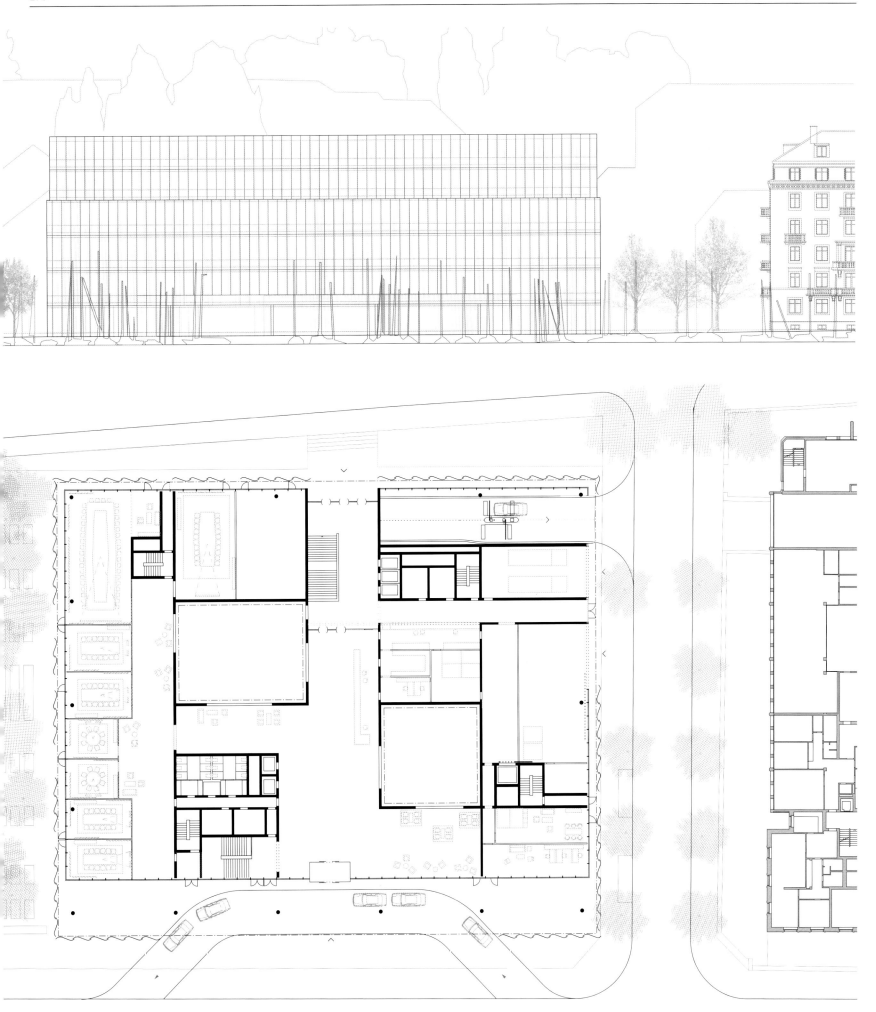

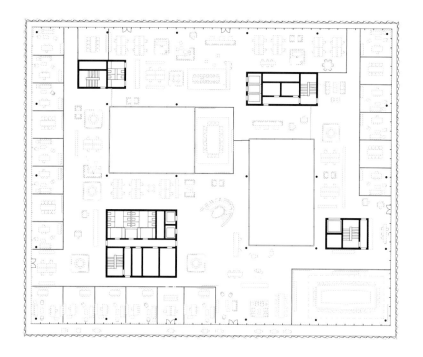

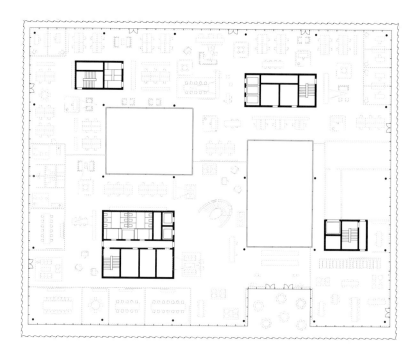

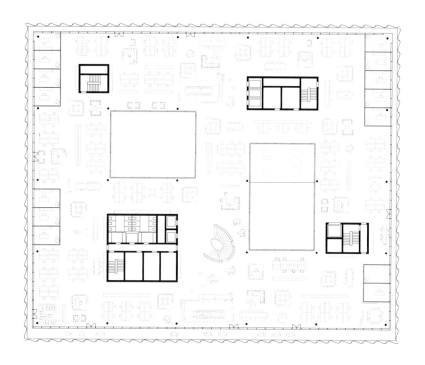

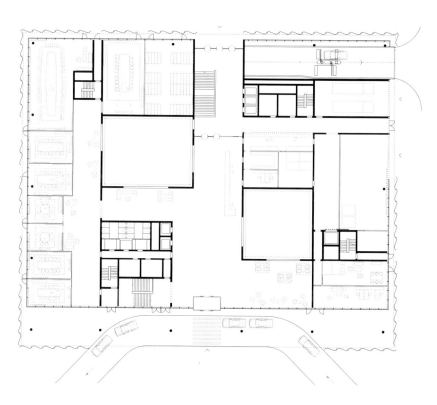

Clockwise from top left:
Fifth-floor plan
Sixth-floor plan
Ground-floor plan
Second- to fourth-floor plan

Opposite:
Glass facade, detail elevations
and plans. The balconies directly
behind the facades vary in depth
from 1 m (3 ft 3 in) to 2 m (6 ft 7 in).

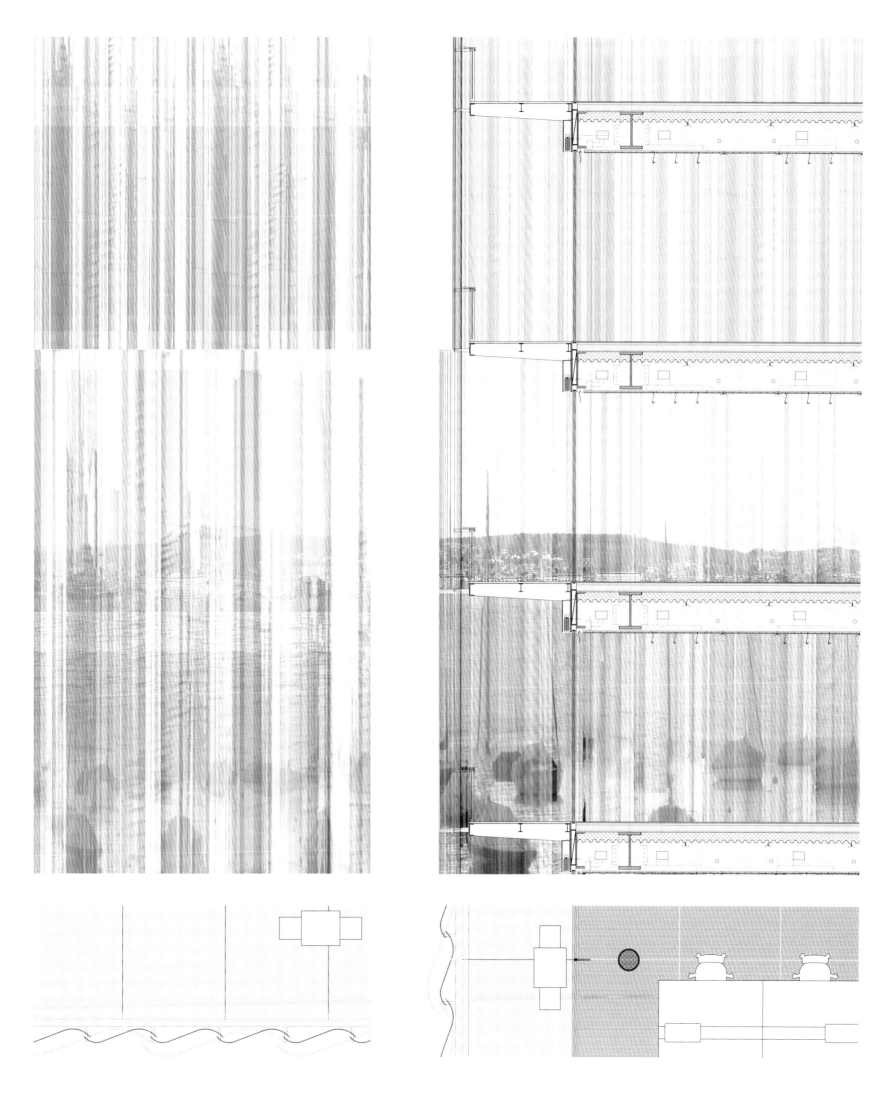

Kunstmuseum Basel Extension
Basel 2009–2010

Competition **2nd prize** *in collaboration with* **Peter Suter, Adam Szymczyk** *Client* **Bau– und Verkehrsdepartement Basel–Stadt** *Structural Engineer* **Gruner AG** *Mechanical Engineer* **Dr. Eicher + Pauli**

The main building of the Kunstmuseum Basel was designed by Rudolf Christ and Paul Bonatz, and completed in 1936. Located at an intersection of five streets, the building addresses the main street of St. Alban-Graben with a representative arcaded facade. It forms a closed front with the other palazzo-type buildings, today occupied by banks, on the boulevards of St. Alban-Graben and Aeschenvorstadt. Dufourstrasse, which cuts through the old town at an oblique angle, was not addressed. A fountain by Swiss sculptor Alexander Zschokke was placed in the remaining space between the side facade and Dufourstrasse.

Originally the Kunstmuseum was not laid out to present large exhibitions. Nowadays, as the requirements of the museum programme have changed, there is no infrastructure to accommodate special exhibitions and, repeatedly, entire collections have to be moved from place to place or stored. Furthermore, the magnificent Beaux-Arts halls are not always appropriate settings for more recently created art. In 2000 the museum moved its administrative functions and library into the neighbouring building to make more space for its expansive and precious collection. In 2009 a site on the other side of Dufourstrasse was acquired, where a new building is anticipated to provide additional spaces for the collection and special exhibitions.

This new building project complements the prominent Christ-Bonatz building and its closed side facade of horizontal layers of stone with a volume that addresses the city with large horizontal openings. Between the two counterparts, a third volume with four large exhibition rooms spans across Dufourstrasse and mediates the incision in the urban fabric. By the sculptural quality of shifted cubes clad in wood, this connecting volume projects the structure of the exhibition rooms to the outside.

The competition brief had suggested an underground passage between the existing and new buildings. Instead, the proposed new building directly adjoins both main exhibition floors of the art museum by exhibition spaces contained in elevated cubes between the two buildings. The majority of the jury had reservations about these connecting cubes, regarding them as an intervention that too profoundly reinterpreted the urban space.

Courtyard of the Kunstmuseum Basel, leading to the main entrance

Opposite:
Rendering of the extension spanning Dufourstrasse, as seen from the boulevard of St. Alban-Graben

Visitors enter the Kunstmuseum through the main building, the deep arcade of nine round arches on St. Alban-Graben giving way to a large interior courtyard. The main foyer with extended facilities, such as information desk, pay desk, cloakroom, bistro and bookshop, serves all parts of the museum, both in the existing and the future building. The new building's entrance area, across the street, houses a lobby for special events and exhibition openings. Complying with the competition brief, the floor assigned to special exhibitions can only be accessed from here on opening nights.

      The splendid staircase from 1936, at the central axis of the courtyard, functions as the stairway for both buildings. From this main staircase, the visitors reach the two upper floors, where the sequences are continuous from the existing to the future exhibition spaces. The cubes spanning Dufourstrasse thus offer the opportunity to show special exhibitions across the whole of the first floor, and the museum's twentieth- and twenty-first-century collection on a single level on the second floor.

First-floor plan

Opposite:
Rendering of the extension,
as seen from Dufourstrasse

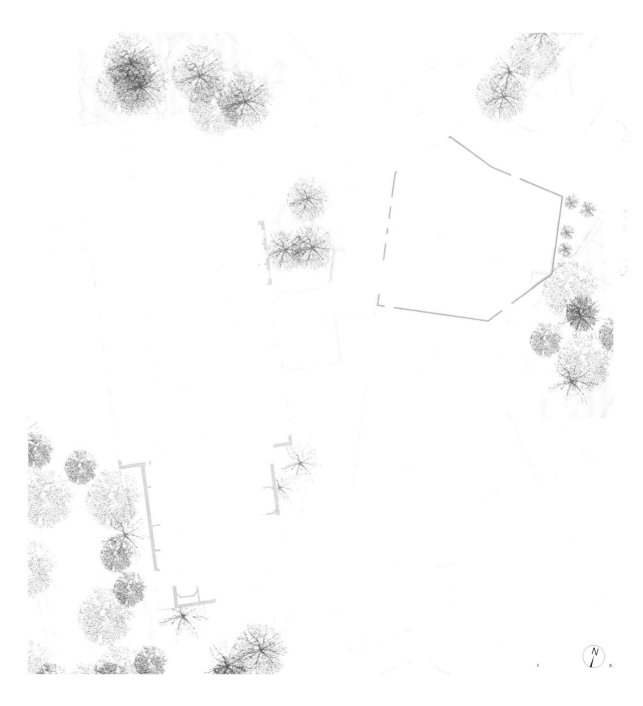

New East Wing Expansion of the Museum of Natural History, Berlin 1995 – 2010

Competition **1st prize** *competition in collaboration with* **Peter Suter** *Client* **Humboldt-University Berlin** *Structural Engineer* **Hildebrandt+Sieber** *Mechanical Engineer* **Dr. Ing. Bernd Kriegel Ingenieure**

South facade of the Museum of Natural History

Opposite:
Detail of the facade of the new east wing

Page 288:
The dinosaurs' exhibition hall

Page 289:
Cross-section of the dinosaurs' exhibition hall

The Museum of Natural History is the central piece of a monumental urban ensemble that was built according to August Tiede's plans between 1875 and 1889 along Berlin's Invalidenstrasse, and extended between 1914 and 1917. During World War II, the museum suffered extensive damage, and its east wing was almost completely destroyed by a firebomb, with only a few facade parts remaining.

In 1995, Diener & Diener won an international competition for the renewal and restructuring of the museum, but the comprehensively conceived redesign could not be realized due to a financial shortfall. In the following years, the concept was revised and now serves as the foundation for a phased renewal process. The variety of measures taken to renovate the museum was required not only due to the richness of architectural forms displayed by this monumental structure, but also because of the multiple uses of the building. One extraordinary aspect of the renovation is the preservation of the historical science collection and modernization of the research facilities as a simultaneous act of conservation and renewal of the science institute.

Between 2004 and 2007, a sequence of exhibition rooms in the centre section of the building was restored and modernized as an initial step in the general renewal. The original conditions of the building were researched and made relevant for the present by crucial interventions such as repairs, maintenance and additions, all traditional historical preservation strategies.

The new east wing houses the zoological specimen collection of embalmed animals, an internationally renowned collection of more than 276,000 glass containers Here, the research pieces and the display objects are one and the same. As they are sensitive to light, air and humidity, the specimens are preserved wet, in 70-proof ethyl alcohol. Placed on transparent shelves on the ground floor, the containers are secured and climate-controlled while the visitors move freely around the glass cube they occupy. The cube is lit from within and stands on a shimmering dark terrazzo floor. The amber colour of the ethyl alcohol is enriched by the surrounding walls, which are painted the dark brownish red colour of *caput mortuum*.

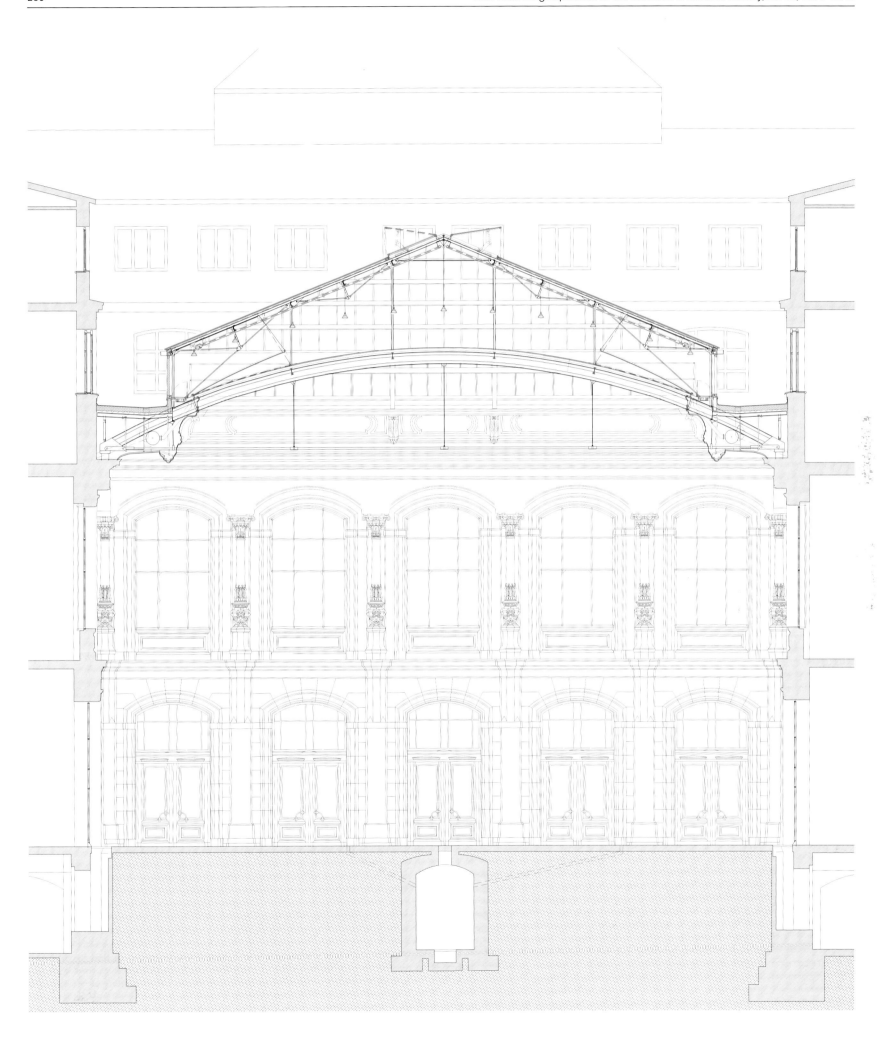

The interior space that the Wet Collection inhabits is a tall, windowless archive. For the first time, on the ground floor, the numerous exhibits of the wet specimen collection are visible to museum visitors, while remaining available for the scientists whose workstations are located inside the structure. In its radical concentration, the newly erected east wing conveys the original impact of the museum as a structure within which the collection, the research institution and public displays are inseparably tied together.

The exterior staging of the reconstruction radically confronts the challenging demands of the museum, which must balance the necessary conditions for the research and display that takes place within the east wing with the urbanistic and architectural desire to fill the empty space in this monumental structure. The result is an edifice whose surfaces accurately absorb and continue the modulation of the architecture – its brickwork, joins, sandstone, cut stone, and cladding – but which is also a homogeneous and closed building envelope, without window openings. To enable this, silicone moulds were made, in order to create cast-concrete pieces that replace those elements of the facade that have been destroyed. The old window openings were bricked up; the new ones are closed by an artificial-stone element. The fragments of the largely destroyed building envelope and its pale grey concrete inserts combine to make a new facade – one that recalls the original entity of the facade without negating its history. This move takes inspiration from *Tierschicksale,* 1913, a painting by Franz Marc, which was damaged in a fire and restored by Paul Klee in 1919, who complemented the destroyed shapes with achromatic additions. The cast relief doesn't repeat the original facade, but allows it to shimmer through, as if something new had been superimposed on it. The overall appearance of the rebuilt wing remains marked by its history, destruction, and renewal.

From left:
The destroyed east wing
Full-size mock up of a cast concrete facade insertion

Opposite:
Ground-floor plan
A – Dinosaurs' hall
B – Exhibition rooms
C – New east wing

Next page:
East facade of the new east wing

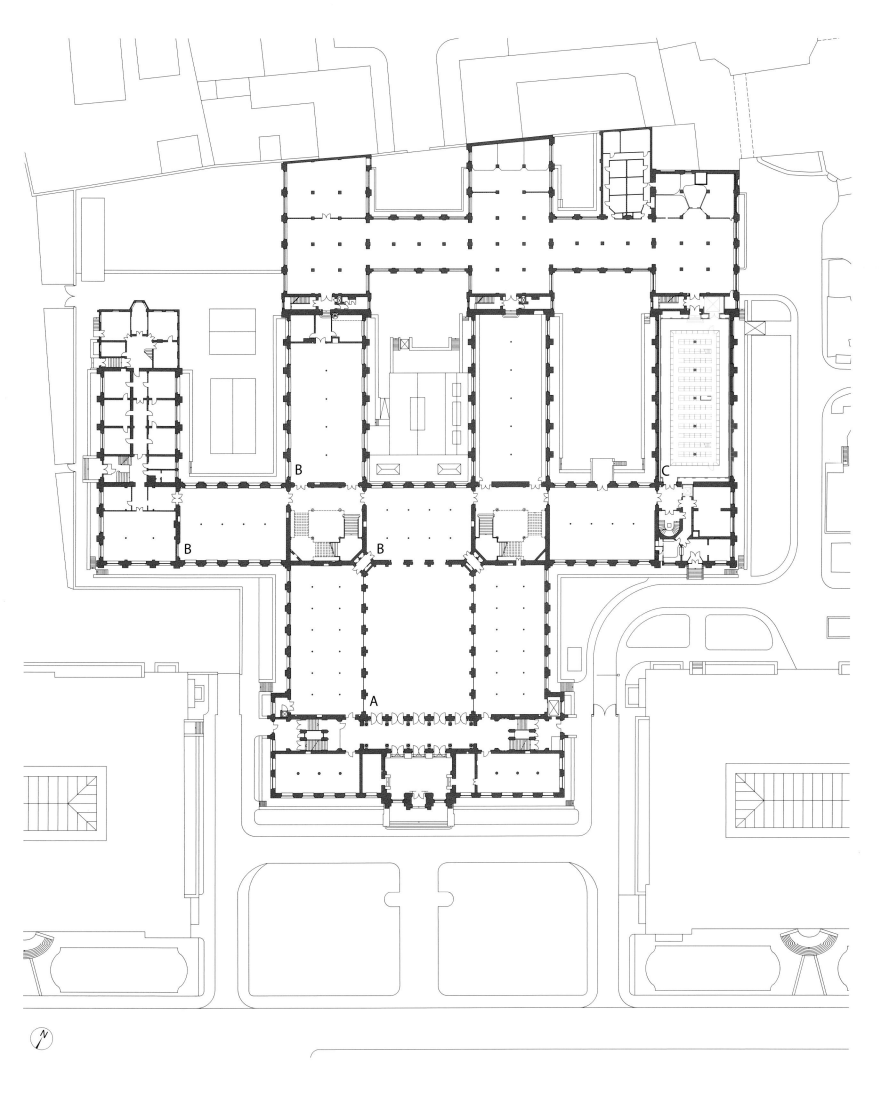

A

B

B

B

B

C

N

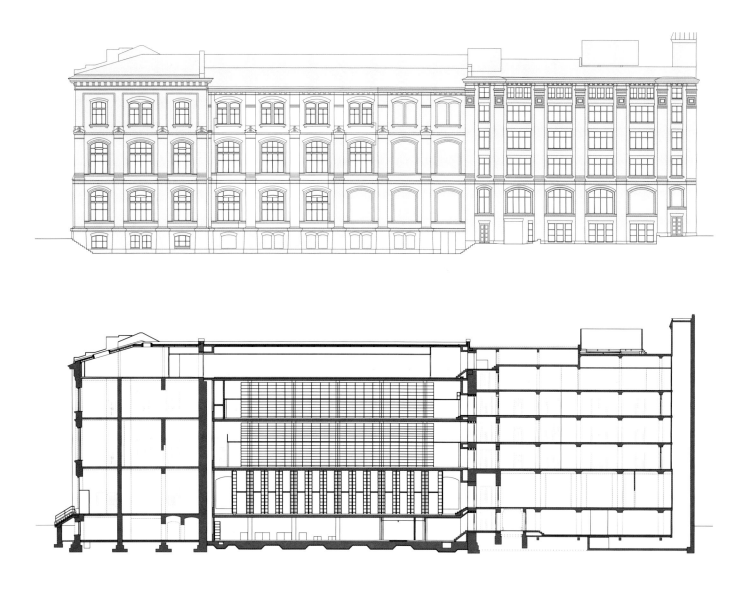

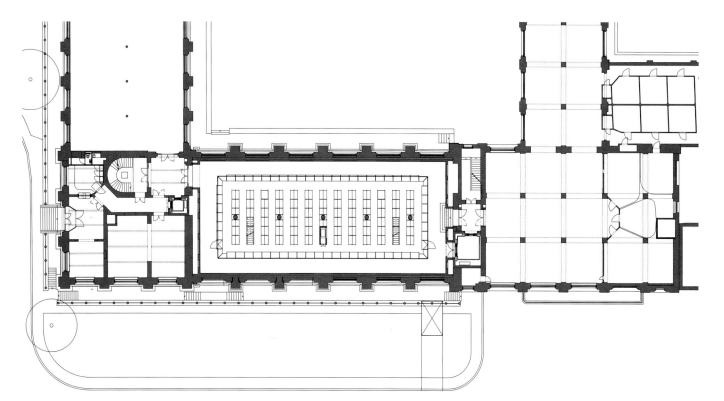

From top:
East elevation
Longitudinal section
Ground-floor plan

Opposite, from left:
Detail of the east
elevation
Detail section of the
east facade

Next page:
View of the east wing
interior, showing the
glass cube housing the
Wet Collection

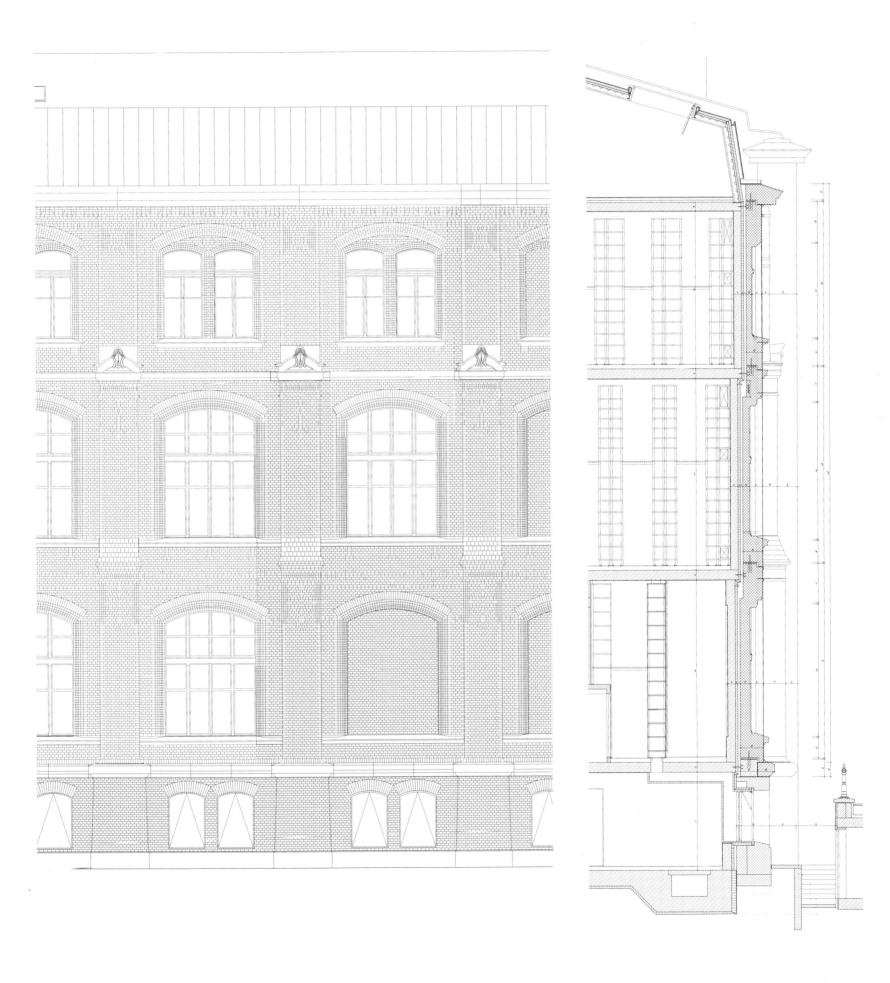

Architecture engagée: Diener & Diener

Martin Steinmann

When taking part in architectural competitions, Diener & Diener often attract attention by submitting designs that go beyond the requirements of the brief, by addressing questions that have not been asked, or by using the exercise to raise such questions. (This will become evident when we come to examine a selection of their projects, both realized and unrealized.) By doing this they are acknowledging a responsibility that goes beyond architecture in a technical sense. The concept of architecture they are staking out in such designs is a social one: it suggests that a building can be expected to make viewers aware of significant elements relating to its social use. This viewpoint guides Diener & Diener's work, and is to some extent the driving force behind their design approach.

We try to use the basic questions associated with the task in hand for our design process. This is because our generation has addressed architecture in terms of social and political questions, and still continues to do so. The idea that architecture relates to a use is part of this. The use is an aspect of the form. If, like us, you have a background in Modernism, then you are at pains to activate the use because it also activates the form.[1]

In thinking about this idea, I think it is permissible to extend the word 'use' to include the intellectual and spiritual aspects of architecture. When designing an art institution, for instance, this would mean not only making it possible in a technical sense to look at works of art, but doing so in a way that is appropriate to them.

Roger Diener tends to start lectures on his work by reflecting about questions shaped by the designs he is presenting. They are prepared in writing, and serve to some extent like surveyors' ranging rods for the points he has to make. What Diener says about his designs can also be applied to the thinking behind them: 'I am not interested in producing statements. It is a searching process – that is why our designs often do not look complete.'[2] These statements are elements from a theoretical discourse, but they are not intended for publication and despite the density of their language they are not in the right form for that. Despite this, in order to give some sense of the designs themselves, the present text frequently draws on passages from these reflections, foregrounding those aspects that deal with urban development.

When a building is erected it changes the relationship between the things that constitute the site. As the architects put it, 'Diener & Diener develop the design by addressing the place in terms of the change in perception that a building will bring about'.[3] They examine the site's qualities so that they can reinforce them with the building they are adding. Here the brief is a key feature:

Even though the particular nature of a building can be established from its form, beyond this there is a sense of coming to terms with the brief somewhere beyond form ... Brief and location relate to each other in a way that has to be redefined from case to case. In the best case it is possible to sharpen the qualities of the location in the brief and then to extend the brief on the basis of these qualities. Here we are developing ambivalent links. We would like to deepen our understanding of the place with a building and at the same time change the way in which it is perceived.[4]

The architecture that results from this process is defined primarily in terms of urban development: in other words, in terms that tie city and society together permanently.

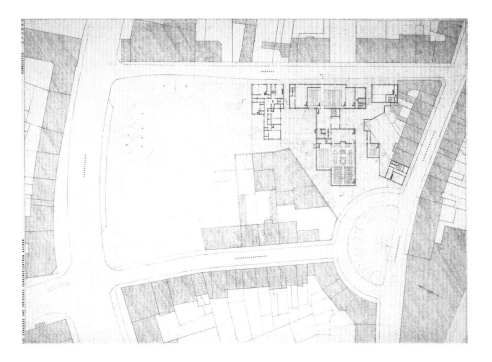

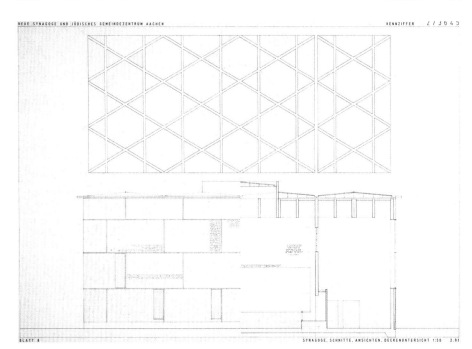

Presentation boards for:

Aachen Synagogue, 1991
(2nd prize)

From top:
Ground-floor plan
Perspective
Roof and facade details

The search for an architecture that will form an integral part of a city's development is undoubtedly crucial for Diener & Diener's work: a building stands within a sequence of measures that constantly change to correspond with new conditions. This means that design must be understood within a continuity of action. If the building is to acquire its form by making itself part of the development of a place, then it should not bring that development to an end. This necessity points backwards, into the past, as well as into the future. This is the reason why these architects keep a building 'open' in terms of form. In describing the Centre Pasqu'Art , Roger Diener explains:

It is possible to imagine building an extension [to the Neo-Classical Bürgerspital dating from 1866, which has housed rooms for an art gallery since 1990] in Biel, which was not imaginable before our own extension. This is often the case with us, because of the insight that one can contribute to a place with a building only for a limited period of time.[5]

Roger Diener's attitude to a listed building like the one in Biel vividly illustrates a fundamental point in his thinking: design that creates something new as a contrast with something old prevents further development. 'We try to take a different path. We try to explore the possibilities fully, to achieve a strong, completed effect for the building with our design.'[6] In this spirit, Diener has commented that in his extension for the Museum of Natural History in Berlin, the new complements the old, offering the prerequisites for further extension without losing the sense of this listed building as a whole entity. The word 'whole' word is important; he is trying to create a whole, but one that can change in response to new conditions. What Diener says about his attitude to listed buildings applies more broadly to cities as well. A building that acquires its form by creating a contrast with the location destroys the continuity that, for Diener, is the most crucial experience we can draw from the city.

Questions that arise from coming to terms with a brief are inevitably contemporary questions: we see – modifying a quotation from Arnold Hauser – only what can be seen from the present. This does not imply a constraint – on the contrary, commitment is shown precisely in the fact that we raise the concerns of our day; by doing this we are placing ourselves firmly in our own time. Jean-Paul Sartre has calls this 'being embarked', in the sense of being confined to a boat that is on a journey: 'I shall say that a writer is committed when he tries to achieve the most

lucid and the most complete consciousness of being embarked ...'[7], and it is possible to add: and if he expresses this awareness in what he writes – in its form or its expression.

Diener identifies Luigi Snozzi as being his most important teacher at the Eidgenössische Technische Hochschule (ETHZ) in Zurich. Snozzi, an architect from Ticino, was a visiting lecturer when Diener was a student. These were 'political' years in the architecture department – a time when meetings, lasting deep into the night, strove to define the architect's social role in order that those ideas could be incorporated into the educational process. It is possible to compare this approach to Sartre's idea of 'littérature engagée' ('committed' or 'engaged' literature), and to then call the resulting architecture 'engaged' or 'committed' architecture. However, Snozzi has pointed out that architecture of this kind does not emerge automatically from political responsibility; the commitment has to be realized within specifically architectural concepts. Architecture does not obey marching orders; its responsibility arises from form. This parallels what Sartre said to those who accused him of placing literature at the disposal of political conflict. And a similar sentiment probably also motivated Diener to include this quote from Adolf Behne in the introduction to a text about Snozzi: 'Anyone who acknowledges the law of society acknowledges the law of form.'[8]

In Snozzi's case, architectural historians and critics have talked about his 'architecture of resistance'. This alludes to his political views, but as discussed above, the responsibility arising from those views must, for architects, be articulated in architecture's own terms. It is a resistance to the way in which the city is treated, a resistance expressed in terms of a different way of approaching urban development. 'For Snozzi, form acquires its significance only from the context it is able to create in a particular place.'[9] Here the context created by the form is inevitably a new one. The city develops as a consequence of changed needs. So an architecture of resistance must make its own development comprehensible; in other words, it must preserve the old context within the new one. And it is around this question that Diener's thinking about urban development revolves. He may have taken this stance from Snozzi, but he has produced quite different works on the basis of it. However, the works often carry the same stamp.

Roger Diener joined his father Marcus Diener's practice in 1976. His first job was to transform an industrial complex into an urban residential area. He chose the form of a hollow block for this project, a form derived from addressing the discourse around the city during that particular period, in the wake of Aldo Rossi's seminal *L'architettura della città* (*The Architecture of the City*), 1966, just as much he chose it from an awareness that the city's form has to satisfy values other than the 'natural' ones of light, air and movement. But the residential scheme – dating from 1978 to 1981, in the Hammer district of Basel – does not simply repeat an earlier image of the city. Its form combines various city experiences: the gardens are like those found in Basel's nineteenth-century courtyards, and are integrated with the residential blocks in just the same way as parks were in early twentieth-century housing estates. A few steps away from the site for this project is a 1950s residential complex that introduced terraced housing into this predominantly nineteenth-century district and, with it, other, alien experiences of city life. But this total break with tradition did not manage to create any meaning other than a functional one.

The Apartment Buildings Hammerstrasse launched the address of the city that is such a distinctive feature of Diener & Diener's work. For that project, it was in part the development of the hollow block form that tied the site into the shape of the district. A measure of this kind was also required in Aachen in 1991, although the means of achieving it were quite different. The aim there was to combine the building of a synagogue with restoring the surrounding area, which still bore signs of war damage. The old synagogue had been burned down on the notorious night of 9 November 1938, and a new one was now to be built on the same site. The building was, as before, to be part of a larger development, but was to embody a new commitment: 'The new synagogue is to be seen as an expression of reconciliation in this context.' However, the architects refused to conform with this plan to use an urban development to reinstate an unquestioned normality.

Diener expressed, in a lecture, the difficulty involved in using a building as a reminder of the crime against the Jews: 'It is unthinkable that architecture should depict the destruction that dominated this place. A new building cannot signify one that has been destroyed, and it cannot even serve as a reminder of an old building that has been destroyed. The act of building excludes that.'[10] This is why the architects proposed a building set back from the building line of the Synagogenplatz. In their

proposal, the site of the old synagogue remains undeveloped, as this is the only way its destruction can be made part of the present. The clarity with which the design tackles this dilemma is an excellent example of Diener & Diener's architectural thinking:

Every building carries its own meaning and justification within it. This is not intended as a statement about urban development. But whole, committed buildings are needed if they are to take on a role in the greater context of the city. We cannot respond to buildings intended to invoke a meaning other than the meaning of the constructed whole itself … For this reason we took pains in Aachen to protect the new synagogue from having to be a vehicle for a particular idea of urban development … A simple building that is contained within itself alone seemed to us to be the only possible way to occupy this place, which is inseparably bound up with destruction … Ultimately it is the absence of a figure tied to an urban development idea that was able to trigger our sense of the place's significant emptiness.[11]

In statements like this, Diener is developing an architecture that is, to a certain extent, permeable to history. This is achieved not through signs, but through forms that engage us precisely because we cannot invest them with definite meanings. How are we to understand the empty space arising from this refusal to fill in the plan in Synagogenplatz? Even if we know, or think we know, we are not basing our reasoning on some thing, but on the absence of something, and we perceive this absence as the form for which we are trying to find a meaning. This is how architecture engages us. Deciding to leave the space empty also creates architecture.

Sartre firmly resisted the reproach that he was committing writers to political conflict with 'littérature engagée'. Literature can only do this at the cost of abandoning art. Émile Zola's famous 'J'accuse …!' open letter to the president of the Third Republic, published in the *L'Aurore* newspaper, is not literature. Of course, architecture serves a purpose, which, as Diener emphasizes, activates its form, but that is not what is meant here. So, in what sense is Diener & Diener's work 'architecture engagée'? In the case of the Aachen design, the commitment does not lie in stating a particular meaning, as a plaque would, but in encouraging viewers to explore what a meaning could be. This is an appeal to viewers' responsibility: they have to give their own meanings to the form. And this process acts as

Die bestehenden und die neuen Räume des Centre PasquArt bilden ein Ganzes. So entfaltet sich erst der Reichtum in der Folge der verschiedenen Ausstellungssäle. Das neue Gebäude ist als ein L-förmiger Körper um das bestehende Haus geführt und mit dem Treppenhaus verbunden. Es entsteht ein System von Raumgruppen, die sich dem Besucher kontinuierlich öffnen. In der gleichen Richtung wie die Treppenanlage angelegt folgt der Gang durch die verschiedenen Geschosse des bestehenden und des neuen Hauses einer fliessenden Bewegung. Es ist die Richtung des Hauskörpers und auch die des Tales. Das bestehende Haus ist von seinem institutionellen Ausdruck bestimmt. Es verschweigt die topographische Lage und seine besondere Bestimmung als Kulturzentrum. Das neue Haus wirkt dagegen gewandter. Es ist von der Lage und von dem Programm geprägt. So lässt sich schliesslich das bestehende Haus durch das neue deuten: die Reihe der drei grossen, hochgestellten Fenster der Ausstellungssäle lässt ahnen, dass sich hinter den kleiner geschnittenen Fenstern des alten Spitals inzwischen ähnliche Räume befinden. Das neue Gebäude ist als eine Stahl-Verbund-konstruktion gedacht, die mit grossformatigen Kunststein-platten verkleidet ist. Ihre Farbe könnte grünlich-grau sein, dem Sandstein des bestehenden Hauses ähnlich. Eine künftige Erweiterung des Centre PasquArt nach Nordosten ist möglich. Das Gewicht der Anlage würde dann verlagert und der Eingang und die neuen Räume ins Zentrum gerückt.

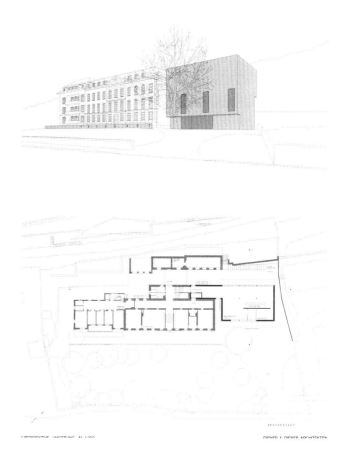

Les nouveaux espaces du Centre PasquArt et ceux existant forment un tout dont la cohérence révèle la richesse de la succession des différentes salles d'exposition...

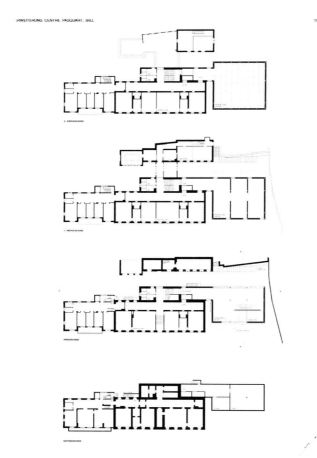

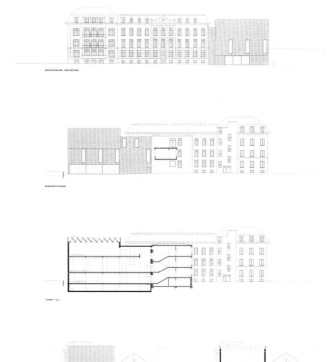

Presentation boards for:

Extension to the Centre Pasqu'Art,
Biel, 1995
(1st prize)

Clockwise from top left:
Text and site plan
Perspective and ground-floor plan
Elevations and sections
Floor plans

an educational impetus. This is why Diener's statement about the effect of buildings in Berlin applies just as much to his own: 'They are put on show in many ways in this open city form. They do not offer themselves to viewers passively, but demand critical appropriation.'[12]

The competition brief in Aachen intended to make amends for the destruction of the synagogue in 1938 by returning to the urban forms of the period that preceded the destruction – an approach that trivializes history in a way that is typical of the present day. This is also true of projects that involve no shameful history, as in the case of the Berlin Schloss.[13] In this sense, Diener & Diener's architecture expresses a commitment that runs like a thread through their work. It is directed against the ability to use form as a means of returning to a certain point in history – to the nineteenth-century city, to Aachen before 1938 – this would be covering up history in the name of history. But this commitment is also directed against another idea, according to which one can express one's own time only in the form of the 'other', or of something different. History is suppressed in this case too, but now in the name of the new, or of novelty.

It is from this twofold resistance that a 'committed architecture' can develop as part of a city into which change is integrated as continuity of action. For Diener, it is probably the most important experience a city can give us. His design for Aachen might seem to contradict such a statement, as it resists the kind of continuity that building on all the available space would express. However, that is not the case, as the urban consequences of the Third Reich are part of history. The concept of the whole that Diener uses is not a superficial one. His designs show what he means: building in such a way that the old becomes a necessary part of the new, or that the new acquires its meaning only in terms of the old, but never in such a way that it is merely a question of forms that symbolically refer back to the old.

The criterion for contemporary architecture intended to hold its own in the context of the city seems to be its value as independent architecture. Each building carries its meaning within itself. Architecture that is not at one with itself is not in a position to take on a committed role in the city. … One building cannot reflect another. At first, a building refers to itself alone. No continuity can be achieved by reflecting architecture.[14]

This does not mean that Diener & Diener eschew elements that they find in the context for their projects. But any elements they work with must have a new *raison d'être* in the buildings they design, not merely function as signs signifying the past. 'The parts we find in a particular place are detached from their immediate local context by being inwardly bound to the other elements [of the design]. In this way, architecture gains independence and escapes from the anecdotal expression of a montage.'[15]

The following sentences characterize, in the briefest possible form, the architecture that results from this approach:

Where we have done our work well the buildings have turned out to be inconspicuous. They look simple, modest, sometimes anonymous. There is no recognizable architect's handwriting. In the early 1980s, references to Modernism were still discernible, but these have receded increasingly in recent years. The buildings do not tell a story of their own. Rather they convey the impression that they are subject to the same history as the buildings that are already there, as their 'other' quality is contained within itself.[16]

I have previously written about Diener & Diener's endeavour to find the most generic form for their facades.[17] Diener calls it 'open'. He recognized in a 1988 lecture, which gave an overview of ten years of their work, that the composition of their facades remains open, and that the effect they make is not conclusive, but that 'the uncertainty is understood as potential'.[18] Though for many people who demand ever more new and powerful stimuli from architecture, this kind of form is seen as a flaw.

Diener speaks of parts that they find in a particular place, not forms; this is significant. If in the Apartment Buildings Hammerstrasse, the windows both on the street side and on the courtyard side are still signs referring to different kinds of city, the architects quickly overcame any postmodernist tendencies in a very few steps, starting with their Administration Building in Basel's Hochstrasse in 1986–8. It forms the end of a row of buildings between the railway line and a road, in the area situated on the 'wrong side of the tracks'. It responds to this very mixed environment with architecture that ensures the building will appear as a whole. Some years after this project Diener stated: 'The use of forms that are taken from the urban context and then reassembled robs a building of its ability to become part of the greater continuity of the city itself.'[19]

There is another crucial reason for having the will to formulate a building as a whole in which the parts are ultimately in a state of dynamic equilibrium: it strengthens its impact as an urban figure, and it is this that Diener & Diener now see as central to their architectural thinking. In reference to the Aachen synagogue, they declare that only simple, sometimes quite meagre, structures can save architecture from being charged with false gestures – 'a simple building that is contained within itself seemed to us to be the only way of occupying this place that is inseparably linked with destruction'.[20] In fact, their design is able to convey significance above all because, as a complete urban structure, it rejects the building line defined by the Synagogenplatz.

The nature of the task makes the Aachen design unique. For this reason we must test the architectural thinking it reveals against other work, starting with the offices for the insurance company Basler Versicherung, which the architects built in Basel's Picassoplatz, following two competitions in the years between 1988 and 1992. The design develops from the urban characteristics of this square, which are determined by buildings set directly on the street as well as buildings that are set back but still relate to the square. The dimension that defines the depth of the square is taken up in the structure of the new office building. This presents itself as two parallel, connected wings forming a complex urban figure. The unity of the building and thus its intended effect as an integral form is ensured by the facades, which run evenly all the way round the building; continuous cornices reinforce this impression.

It is, above all, these efforts to integrate a new building into its urban context and to clarify the qualities of the site through its design, that brings into play what I am calling 'social responsibility'. Diener & Diener's architecture shows how seriously they take this responsibility. I once described it as 'architecture for the city', in order to distinguish it from architecture that uses the city as a background against which it can stand out as 'different' (which could be described as 'architecture against the city', to allude to an important essay by Bernard Huet).[21] So the taking of responsibility is related to the city as a place where action can be taken. I have already mentioned Diener's conviction that this action should be continuous. This does not exclude formal breaks, as the Aachen design shows, so long as something is contained within them in the Hegelian sense – something against which the action turns. That is, action of this kind is not aimed at the form; the form

itself expresses it, by the connection between the old and the new that is discernible within it.

Is it necessary to say that this is a dialectical relationship? A question arises in relation to architecture like Diener & Diener's that owes its existence to addressing the city: to what extent can it be said that its form is derived from the qualities of a site? This would necessitate knowing these qualities – on the basis of thorough investigations – before starting to design. But is it not rather the case that certain qualities emerge as significant only during the design process? A place is 'open': its qualities are given, but they do not become relevant until the design interprets them by assigning them a place in a new whole. The design makes them new qualities, of a changed place. 'The consequences of a process like this … in which old and new parts are activated, as it were, cannot be predicted. Sometimes it produces new aspects, sometimes the new parts are dominated by the reactivated old ones. Designs of this kind are authentic only if we are prepared to take this risk.'[22]

To see what this can mean, let us look at the housing and office buildings in the former Warteck Brewery (1993–6) in Basel. In several ways, this is one of Diener & Diener's crucial works. The Warteck Brewery buildings have put their stamp on this district since the late nineteenth century; the large volumes, clad in yellow and red brick, are an important example of industrial architecture. Originally, after the brewery closed in 1991, it was to be demolished and the whole site redeveloped as residential and commercial premises by other architects. This would have meant losing the striking brewery buildings, and would also have removed the site's distinctive urban planning features (which were those of an industrial area, not a residential one), and replaced them with a perimeter block. However, adherence to the principle of continuity of action requires that although the old is replaced, it is preserved by the way in which it is replaced, and to a certain extent it requires that the old forms the background for the new.

The basis for the form that the new development took was found first of all in something else – namely, in the fierce resistance put up by the district's residents against the destruction of buildings that determined its appearance. Given this situation, Diener suggested that the brewery buildings should be listed and used for non-commercial purposes. This would not impair full use of the site, as it would be compensated by developing greater density in the remaining areas. In this way, the con-

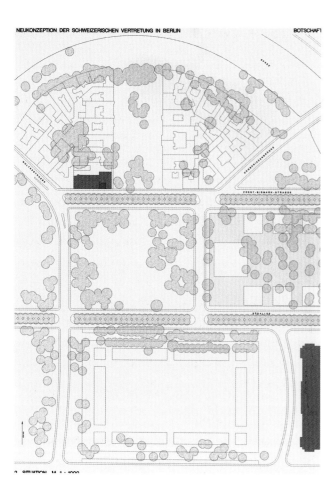

3 SITUATION M. 1 : 1000

„Als Individualität steht jeder Denkmalgegenstand über die Raumbezüge hinaus in Zeitbezügen, und über Raum- und Zeitbezüge hinaus in Bezügen zu einem allgemeinen Typus, dem sich kein Ding entziehen kann."
Tilmann Breuer, Baudenkmalkunde, München 1981.

Die Fotomontage zeigt die projektierte Erweiterung des Stadtpalais an der Fürst Bismarck-Strasse um 1911. Die aktuelle Erweiterung der Schweizer Vertretung ist geeignet, den ursprünglichen Zusammenhang des Palais als Teil des geschlossen bebauten Alsenquartiers wieder verständlich werden zu lassen. Die ganze Anlage soll sich zugleich zu einem eigenständigen Ensemble schliessen.

Das Palais wird weitgehend unverändert erhalten und genutzt. Die Art und Dichte der Funktionen in dem Gebäude gewährleisten eine Kontinuität, die über die Erhaltung der Räume hinausreicht. Sie bewahren ihre ursprüngliche Bestimmung in ihrem Gebrauch und der Aneignung durch die Bewohner.

Die Erweiterung ist als ein zweites Gebäude neben das Palais gesetzt. In ihm sind die diplomatischen und konsularischen Dienste angeordnet. Ein Hof ordnet die nach Norden und Osten gerichteten Räume des neuen Hauses. Die Komposition der neuen Fassade folgt einer freien Symmetrie, wie sie bei der Erweiterung des Göteborger Rathauses ausgeführt ist. Doch im Unterschied dazu sind die Öffnungen nach aussen gerückt und verschieben das Gewicht der Komposition zum Eingangshof des neuen Hauses hin. Die alte Fassade, für sich genommen fest gefügt, verliert als Teil der ganzen Komposition von ihrer Schwere und gerät in Bewegung. Die Erweiterung setzt der schematischen Fassadenordnung des neuklassizistischen Palais eine elementare Figur von Wand und Öffnung entgegen. Das Wechselspiel der leeren und ausgefachten Maueröffnungen entspricht dem Aufbau des Hauses. Ihre Grösse monumentalisiert keine Fassadenordnung, vielmehr sprengt sie die Regel, wie im Haus Tristan Tzara. In einer solchen Figur stehen die Teile nur noch für sich selbst.

Eine architektonische Fassung der Brandwand ergänzt das Ensemble auf der Westseite. Sie wurde in Zusammenarbeit mit einem bildenden Künstler entwickelt. Die Regel der Blockrandbebauung bleibt nachvollziehbar, aber die Brandmauer wird eindeutig dem Palais zugeordnet. Die Scheidemauer steht nicht länger für das abwesende, zerstörte Haus. Die einzelnen Kassetten des Rasters sprechen mehr von den gebauten Räumen im Innern des Gebäudes als von deren Öffnungen. So gesehen ist das Raster eher Grundriss als Ansicht. Der Reliefcharakter ist nur gerade soweit als Abbild der baulichen Dimension ausgebildet, als er die Scheidemauer nicht zur Skulptur werden lässt.

In der Ostansicht des neuen Gebäudes lässt ein feiner Versatz die Fenster wie ausgestanzte Löcher in der Wand erscheinen. Das Bild der giebelständigen Lage bestimmt den Ausdruck auf der Ostseite. Eine anekdotische Rekonstruktion des Stadtgrundrisses mit einer Strassenfassade an dieser Stelle wurde vermieden. Die Fenster auf der Nordseite fügen sich in das Bild der bestehenden Hoffassade.

Das Material für die Tragstruktur der neuen Gebäudeteile ist Beton. Eine Zementmischung mit Muschelkalkstein setzt auch die Materialität von Palais und Erweiterung in Beziehung zueinander. Ein unterschiedlich intensives Auswaschen (Druckbestrahlung) des Kunststeins lässt die braun- und ockerfarbigen Steinanteile gegenüber dem grauhaltigen Zement verschieden stark hervortreten. Das Verfahren erlaubt, Tonalitäten einzuführen und die neuen Teile so vom Palais und auch voneinander abzusetzen.

Die Gartenanlage ist einfach gehalten. Lichte Baumgruppen sind angeordnet, um das Gebäude-Ensemble in den Park einzubinden. Sie setzen sich in ihrer Anordnung bewusst über die ausgeschiedene Parzelle hinweg. Die Einzäunung ist als eine massive Holzkonstruktion gedacht.

Erweiterung des Stadtpalais, Paul Baumgarten, Fotomontage 1910/11.

Erweiterung Rathaus Göteborg, Gunnar Asplund 1934/37.

Haus Tristan Tzara Paris, Adolf Loos 1926.

Entwurf für die Erweiterung der Schweizerischen Vertretung, Fotomontage 1995.

1

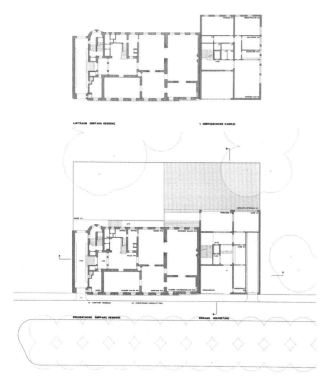

LUFTRAUM EMPFANG RESIDENZ　　1. OBERGESCHOSS KANZLEI

ERDGESCHOSS EMPFANG RESIDENZ　　　EINGANG VERTRETUNG

3　GRUNDRISSE　M. 1 : 200

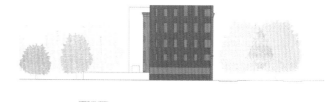

ANSICHT VON WESTEN

ANSICHT VON OSTEN

SCHNITT A - A

7　FASSADEN / SCHNITTE　M. 1 : 200

Presentation boards for:

Swiss Embassy, Berlin, 1995
(1st prize)

Clockwise from top left:
Site plan
Perspective, text and references
Extension, west elevation, east
elevation and cross-section
Extension, ground-floor plan and
first-floor plan

flicting interests of the residents and the developers could be brought in line with each other. Diener & Diener's design reflects this overlap, which is both an overlap of two different uses and an overlap of two important elements in the district's history.

This large urban quarter is structured as three massive building complexes: a deep commercial block with a small inner courtyard, a residential block with a large courtyard, and the brewery buildings, which are now listed and, together with the Warteck bar and restaurant, make up a heritage conservation area. The gaps among these groups of buildings open up the site for the quarter's residents; in contrast with the courtyard of a peripheral block, this plan has produced an urban space with a public feel to it. Other than those along the main road, the buildings are set back from the street line, so the paved area feels like a large square occupied by gigantic volumes.The volumes themselves – large buildings made up of greenish concrete for the commercial premises and brownish-red brick for the residential block – look heavy and solid, but they also seem 'mobile', to use a word that Diener loves, and which I understand to suggest that his buildings do not settle for a fixed meaning. That is the case here, in part because the volumes withdraw from the regime of the street line.

Many of Diener & Diener's designs stand out because of this distinctive quality: the fact that they cannot be pinned down to a single meaning conveyed by form. This is intentional, because it makes it possible for them to absorb the city, or to exist in a kind of superimposition with the city. In the case of the Warteck design the old use fades but is still alive – as remembered experience – within the new use, a connection we can easily make because we are familiar with spaces like this from factories. New uses have emerged from the existing building stock. The design has to work as hard to preserve such existing stock as to replace it. In the case of the Warteck development the two new buildings owe their strength to the suggestion that substantial sections of the brewery should be retained and financially liberated from the overall development imperatives by giving them listed status. 'Even though this design incorporates urban planning aspects that are important to us,' says Diener on this subject, 'in this case we were probably more concerned with social use aspects.' He adds: 'This also applies to the residential blocks that were built there ... The new buildings correspond with the old factory buildings: they are robust structures suitable for flexible use.'[23]

Diener says of Snozzi that his position is very simple and also very poetic.[24] But it is also idealistic, because it tries to set an imagined 'good' reality against the existing 'bad' one. In contrast with this, it is possible to say that the position expressed in the work of Diener & Diener is realistic, in that it dialectically inscribes the buildings into the given city. Vittorio Lampugnani describes it as follows: 'The designs represent additions that continue the structure of the city to a certain, changing extent.'[25] Sometimes the severity with which Diener & Diener demand (social) significance here can be alarming. This is why Diener talks about designs whose effect could be seen as controversial because they have not met certain expectations associated with a new version of a place. One example of this could be the housing they proposed for the Ministergärten in Berlin in 2002.

The Ministergärten is a place defined by sharp contrasts: it is situated between the last housing estate in central Berlin built of concrete slab construction and Peter Eisenman's Memorial to the Murdered Jews of Europe.

We could not imagine ... removing the slab buildings from the Berlin scene. This is why we suggested that the slab construction estate should be extended; in other words, that the unfinished model of the GDR estate should be completed. The repertoire of prefabricated parts was not to be taken literally: articulated buildings, freshly conceived ground plans and larger windows would have left no doubt about the contemporary nature of the version, but the new buildings would have been seen as part of the slab estate. The residential buildings were not intended to acquire their form from their proximity to the memorial. An unrelated juxtaposition seems more promising to us than a proximity taking account of the memorial, as the brief required.[26]

Designs of this kind take reality as it is, but they transform it. In the case of the Ministergärten, rather than the new housing deriving its form from a contrast with the slab construction blocks, revealing how ugly the latter are, the design draws them into a new whole, making people look at the slab construction blocks in a new way.

An ordinary building can achieve a poetic dimension if it is seen in combination with a new one that does not disown it from the outset, that certainly is different, but shaped by a reality determined by everyday things. The new building makes it

*possible to understand the place. I do not mean that in a dia-
lectic spirit. It is not about teaching – it is about the possibility
of discovering a poetic dimension in this place.*[27]

So, with their realistic approach, Diener & Diener do not reject
any of the steps within a city's development; the amalgama-
tion of these steps indicates the city's changing social use.
Housing estates of the 1950s are just as much part of this as
ones from the 1920s, even if these days, when thinking about
city development, they are often not thought of very highly.
Given the fierce debates that have raged in Berlin in particular, Diener has said, with reference to the different stances
adopted under Neues Bauen, that they were all contributions
to finding an appropriate model for the city: 'Every attempt
… to restrict the various facets of this open form for Berlin
threatens to blur the continuous trail of its development.'[28]
He significantly called his lecture 'Weiterbauen' (continuing to
build), an allusion to a modest journal published in Switzerland
in the 1930s whose aim was to further develop Neues Bauen
architecture despite the difficult conditions imposed by that
period.

If a building is to be preserved, then its redesign means finding
a use that can be integrated into its existing structure as
a new meaning. However, it can also be that refusing to use a
building in a new way is the only possible answer to the question posed. The instance of the large hall in Weimar, which
originated from the Third Reich, demonstrates the radical way
in which architects' responsibility to history – and to society,
whose history it in fact is – sometimes has to manifest itself in
refusal. This is evident in the report commissioned from Diener
& Diener in 2002. The Halle der Volksgemeinschaft (Public
Community Hall) was built in 1944 and, together with a parade
ground, formed the Weimar Gauforum; the plan was to convert
it into a shopping centre.

Complexes of this kind were intended to symbolize the power
of the National Socialist party in German cities, though the
Gauforum in Weimar was the only example to be largely completed by 1944. The concrete structure had been converted
into a multipurpose hall in 1974; then, in 2001, plans were
made to turn it into a shopping centre. Diener & Diener refused
to trivialize the history of the place in this way. They proposed
instead that the hall should be stripped of its facilities added
during the German Democratic Republic and shown as an over-
whelming naked structure: as a monument against Nazism.

The shopping centre was to be built on the large square by the
hall that served as a car park – a square whose sequence
of names reflects history: Karl August Platz, Adolf Hitler Platz,
Karl Marx Platz and finally, with no historical associations,
Weimarplatz.

The proposed measure – restoring the Halle der Volksgemeinschaft to its 1944 condition – lays the building open to experience in both its architectural and its political dimension, 'as
a monument in the open air', wrote Diener & Diener, and it is
'only by laying it bare that that the meaning, now blurred, of the
existing building is revealed again: the hall, never handed over
to serve its purpose, simply stands there, without a use', that
is, without any other use than that of reminding us of the delu-
sions of the Third Reich. Instead of disposing of history, history
is recalled by this impressive monument to National Socialist
delusion and its failure – would have been recalled, we have to
say, as Diener & Diener's design was not carried out.

According to the view reflected in this design, architectural
thinking is not restricted to finding an appropriate form for the
task in hand; it includes the task itself, its social significance
and the responsibility taken for this significance. In the case of
the hall in Weimar, it was this responsibility that moved Diener
& Diener to reject a use that undermined this significance –
and any use other than that as a monument would do this.
This is an extraordinary case, but the attitude that their design
expresses is typical of these architects' thinking in general. It
sometimes leads them, as I stated fleetingly at the beginning
of this essay, to go beyond the brief, or more precisely, to
expand the brief's conditions in such a way that its underlying
implications can be brought to light.

In other words, Diener & Diener lay claim to a responsibility
that includes taking on the brief and describing it: a belief
that designing begins with explaining the brief. It is not about
proposing something different at all costs, and looking for
meaning in the resulting 'difference'. That would be a kind of
Dadaist approach that is entirely alien to these architects.
When Diener says they try to look at a brief differently, this is
with the intention of identifying questions that have been obscured. A few lines from a poem by Günter Eich present a vivid
picture of what is meant here: 'Mit List / die Fragen aufspüren /
hinter dem breiten Rücken der Antworten' (cunningly / detecting
the questions / behind the broad backs of the answers).[29]
It would also be possible to use the Russian Formalist term

Villa Farnese, Caprarola, 1955. Aufstockung von Giacomo de Vignola. Festung um 1500 von Antonio da Sangallo und Baldassare Peruzzi

Kohlenwäsche, Innenansicht

Aufstocken der Kohlenwäsche

Aufstockungen sind ein oft wiederkehrendes, etwas unbeachtetes Thema in der Architekturgeschichte. Die schönsten Erweiterungen vermögen die Qualität des Baudenkmals zu steigern, ohne den Bestand in seiner Wirkung zu schmälern. Der architektonische Ausdruck solcher Aufstockungen ist beziehungsreich, dennoch versucht das Neue die Grenze zum bestehenden Bauwerk nicht aufzulösen. Schönes Beispiel dafür ist die Villa Farnese in Caprarola von Giacomo de Vignola. Ursprünglich als Festung über einem fünfeckigen Grundriss errichtet, wurde das Bauwerk um die beiden, über der Bastion liegenden Geschosse zu einer Sommerresidenz erweitert. Der Gebäudeschaft ist nach oben projiziert, die Mauern in den oberen zwei Geschossen wirken durchlässiger, ohne die Ordnung der alten Basis aufzulösen. Die Aufstockung der Kohlenwäsche folgt ähnlichen Regeln. Die neuen Geschosse sind ebenfalls exakt über dem bestehenden Gebäudekörper gelegen. Der Kopfteil ist proportional leicht erhöht. Damit wird die Fassung der Eckrisalite für die Erweiterung in eine räumlich architektonische Form übergeführt, in den übrigen Teilen führt die Erweiterung jene Themen fort, die bereits in der heutigen Fassung angelegt sind, so die dünne Fassadenhaut, die in der Aufstockung aus Gussgläsern besteht, die ohne Rahmen gefügt sind und den ruhigen Ausdruck des Gebäudes weitertragen.

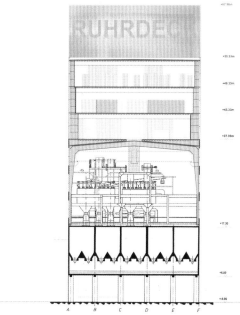

Kohlenwäsche und Museum Zeche Zollverein

Die Besichtigung der Kohlenwäsche bleibt eine wichtige Station des Museumspfads, auf dem der Besucher den Komplex der Zeche Zollverein kennenlernt. Im historischen Gebäudeteil werden Kohle und Berge nach den Gesetzen der Schwerkraft voneinander getrennt. Über der Maschinerie wird dem Besucher das gewaltige Haus erst verständlich, denn der Weg der Kohle führt durch das ganze Haus. Die Maschinen vergegenwärtigen die Produktionsbedingungen grosstechnischen Bergbaus eindringlich. Die Zeit scheint in den kalten Hallen still zu stehen. Hier unterscheidet sich die Wahrnehmung radikal von jener im Kesselhaus. Der Besucher erlebt das Gebäude, die Kohle und die Maschinen unmittelbar – ohne eine didaktische oder interpretierende Schicht, die dazwischen gelegt ist. Im Kesselhaus dagegen hat das neue Programm vom Bauwerk Besitz ergriffen. Die Maschinen sind ebenso manifest, aber sie sind als ein Denkmalfragment in einem neuen Ganzen aufgehoben. Die alten Dampfkessel im Design Zentrum sind domestiziert.

Die besondere Wirkung des Industriedenkmals Zeche Zollverein hat viel mit der unspektakulären und direkten Präsentation durch die Museumsorganisation zu tun. Gruppen von Besuchern gehen den Weg der Kohle nach und werden vor die still gelegten Maschinen geführt. Oft sind es authentische Schilderungen des erst kurz zurückliegenden Alltags auf Zeche Zollverein. Die Besucher erkennen, wie aktuell diese Industriedenkmal im Bewusstsein des Ruhrgebiets noch ist. Dabei scheint es nicht das Wichtigste, dass die technischen Fertigungsprozesse in allen Teilen verstehen. Vielmehr gilt es, diese besondere Authentizität des Denkmals und seiner Vermittlung zu bewahren, mindestens für diese und die nächste Generation.

Kohlenwäsche, Ansicht Portalträger

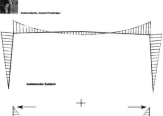

bestehender Zustand

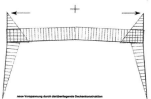

neue Vorspannung durch darüberliegende Deckenkonstruktion

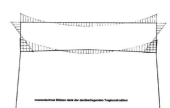

momentenfreie Stützen dank der darüberliegenden Tragkonstruktion

Portalträger und Aufstockung

Die Idee besteht darin, die heute mit Biegemomenten belastete Konstruktion mit Hilfe der darüberliegenden Tragwerks der Aufstockung so zu entspannen, dass keine Verstärkung notwendig wird. Die bestehenden Rahmen (Portalträger) werden aufgestockt. Der Rahmenriegel wird durch die Transformation vom Satteldach zur Geschossdecke zwangsläufig gegen die Rahmenecken hin höher. Diese zusätzliche Höhe wird als statische Verstärkung genutzt. Die grösseren Rahmenmomente werden dann auch wenn diese abgeleitet. Soitt ist eine horizontale Vorspannung der rückst höheren Decke notwendig. Mit diesen Massnahmen werden die Biegemomente in den bestehenden Rahmenstielen praktisch eliminiert. Deren Querschnitt steht somit ganz für die Aufnahme der Normalkräfte zur Verfügung. Er ist stark genug, das Gewicht der zusätzlichen Geschosse ohne Verstärkung aufzunehmen.

Trotz der Erweiterung der Portalträger nach oben kann das bestehende Betondach beibehalten werden. So bleibt der Innenraum in seinem originären Bestand bewahrt. Lediglich in den Binderachsen wird die Betondecke aufgeschnitten, um die neuen Stahlstiele mit der bestehenden Konstruktion verbinden zu können. Die neue Decke direkt über den bestehenden Bindern besteht aus Rahmenträgern mit dazwischen liegenden Spannbund Beiten. Die Decken werden in einer mehrschichtigen Lage aus Holz und Isoliermassen aufgebaut und mit einem Industrie-Gehbelag belegt.

ZECHE ZOLLVEREIN ESSEN Ruhrdeck und Bahnhof Museum Zeche Zollverein · Kohlenwäschemuseum – Plattform Design Diener & Diener Architekten Conzett Bronzini Gartmann Ingenieure 11.00 Spannungsverlauf Portalträger

Presentation boards for:

Ruhr Museum, Zeche Zollverein, Essen, 1999
(1st prize)

Clockwise from top left:
Perspective of the Ruhr Museum
Cross-section
Structural concept
Perspective of the main entrance of the Zeche Zollverein, showing the Ruhr Museum in the background

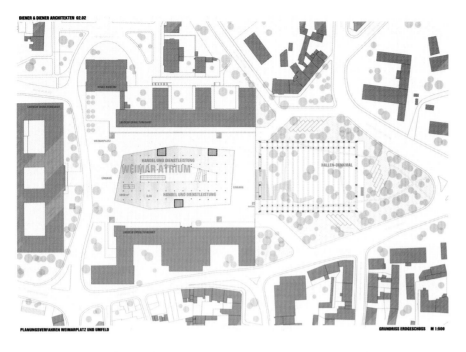

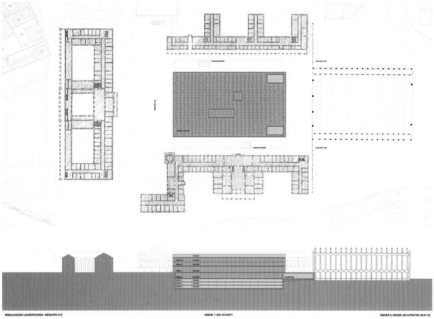

Presentation boards for:

'Gauforum' Weimar, 2002

From top:
Site plan
Ground-floor plan and section
Perspective

'dis-automatization' to describe this process, or to say that it is disturbing our normal habits, rather than striving to create something 'different', that is more likely to create genuinely new experiences. 'In the best case, it means that one comes across possibilities that one had not thought of, because they only show up when these questions are asked again.'[30]

Design that runs counter to expectations in this way often comes up against political obstruction, during the competition stage or later. An example of the latter took place in 1999, when Diener & Diener won first prize in a competition for the design for a museum of natural and cultural history of the Ruhr region (the Ruhr Museum) to be established in the former coal washing plant of the Zollverein Coal Mine in Essen. The world's largest coal-mine, commissioned in 1932, and seen as a model of rationalization, Zollverein Coal Mine was closed in 1986.

The creeping death of the coalfield was finally sealed. What remained was the coal industry's most important structural and technological monument. ... Production processes determined the organization and disposition of the cubic buildings, which were shaped according to very strict rules and fitted together as a rational whole that is all of a piece.[31]

Diener & Diener saw the coal washing plant as an inseparably joined sequence of buildings, rooms and machines that were used to process the coal. They felt that interrupting this continuum would mean robbing the plant of its power and effectiveness. For this reason, they explained that the coal washing plant cannot be divided and not put to a different use; instead, they proposed housing the museum by adding an upper floor to the building.

This additional storey continues the building according to the rules of construction, form and material that are integral to it. The cladding for this story is made of sheets of cast glass, which create a transparent covering that is visible from a distance and signals the transformation of this impressive mining landscape. The new museum on the roof of the coal washing plant enhances the quality of the monument without diminishing the impact of the existing buildings. On the contrary: as no machines had to be removed, the coal extraction processes can be presented with unique clarity. It is precisely this addition of a storey to the plant in the name of being faithful to the existing structure that led to the design's downfall. Because

it was thought that the addition would put at risk the pit's acceptance to the UNESCO World Heritage List, this design, extraordinary in its form and its significance, was withdrawn. Instead, the coal washing plant was cleared of its contents to make room for a museum designed by OMA, putting to waste the very elements that had made the building a monument!

'We read the city attentively, mark points of fracture, try to identify starting points in it and to design them as such; these are interpretations of complex states of affairs, and the means available for addressing them are equally complex.'[32] In other words, Diener & Diener's designs commit themselves by not removing these points of fracture, but by giving them a form by which they can become an insight for viewers, even if, at first, they find this experience disquieting. As Diener commented on their extension to the Swiss Embassy in Berlin, 'The fact that we took up the fundamental conditions of the palace that was to be extended, that we drew conclusions from them – in a word, that we expressed reality – that alarmed people.'[33]

The conditions to which Diener is referring are embedded in the history of the Alsen district, where the original villa had been built in 1871. It was the only building to survive wholesale demolition, from 1938 onwards by heavy machinery, to make room for Albert Speer's vast Volkshalle (People's Hall) – 'even before 1939, countless buildings around the Reichstag had been pulled down ... to establish the foundations for the monument to Fascist power'[34] – and from 1943 by air raids. After World War II it stood alone on its site northwest of the Reichstag; the Alsen district was not rebuilt. The form of the 1995 design for the Swiss Embassy extension encapsulates this history.

In their explanations, Diener & Diener write laconically: 'Various parts are set against each other. The wall created by Helmut Federle, the old villa and our new building create a singular kind of urban density. They are not apparently related, and yet they belong together. Two concepts were linked together: showing the villa as part of an earlier, complete development and creating a whole that was complete in itself.'[35] Even though this explanation was presumably written after the event, it captures the path that the work followed from the outset. For these architects, design means identifying paths of this kind via their questioning of the brief. 'Form emerges only from addressing a brief; it is only by addressing it that it is possible to discover the trails one would like to follow.'[36] Design of this kind resists, for as long as possible, any form that, beyond a certain extent, affects the work from the outside by prescribing rules that are not based in the process itself.

In accordance with this statement, Diener & Diener work on their designs over a long period, through a process of discussion: 'We cannot imagine designing by drawing. We use drawing only to capture what we have found. We think about the design, we talk about it. In this way it is developed in the form of ideas until we are in a position to capture it in drawing. And drawing means: ground plan, elevation, section.'[37] References play a major part in this process: 'In any case, it is possible to speak very precisely about architecture based on architecture that already exists and that one can remember.'[38] References contain concrete architectural experience, and as it is not possible to think out a design other than on the basis of such experience, they are a necessary device for approaching new form.

Statements and pictures, of buildings but also of other things, are to be found on the lower portion of the presentations that the architects submit for competitions. These are not there simply to convey the design decisions; they are part of it, because these decisions are inconceivable without them. So Diener calls these references 'vermutungen' ('speculations'). They illustrate questions the design is supposed to answer. For example, Gunnar Asplund's 1937 extension to the courthouse in Gothenborg, Sweden, was one of the references for the extension to the Swiss Embassy in Berlin, although they are not particularly similar in form. But what they have in common is the question of how a Neo-Classical building can be extended without subjugating the extension to the monumental form of the original, but also without ignoring it.

Undoubtedly some of these references explain the design presented in the plans. In the case of the coal washing plant, the architects linked their project for the added storey with a picture of the Villa Farnese in Caprarola. This was originally built as a fortified castle in around 1500, then extended in 1560 into a villa by Giacomo Vignola, who added two storeys. The walls of the upper storeys are more permeable, appropriate to the new function. In this way, the villa integrates itself with the changing use of the place. However, in a contrary movement, it is the design for the plant that explains the villa, in that we see a comparable relationship between old and new within it. This creates the dialectic that Arnold Hauser formulated for analysing the development of art: the new should emerge from the old, but the old should change in the light shed by the new.[39]

When Diener & Diener relate to other architecture in this way, it is on grounds of more than mere usefulness. The references are not restricted to making a problem visible. They stake out the field of research in comparison with which the architects are going to 'calibrate' their own work, as Diener puts it (using a word that he often cites): their view of architecture always leads them to 'recalibrate the design within architecture and within the social conditions. We are reminded of a requirement stated by Aldo Rossi, in his essay 'Architettura per i musei' (Architecture for Museums), that is central to his thinking: 'We must be in a position to identify what architecture makes our own architecture come into being.'[40]

The statements that Diener & Diener write on their plans are not restricted to explaining their decisions either. They sometimes refer to the design in a way that is not limited to the literal meaning of the words: they explain it poetically. And so they lend colour to the design, or to the way in which we see it. So, for example, they say about the structures in Zollverein Coal Mine in Essen that they give a sense of the enormous power of mining, and 'at the same time we recognize the beauty of the way they fit together to form a rational structure'. By listing all the elements with their technical names, the logic of the construction is reinforced through the medium of language. But the design makes the structure of the plant that is being illustrated its *raison d'être*; it does not intervene in the way the parts fit together, but continues the pattern by incorporating an additional use. It is also possible to see the extent to which language of this kind determines the perception of a design from the fact that articles about Diener & Diener's work often do not escape them: we sometimes find them there on the presentation boards without quotation marks.

In other words, Diener & Diener's approach is about making the site that the design must change comprehensible, precisely by changing it. Diener himself provides the keyword when he talks about a 'controversial' effect, by which he means an effect that does not become a foregone conclusion. When we understand the residential blocks in the Ministergärten – thanks to Diener's explanations as much as to our own attention – it does not mean that they will stop asking us questions. It is the form – perhaps seen as alien within its context – that gives the initial impetus for our interest, but beyond that the memory of the place in which the form emerges is always clearly addressed. This approach, which situates the design in a particular relationship with the elements that constitute the site, is necessarily a social one. But as it takes on concrete form as architecture, it is equally an architectural concern, in that the design acquires its form – and consequently its meaning – from this relationship with place. 'We work on the basis that the design can develop only if it is rooted in the time and the memory of a city. That is what we try to do again and again: to tie a design down in a place and in time. That is how we gain space for creative action as designers.'[41]

1 Roger Diener in conversation with Martin Steinmann, 26 June 2009.
2 Roger Diener in conversation (as note 1).
3 Roger Diener in conversation (as note 1).
4 Roger Diener, lecture, Florence, 2004.
5 Roger Diener in conversation (as note 1).
6 Roger Diener, lecture, Basel, 1994.
7 Jean-Paul Sartre, 'For Whom Does One Write?' in *What is Literature?* (Cambridge: Harvard University Press, 1988), p. 77.
8 Roger Diener, 'Die Verführung des Architekten', in Peter Disch, *Luigi Snozzi – Bauten und Projekte 1958–1993* (Lugano 1994), 414.
9 Ibid., 414.
10 Roger Diener, lecture, Erfurt, 1994.
11 Roger Diener, lecture, Erfurt, 1994.
12 Roger Diener, lecture ('Berlin, ein Ort für Architektur'), Berlin, 1993.
13 Many people in the newly reunified Germany argued for the reconstruction of the Berlin Schloss, a palace on the central Museum Island, which had been destroyed and replaced with a state parliament building for the GDR in 1964. The German government demolished the parliament building, and the future of the now-empty lot is still in debate.
14 Roger Diener, lecture, Vienna, 1992.
15 Roger Diener, lecture, Dresden, 1992.
16 Roger Diener, lecture, Dresden, 1992.
17 Martin Steinmann, 'Die allgemeine Form', in Ulrike Jehle and Martin Steinmann, *Diener & Diener – Bauten und Projekte 1978–1990* (Basel, 1991), 25–31.
18 Roger Diener, lecture, 1988.
19 Roger Diener, lecture, Vienna, 1992.
20 Roger Diener, lecture, Erfurt, 1994.
21 Martin Steinmann, 'Die Architektur von Diener & Diener – Ein Architektur für die Stadt', in *Faces*, no. 41 (1997), 26–7.
22 Roger Diener, lecture ('Continuity and Discontinuity'), Copenhagen, 2006.
23 Roger Diener, lecture, Florence, 2004.
24 Roger Diener in conversation (as note 1).
25 Vittorio Magnago Lampugnani, 'Anmerkungen zum Städtebau von Diener & Diener', in *Stadtansichten Diener & Diener* (Zurich, 1998), 8.
26 Roger Diener, lecture ('L'architecture face à l'histoire'), Lausanne, 2005.
27 Roger Diener in conversation (as note 1).
28 Roger Diener, lecture ('Weiterbauen'), Erfurt, 1994.
29 See Max Frisch, 'Skizze (zu Günter Eich)', in Max Frisch, *Forderungen des Tages* (Frankfurt, 1983), 97.
30 Roger Diener in conversation (as note 1).
31 Ulrike Steiner in Winfried Nerdinger and Ulrike Steiner, *Von innen und aussen bewegt: Diener & Diener* (Munich, 2004), 29.
32 Roger Diener, lecture, 1988.
33 Roger Diener in conversation (as note 1).
34 Werner Durth, *Deutsche Architekten – Biografische Verflechtungen 1900–1970* (Braunschweig, 1986), 144.
35 Diener & Diener, lecture, Entwurf, 1995.
36 Roger Diener in conversation with Mathias Müller and Daniel Niggli, 2009.
37 Roger Diener, lecture, London, 1992.
38 Roger Diener, lecture, Vienna, 1992.
39 Arnold Hauser, *Kunst und Gesellschaft* (Munich, 1973), 103.
40 Aldo Rossi, 'Architettura per i musei', in Aldo Rossi, *Scritti scelti sull architettura e la città* (Milan, 1975).
41 Roger Diener, lecture, Lausanne, 2005.

Page 34
Apartment Buildings Hammerstrasse
N° 525 HAM / 1978–1981
Hammerstrasse 164,
Bläsiring 150–160, Efringerstrasse 25
Basel, Switzerland

Hotel Metro
N° 528 MET/ 1978–1981
Elisabethenanlage 5
Basel, Switzerland

Study of a Private Hospital
N° 550 PKM/ 1979
Münstertal, Germany

Page 40
Apartment Buildings Riehenring
N° 530 RIH / 1980–1985
Riehenring 169–175,
Amerbachstrasse 100–104,
Efringerstrasse 22–32
Basel, Switzerland

Indoor and Open Air Swimming Pool
N° 555 HFR/ 1980
Competition 2nd prize
Riehen, Switzerland

Page 46
Apartment Buildings St. Alban-Tal
N°562 STA/ 1981–1986
Competition 1st prize
St. Alban-Rheinweg 94, 96
Basel, Switzerland

'Basel' Door handle
N° 569 GLU/ 1981

Apartment Building with Bank
N° 557 BKB/ 1982–1985
Missionsstrasse 86,
Sankt-Johanns-Ring 145
Basel, Switzerland

Extension Restaurant Le Relais
N° 571 RLR/ 1983
Elsässerstrasse 138
Basel, Switzerland

Bar Restaurant Kunsthalle Basel
N° 576 BRK/ 1984–1985
Demolished in 2001
Steinenberg 7
Basel, Switzerland

Residential Building
Allschwilerstrasse
N° 588 ALL/ 1984–1986
Allschwilerstrasse 94
Basel, Switzerland

Page 56
Office Building Steinentorberg
N° 543 STE / 1984–1990
Steinentorberg 8–12,
Innere Margarethenstrasse 5
Basel, Switzerland

Architecture Museum at
Domus-Haus
N° 596 AMB / 1984–1985
Pfluggässlein 3
Basel, Switzerland

Page 64
Showrooms and Administration
Building for Manor
N° 595 REB / 1984–1990
Rebgasse 34
Basel, Switzerland

Contribution to 'Architektur & LEGO'
Exhibition
N° 603 LEG/ 1984

Apartment Buildings Bener Areal
N° 605 CHU / 1985
Competition 3rd prize
Chur, Switzerland

Page 68
Administration Building Hochstrasse
N° 597 HOC / 1985–1988
Hochstrasse 31
Basel, Switzerland

Page 76
Training and Conference Centre
Viaduktstrasse
N° 650 ABZ / 1985–1994
Viaduktstrasse 33
Basel, Switzerland

Music Pavilion at Eden Hotel
Rheinfelden
N° 619 EDE/ 1986
Competition 2nd prize
Rheinfelden, Switzerland

Residential Buildings
Hans-Sachs-Hof
N° 617 SAC/ 1986–1989
Competition 1st prize
Hans-Sachs-Gasse 5
Salzburg-Lehen, Austria

Arts and Training Centre
N° 625 FRB/ 1986
Competition
Freiburg im Breisgau, Germany

Renovation and New Staircase
Basel Synagogue
N° 577 SYN/ 1987, 1988
In collaboration with Jonas Hechel
Leimenstrasse 24
Basel, Switzerland

Page 84
Administration Building
Picassoplatz
N° 591 BAL / 1987–1993
Competition 1st prize
Picassoplatz 5/6
Basel, Switzerland

Training Centre Bleicheliareal
N° 629 GAL/ 1987
Competition
Saint Gall, Switzerland

Page 90
Gmurzynska Gallery
N° 636 GMU / 1988–1991
Goethestrasse 65a
Cologne, Germany

Manor Departement Store
Schlossbergplatz
N° 637 BAD/ 1988
Competition
Baden, Switzerland

Regent Factory and Warehouse
N° 646 REG/ 1989–1992
Domacherstrasse 377
Basel, Switzerland

Police Administration Building
N° 643 LAG/ 1989
Competition, Honorary Mention
Saint Gall, Switzerland

Residential Buildings Luzernerring
N° 647 LUZ/ 1989
Competition
Basel, Switzerland

Study Triple Gym Gotthelf School
N° 648 GOT/ 1989–1990
Basel, Switzerland

Panoramarestaurant Parpaner
Rothorn
N° 651 PAR/ 1990
Competition 1st prize
Rothorn, Switzerland

Study Admes Commercial Buildings
N° 652 ADM/ 1990
Pratteln, Switzerland

Masterplan Ilôt Beleignat
N° 654 BEL/ 1990
In collaboration with
Gilles Barbey Colombier
Competition 1st prize
Monthey, Switzerland

Entrée de Ville Nord
N° 662 MON/ 1990
In collaboration
with Gilles Barbey Colombier
Competition 1st prize
Monthey, Switzerland

Study Residential Buildings
Gutenberghof
N° 659 GUT/ 1990–1991
Münchenstein, Switzerland

Aachen Synagogue
N° 661 AAC/ 1991
Competition 2nd prize
Aachen, Germany

Hotel 'Place Centrale'
N° 662.1 HPC/ 1991
In collaboration with
Gilles Barbey Colombier
Competition
Monthey, Switzerland

Extension of the FHBB, the Basel
School of Technology
N° 677 MUT/ 1992
Competition 3rd prize
Muttenz, Switzerland

Wipkingen Bridge Zurich
N° 679 WIP/ 1992
In collaboration with Meili,
Peter Architekten AG
Competition
Zurich, Switzerland

The Biel Gas Works
N° 664 GAS/ 1992
In collaboration with
Gilles Barbey Colombier
Competition
Biel, Switzerland

Refurbishment Basel Zoo
Restaurant
N° 674 ZOO/ 1992–1993
Bachlettenstrasse 75
Basel, Switzerland

Project for the Basel Stadtcasino
N° 686 CAS/ 1992–1995
Basel, Switzerland

Page 98
Office Building Kohlenberg
N° 632 KOH / 1992–1995
Steinenvorstadt 2, Kohlenberg 1
Basel, Switzerland

Roquette Residential Buildings
N° 689 ROQ/ 1992–1996
Courtyard in collaboration with
Dani Karavan
177, 179, Rue de la Roquette
Paris, France

Page 102
Vogesen School
N° 684 VOG / 1992–1996
St. Johanns-Ring 17
Basel, Switzerland

Page 106
Housing and Office Buildings
Warteck Brewery
N° 665 WAR / 1992–1996
In collaboration with Suter & Suter
Grenzacherstrasse 62, 64,
Fischerweg 6, 8, 10,
Alemannengasse 33, 35, 37
Basel, Switzerland

Residential and Office Building
Greifengasse
N° 673 GRE / 1993–1996
Greifengasse 23
Basel, Switzerland

Residential Building
Hochbergerstrasse
N° 645.5 WOH / 1993–2002
In collaboration with August Künzel
Landschaftarchitekten
Hochbergerstrasse 72, 74, 76
Basel, Switzerland

Extension of the Berlin Water
Company BWB
N° 690 WAS/ 1993
In collaboration with August Künzel
Landschaftarchitekten
Competition 2nd prize
Berlin, Germany

School of Architecture Nancy
N° 687 NAN/ 1993
Competition 2nd prize
Nancy, France

Facade on Mönkedamm
N° 702 MOE/ 1993
Competition
Hamburg, Germany

Study Nielsen Bohny Residential Buildings
N° 703 NIE/ 1993
Basel, Switzerland

Federal Institute of Technology Lausanne
N° 700 EPFL/ 1993
In collaboration with
Martin Steinmann
Competition 2nd prize
Lausanne, Switzerland

Neanderthal Museum
N° 704 NEA/ 1993
Competition 3rd prize
Mettmann, Germany

Photo Studio Murtengasse
N° 705 MUR/ 1993
Murtengasse 9
Basel, Switzerland

Masterplan for Baden–Nord
N° 691 CBN / 1994–1998
Competition 1st prize
Baden, Switzerland

A + T Residential Buildings Potsdamer Platz
N° 697 KÖT/ 1994
Competition 2nd prize
Berlin, Germany

Page 112
Apartment Buildings Parkkolonnaden
N° 697.2 KÖB/ 1994–2000
Competition: 2nd prize
Haus 5/ Gabriele–Tergit–
Promenade / Köthener Strasse
Berlin, Germany

Music College 'Schloss Belvedere'
N° 710 SBW/ 1994
Competition 2nd prize
Weimar, Germany

Migros Supermarket Eglisee
N° 692 RIE/ 1994–1996
Riehenstrasse 315
Basel, Switzerland

Hypo–Bank Theatinerstrasse
N° 708 HYP/ 1994
Competition 2nd prize
Munich, Germany

Page 118
Extension to the 'Centre Pasqu'Art'
N° 715 PAS / 1995–1999
Competition 1st prize
Seevorstadt 71–75
Biel, Switzerland

Page 126
Hotel Schweizerhof, Migros Supermarket, Migros School
N° 721 SCH / 1995–2000
Competition 1st prize
Schweizerhofquai 3,
Hertensteinstrasse 9,
Töpferstrasse 3
Lucerne, Switzerland

Page 132
Apartment Buildings KNSM and Java Island
N° 722 JAV / 1995–2001
Competition 1st prize
'Hoogkade' Bogortuin 3–255,
'Hoogwerf' KNSM Laan 8–98
Amsterdam, The Netherlands

Gerling Residential and Office Buildings
N° 723 GER/ 1995
Competition 2nd prize
Cologne, Germany

Page 140
Swiss Embassy Berlin
N° 724 BOT / 1995–2000
In collaboration with Helmut Federle
Competition 1st prize
Otto von Bismarck Allee 4A
Berlin, Germany

Page 286
Renovation of the Museum of Natural History
N° 727 HUB / 1995–
Competition 1st prize
In collaboration with Peter Suter
Invalidenstrasse 43
Berlin, Germany

Study Gstühl-Platz
N° 691.2 GST/ 1996–1998
Baden, Switzerland

Foreign Office Berlin
N° 728 AUS/ 1996
Competition, Honorary Mention
Berlin, Germany

Schönau Appartmenthouse
N° 658.1 SCÖ/ 1996–2002
Schönaustrasse 33
Basel, Switzerland

Residential and Office Building Elsässerstrasse
N° 683 LAN/ 1996–1997
Elsässerstrasse 57/ Landskronstr. 1
Basel, Switzerland

'Twogether' Prefab
N° 725 NEW/ 1996
New Standard Düsseldorf

Police School Zürich Barracks
N° 731 KAS/ 1996
Competition
Zurich, Switzerland

Residential and Office Building 'Unter den Linden'
732 LIN/ 1996
Competition 4th prize
Berlin, Germany

Residential Tower Spandau
N° 733 HEE/ 1996
Competition 1st prize
Berlin, Germany

Office and Residential Buildings 'Quartier 110'
N° 739 FRI/ 1996–2004
Competition 1st prize
Friedrichstrasse 180–184,
Mohrenstrasse 51–61,
Taubenstrasse 11–13
Berlin, Germany

Café 'Kunstmuseum Basel'
N° 738 UKK/ 1997
Sankt Alban-Graben 14
Basel, Switzerland

Basel Theatre
N° 750 BAS/ 1997
Competition, Honorary Mention
Basel, Switzerland

Längfluh Mountain Station
N° 741 SAF/ 1997
Competition 5th prize
Saas-Fee, Switzerland

Residential and Cultural Buildings 'Streichhan-Kaserne'
N° 742 WEI/ 1997
Competition 1st prize
Weimar, Germany

Row Houses Isteinerstrasse
N° 658.3 SCA / 1997–2003
In collaboration with August Künzel
Landschaftsarchitekten
Isteinerstrasse 90–96a
Basel, Switzerland

'Classic' Light Switch Levy Fils
N° 744 LEV/ 1997

'Kunsthaus Teufen'
N° 745 TEU/ 1997
Competition
Teufen, Switzerland

Page 166
Masterplan for the University Harbour
N° 746 MLO / 1997
Competition 1st prize
Malmö, Sweden

Project for Centralbahnplatz
N° 749 CEN/ 1997
In collaboration with August Künzel
Landschaftsarchitekten
Basel, Switzerland

Projects for Niagara Library and Orkanen Teacher Training's Centre
N° 746.1 MLN / 1998
Malmö, Sweden

Show and Exhibition Concept for Audi AG
N° 757 ING/ 1998
In collaboration with Peter Suter
Competition 2nd prize
Ingolstadt, Germany

Residential and Office Building Unter den Linden
N° 758 UDL/ 1999
Competition 2nd prize
Berlin, Germany

Hotel Bellevue
N° 761 RIG/ 1999
Competition 1st prize
Rigi-Kaltbad, Switzerland

ABB Power Tower Engineering Building
N° 691.7 ABB/ 1999–2002
Competition 1st prize
Bruggerstrasse 66–72
Baden, Switzerland

Sachsenhausen Monument
N° 763 SAO/ 1999
Competition
Oranienburg, Germany

Mainz Synagogue
N° 764 SYM/ 1999
Competition 3rd prize
Mainz, Germany

Leipzig Monument
N° 765 LEI/ 1999
Competition
Leipzig, Germany

Page 178
Presentation of the 'Guest of Honour 1998 Switzerland' at Frankfurt Book Fair
N° 737 FRA / 1998
In collaboration with Peter Suter
Frankfurt am Main, Germany

Rollerhof
N° 767 MUK/ 1999–2000
In collaboration with Peter Suter
Münsterplatz 20
Basel, Switzerland

Page 182
Apartment and Office Building Bäumleingasse
N° 769 BÄU / 1999–2005
Bäumleingasse 14
Basel, Switzerland

Page 188
Collection Rosengart
N° 771 ROS / 1999–2002
Pilatusstrasse 10
Lucerne, Switzerland

Residential and Office Buildings Gartenstrasse
N° 775 ZUG / 1999–2009
Gartenstrasse 6, Rigistrasse 3,
Bundesplatz 7/9
Zug, Switzerland

Page 192
Ruhr Museum at Zeche Zollverein
N° 774 ZZE / 1999
In collaboration with Conzett,
Bronzini, Gartmann
Competition 1st prize
Essen, Germany

Dorint Hotel
N° 658.2 SCD/ 2000–2004
Schönaustrasse 10
Basel, Switzerland

Page 198
**Extension to the National Gallery
of Modern Art**
N° 776 ROM / 2000–
In collaboration with Peter Suter
Competition 1st prize
Viale delle Belle Arti 131
Rome, Italy

Berlin National Library
N° 777 SBB/ 2000
In collaboration with
Adolf Krischanitz
Competition 3rd prize
Berlin, Germany

Page 212
Masterplan for the Maag Areal Plus
N° 778 MAA / 2000
In collaboration with
M. & E. Boesch Architekten
Competition 1st prize
Zurich, Switzerland

Study for Schällemätteli
N° 779 SCA/ 2000
Competition
Basel, Switzerland

Page 202
Extension to the Pergamon Museum
N° 780 PER / 2000
In collaboration with Peter Suter
Competition 2nd prize
Berlin, Germany

**Residential Building Meierhof
Gamander**
N° 781 GAM/ 2000
Competition
Schaan, Liechtenstein

Page 206
Residential Buildings Ypenburg
N° 754 YPE / 2000–2003
In collaboration with West 8
Weidevogellaan / Spenwersingel
The Hague, The Netherlands

Residential Buildings Im Forster
N° 784 FOR/ 2000
Competition
Zurich, Switzerland

Study for Toni
N° 793 SZH/ 2000
Zurich, Switzerland

Musterhaus
N° 792 HAD / 2000–2007
In collaboration with
Architekt Krischanitz
Friedhofstraße 169
Hadersdorf, Vienna, Austria

Stuker Auction House
N° 790 ROB/ 2001–2003
Alter Aargauerstalden 30
Bern, Switzerland

Hi –Fi Furniture
N° 793.1 SZH/ 2001
Villa zum Delphin
Zurich, Switzerland

Page 222
Stücki Shopping Centre
N° 645.8 STU / 2001–2009
Hochbergerstrasse 68/70
Basel, Switzerland

Office Building Theresienhöhe
N° 799 MUT/ 2001
Competition
Munich, Germany

Residential Building Wasserstadt
N° 800 WSB/ 2001
Competition
Berlin, Germany

Endress & Hauser Office Building
N° 801 EHR/ / 2001
Competition
Reinach, Switzerland

Gerling Office Building
N° 802 GER/ 2001
Competition
Cologne, Germany

Masterplan Siemens Hofmannstrasse
N° 804 SIM/ 2001
Competition
Munich, Germany

Residential Buildings Ministergärten
N° 806 MGB/ 2001
Competition
Berlin, Germany

'Neue Markthalle' Basel
N° 808 MHB/ 2001
Competition
Basel, Switzerland

Maag Residential Building
N° 778.3 MAA/ 2002–
Turbinenstrasse 31, 35, 39, 43
Zurich, Switzerland

Page 216
Mobimo Tower
N°778.1 MAA/ 2002–2011
Turbinenstrasse 18 and 20
Zurich, Switzerland

**Showroom and Administration
Building Slam Jam**
N° 803 FER / 2002–2005
Via Luigi Francesco Ferrari 37 A
Ferrara, Italy

Bocconi University
N° 807 MIL/ 2002
Competition
Milan, Italy

'Gauforum' Weimar
N° 809 WPM/ 2002
Competition
Weimar, Germany

Hochbergerplatz
N° 811 HBG/ 2002
Competition 1st prize
Basel, Switzerland

Page 230
Novartis Campus Forum 3
N° 814 NOH / 2002–2005
In collaboration with artist Helmut
Federle, architect Gerold Wiederin
Competition 1st prize
Basel, Switzerland

Masterplan for Citygate
N° 819 MIB / 2002–2010
In collaboration with August Künzel
Landschaftsarchitekten
Competition 1st prize
Sankt Jakobs-Strasse 187–201
Basel, Switzerland

House 'C' at Citygate
N° 819.1 MIB/ 2002– 2010
St. Jakobs-Strasse 199
Basel, Switzerland

Masterplan Droogdokkeneiland
N° 821 MAS/ 2002
Antwerp, Belgium

Hotel Zeche Zollverein
N° 822 HZE/ 2002
Competition
Essen, Germany

Page 170
University Building
N° 746.3 MLÖ / 2003–2005
Nordenskiöldsgatan 10
Malmö, Sweden

Athletics Stadium Letzigrund
N° 825 LET/ 2003
Competition
Zurich, Switzerland

Saint Andreas Castle
N° 828 CHA/ 2003–
Cham, Switzerland

Page 246
Casa A1 at the Olympic Village
N° 830 TUR / 2003–2006
In collaboration with Steidle + Partner
Via Giacomo Bruno / Zino Giacomo Zini
Turin, Italy

'Hessisches Landesmuseum'
N° 831 DAR/ 2003
Competition
Darmstadt, Germany

Table Prototype for Vitra
N° 833 TIS/ 2003

Apartment Buildings Riedbergstrasse
N° 834 RBS/ 2003–2007
Riedbergstrasse 1–7
Basel, Switzerland

'Autobahneinhausung'
N° 836 ASZ/ 2003
Competition
Schwamendingen, Switzerland

Masterplan 'Schlachthof Letzi'
N° 832 ELZ/ 2004
Zurich, Switzerland

**Residential and Office Buildings
Arnulfpark**
N° 842 AFP/ 2004
Competition 2nd prize
Munich, Germany

Office Building Spreedreieck
N° 845 SDP/ 2004
Competition 1st prize
Berlin, Germany

Maihof Center for Media
N° 850 NLZ/ 2004
Competition 1st prize
Lucerne, Switzerland

**East Wing Expansion of the
Museum of Natural History**
N° 727.2 HUB / 2004–2007
Invalidenstrasse
Berlin, Germany

Page 250
Westkaai 1 + 2 Apartment Buildings
N° 817 ANT / 2005–2009
In collaboration with Michel
Desvigne Paysagiste
Kattendijkdok, Westkaai 41, 51
Antwerp, Belgium

**Masterplan for Residential and
Office Buildings 'Ile Seguin'**
N° 860 BIL/ 2005–2009
In Collaboration with
Vogt Landschaftsarchitekten
Competition 1st prize
Cour de L'Ile Seguin
Boulogne Billancourt, France

Page 258
Convention Centre 'ZürichForum'
N° 862 ZFZ / 2005
In collaboration with Peter Suter
Competition
Zurich, Switzerland

Residential Buildings 'Parc du Hamoir'
N° 864 HAM/ 2006–2010
Brussels, Belgium

The Bauhaus Collection
N° 866 BAB/ 2005
Competition 3rd prize
Berlin, Germany

**Sulzer Smithy Hall on 'Katharina
Sulzer Platz'**
N° 869 SUL/ 2005
Competition 1st prize
Winterthur, Switzerland

Siemens Residential Buildings Obersendling
N° 872 SOM/ 2005–
In collaboration with
Vogt Landschaftsarchitekten
Competition 1st prize
Munich, Germany

Office Building Stänzlergasse
N° 873 STÄ/ 2005–2007
Stänzlergasse 4
Basel, Switzerland

Three Villas Chäppeli
877 MEG/ 2005–2007
Käppelistrasse 21
Meggen, Switzerland

Masterplan Sihl Manegg
N° 858 SIH/ 2006–2010
Zurich, Switzerland

Residential Buildings Deux Alice
N° 865 DAB 2006–2007
Brussels, Belgium

Page 262
Shoah Memorial Drancy
N° 878 SHO / 2006–2011
In collaboration with Eric
Lapière and J.L. Cohen
Competition 1st prize
110–112, Avenue Jean Jaurès
Drancy, France

Town Hall Sarnen
N° 880 SAR/ 2005
In collaboration with
Joos Mathys Architekten
Competition 1st prize
Sarnen, Switzerland

Dining Table for 8
N° 882 TAB/ 2006

Page 266
Music House for Instrumental Practice and Choral Rehearsal
N° 885 MKE / 2006–2010
Benedictine Monastery Einsiedeln
Einsiedeln, Switzerland

Extension to Paulaner Brewery
N° 886 FPM/ 2006
Competition 2nd prize
Munich, Germany

Study 'Deutsches Theater'
N° 887 DTM/ 2006
Munich, Germany

Karlin Residential and Office Buildings
N° 888 KAR/ 2006
Competition 1st prize
Prague, Czech Republic

Apartment Building and Hotel 'Kantonsspital Zug'
N° 857 KAZ/ 2005
Competition 1st prize
Zug, Switzerland

Extension to the Town Museum 'Schlössli'
N° 891 SSA / 2007–
In collaboration with Martin Steinmann, and artist Josef Felix Müller
Competition 1st prize
Schlossplatz 23
Aarau, Switzerland

Apartment Buildings Schwamendingen
N° 892 AHS/ 2006
Competition
Zurich, Switzerland

Residential Buildings Schönwilpark
N° 896 SPM/ 2006–
Competition 1st prize
Meggen, Switzerland

Siemens Office Building
N° 897 SBT/ 2006–
Competition 1st prize
Zug, Switzerland

Study 'Wohnstadt Luzern'
N° 900 BZO/ 2006
Lucerne, Switzerland

Masterplan for Malters
N° 893 HUG/ 2007–
In collaboration with August Künzel
Landschaftsarchitekten
Competition 1st prize
Malters, Switzerland

Residential Buildings Cloche d'Or
N° 898 LUX/ 2007
Competition
Cloche d'or, Luxembourg

La Maison du Savoir 'Cité des Sciences'
N° 899 MAI/ 2007
Competition
Belval–Ouest, Luxembourg

Pisa University Lecture Hall
N° 904 PIA/ 2007–2009
In collaboration with Heliopolis
Competition 1st prize
21-Architetti Associati
Via Nicola Pisano, Via Risorgimento
Pisa, Italy

Markthalle Basel Residential Building
N° 907 MBH/ 2007–2012
Viaduktstrasse 10, Steinentorberg 18
Basel, Switzerland

Schoren Residential Buildings
N° 908 SCN/ 2007
Competition
Basel, Switzerland

Laboratory Building Novartis Campus Shanghai
N° 910 NCS/ 2007–
In collaboration with Sevil Peach
Gense Associates
Competition 1st prize
C11–2, Jinke Road
Shanghai, China

Wertheim Residential and Office Buildings Leipziger Platz
N° 911 WAB/ 2007
Competition
Berlin, Germany

Building for a Law Firm
N° 912 AML/ 2007–
39 Avenue John F. Kennedy
Competition 1st prize
Kirchberg, Luxembourg

Study School of Sports and Hotel Management
N° 913 PFA/ 2007–2008
Pfarrkirchen, Germany

Vision Suvretta House 2025
N° 914 VIS / 2007–
Competition 2nd prize
Saint Moritz, Switzerland

Industrial Buildings for Leica at Leitz–Park
N° 915 LEW/ 2007
Competition
Wetzlar, Germany

Apartment Buildings 'Entrepots Boulevard Macdonald'
N° 917 RBM/ 2007
Competition
Paris, France

Bäumlihofpark
N° 920 OST / 2007–
In Collaboration with August Künzel
Landschaftsarchitekten
Competition 1st prize
Basel, Switzerland

Masterplan Yuntolovo
N° 921 PET/ 2007
In collaboration with
Milica Topalovic, James Melsom
Competition
Saint Petersburg, Russia

Station Building Oerlikon
N° 922 BFÖ/ 2008–2009
Oerlikon, Switzerland

Residential Buildings 'Eichhof West'
N° 924 AEW/ 2008 –
Competition 1st prize
Lucerne, Switzerland

Roquebrune Residential Buildings
N° 925 ROA/ 2008
Study
Roquebrune sur Argens, France

Page 272
'Kunsthaus Zürich' Extension
N° 927 KEZ / 2008
In Collaboration with Peter Suter
Competition, Special Commendation
Zurich, Switzerland

Refurbishment Administrative Court Building Lucerne
N° 928 LUS/ 2008–2010
Adligenswilerstrasse 24
Lucerne, Switzerland

Residential Buildings 'Richti' Wallisellen
N° 929 RAW/ 2008–
Zurich, Switzerland

Monastery Archive and Library
N° 905 MKE/ 2008–2010
Benedictine Monastery Einsiedeln
Einsiedeln, Switzerland

Masterplan Rosental Basel
N° 934 RAM/ 2008–
Competition 1st prize
Basel, Switzerland

Apartment Buildings Champfèr
N° 939 CHF/ 2008–
Via Suot Chesas
Champfèr, Switzerland

Page 276
Swiss Re Headquarters
931 SRH/ 2008–
Competition 1st prize
Mythenquai 50
Zurich, Switzerland

Bukdahl's Bench
N° 894 BUK/ 2009
Royal Danish Academy of Fine Arts,
School of Visual Arts
Copenhagen, Denmark

Apartment Building with daycare centre, Macrolot A2
N° 860.1 BIL/ 2005–2009
In Collaboration with Peter Suter
Boulogne–Billancourt, France

Masterplan for 'Dräger' Industrial Works
N° 933 DSL / 2009–
Competition 1st prize
Moislinger Allee 53–55
Lübeck, Germany

Study for High Rise Buildings Baden
N° 936 HKB/ 2009
Study
In Collaboration with
Martin Steinmann
Baden, Switzerland

Office Building CSS Assurances
938 CSS/ 2009
Competition
Lausanne, Switzerland

Page 282
'Kunstmuseum Basel' Extension
N° 943 KUM/ 2009
In Collaboration with Peter Suter and
Adam Szymczyk
Competition 2nd prize
Basel, Switzerland

Page 286
New East Wing Expansion of the Museum of Natural History
N° 727.3 HUB / 2005–2010
Invalidenstrasse
Berlin, Germany

Diener & Diener

The firm Marcus Diener Architect became the architecture office of Diener & Diener in 1980.
Today Diener & Diener has offices in Basel and Berlin.

From the outset, conversation and discussion has played an integral role in the design process.
Roger Diener has consistently collaborated on the architectural designs with his long-standing coworkers Laurène Dubuis, Jens Erb, Terese Erngaard, Isabel Halene, Aja Huber, Dieter Righetti, Michael Roth, Andreas Rüedi, Wolfgang Schett.

Roger Diener

In 1976, the Basel architect Roger Diener (born 1950) graduated from the Swiss Federal Institute of Technology Zurich (ETHZ) and joined the firm Marcus Diener Architect, the company his father had founded in Basel. He was made partner in 1980.

From 1987–1989 Roger Diener was a professor at the École Polytechnique Fédérale de Lausanne (EPFL). He has been a professor at the ETHZ, the Swiss Federal Institute of Technology Zurich (Studio Basel) since 1999.

The Académie d'Architecture in Paris honoured his work with the Grande Medaille d'Or in 2002.
He was awarded the Prix Meret Oppenheim in 2009.
In 2011 he received the Heinrich Tessenow medal.

Chronological List of Selected Publications

Jehle-Schulte Strathaus, Ulrike and Martin Steinmann, *Diener & Diener, Projekte / Projects 1978 – 1990* (New York and Basel, 1991)

Wang, Wilfried, *From City to Detail* (London and Berlin, 1992)

Diener & Diener, *Diener & Diener* (Lugano, 1994)

Bürohaus Picassoplatz Basel (Berlin, 1994)

Steinmann, Martin and Roger Diener, *Das Haus und die Stadt / The house and the city* (Basel, Boston and Berlin, 1995)

Lampugnani, Magnago Vittorio and Martin Steinmann, *Stadtansichten,* (Zurich, 1998)

Diener & Diener, Winfried Nerdinger and Ulrike Steiner, *Von innen und aussen bewegt*, Architekturmuseum der Technischen Universität München, Pinakothek der Moderne (Munich, 2004)

Lampugnani, Magnago Vittorio, Jehle-Schulte Strathaus, Ulrike Steiner, Martin Steinmann and Jan Thorn-Prikker, *Novartis Campus– Forum 3, Diener, Federle, Wiederin, Schweizerisches Architekturmuseum* (Basel, 2005)

'Adam Szymczyk in conversation with Roger Diener', in: *Prix Meret Oppenheim* (Zurich, 2010)

Diener, Roger, Tony Fretton and Peter Zumthor, 'Das Haus / The House', *Lectures on Architecture at the ETH Zurich, Department of Architecture,* vol. 9 (Zurich, 2010)

Solo Exhibitions

1992–1993
From City to Detail, The Architecture Foundation, London

Von der Stadt zum Detail, Galerie Aedes, Berlin

De la Cité au Détail, Département d'Architecture, Ecole Polytechnique Fédérale à Lausanne (EPFL), Lausanne, Museo d'arte e Architettura, Museo Cantonale d'Arte Lugano, Lugano, Centre Pasqu'Art, Biel

1994
Galerie Gmurzynska, Architekturforum, Biel

1995
Drei Projekte für Basel und Berlin, Galerie Aedes West, Berlin, Architekturforum Zürich, Zurich

1995–1998
Das Haus und die Stadt, Architektur-galerie Luzern, Lucerne, Architectur Centrum (ARCAM), Amsterdam, Universitat Polliñentca de Catalunya (ETSAB), Barcelona, Col·legi d'Arquitectes de Catalunya (COAC), Girona, Fundacio Cultural Colegio Oficial de Arquitectos de Madrid (COAM), Madrid, Colegio Oficial de Arquitectos, San Sebastian, The Royal Danish Academy of Fine Arts, School of Architecture, Copenhagen, Architecture Gallery, Rome, Architekturmuseum TU, Munich, Architekturmuseum, Augsburg, Museum of Finnish Architecture, Helsinki

1997
Centralbahnplatz-Von der Drehscheibe zum Arboretum, Architekturmuseum, Basel

1998–1999
Stadtansichten, Swiss Federal Institute of Technology Zurich (ETHZ), Zurich, University Library, Malmö, De Singel, International Kunstcentrum, Antwerpen,

Stadtansichten, La Première Rue, Unité d'habitation Le Corbusier, Briey-En-Forêt

2001
Diener & Diener. Die Schweizer Botschaft in Berlin im Spiegel anderer Projekte, Galerie Aedes East, Berlin

Diener & Diener, Seit / Depuis Pasqu'art, Kunsthaus Centre Pasqu'Art, Biel

2003
Diener & Diener, Recent Work, Galleri AHO, Oslo

Diener & Diener, Dentro il Volume. Interior Volume, Spazio Espositivo di Santa Verdiana (SESV) Facoltà di Architettura–Università di Firenze, Florence

2004
Von innen und außen bewegt. Diener & Diener, Architekturmuseum der Technischen Universität München, Pinakothek der Moderne, Munich

2005
Novartis-Campus - Forum 3. Diener, Federle, Wiederin. Schweizerisches Architekturmuseum (SAM), Basel

2009
The House and the City. Architecture by Diener & Diener, Tokyo Opera City Art Gallery (TOCAG), Tokyo

2010/11
Carte Blanche VIII: Diener & Diener Architekten, Architekturforum Zürich, Zurich

Group Exhibitions

1984
Architektur & LEGO, Paris, Geneva, Basel, Milano, Frankfurt, Hamburg, Berlin, London, Edinburgh, Liverpool, Helsinki, Rotterdam

1996
Architekturmodelle für Berlin, Galerie Max Hetzler, Berlin

2002
Effet Camouflage, Musée de Design et d'Arts Appliqués Contemporains, Lausanne

Exemplarisch. Konstruktion und Raum in der Architektur des 20. Jahrhunderts, Munich

Next, La Biennale di Venezia Società di Cultura Architecture a Venezia, Venice

2003
Berlin, Experimentierfeld der Architektur: Die Stadt nach 1989, Fundacio Cultural Colegio Oficial de Arquitectos de Madrid (COAM)

A Matter of Art: Swiss Architects in China, Shanghai

Page numbers in **bold** *type refer
to principle descriptions of projects,
in italic to illustration captions.*

Aachen Synagogue *300*, 302, 304, 305
Administration Building Hochstrasse
 10, *11*, 13, 14, 15, **68–75**, *152, 158*,
 159, 304
Administration Building
 Picassoplatz *9*, 10, 11, **84–9**, *161*
Adorno, Theodor 31
Albert, Bruno 133
Alexander, Christopher 150, 160
Amsterdam, Netherlands
 see Apartment Buildings KNSM
 and Java Island
Angelico, Fra 14
Antwerp, Begium
 see Westkaai 1 + 2 Apartment
 Buildings
Apartment Buildings Hammerstrasse
 9, 10, **34–40**, 151, 302
Apartment Buildings KNSM and
 Java Island 11–12, *24*, 25,
 132–9, 163–4, 164
Apartment Buildings
 Parkkolonnaden 11, 13, *27*, **112–17**
Apartment Buildings Riehenring
 9, 10, **40–6**
Apartment Buildings St. Alban-Tal
 9, 11, **46–56**
Apartment and Office Building
 Bäumleingasse **182–7**
Arendt, Hannah 7
Asplund, Gunnar 20, 141, 312

Bacon, Francis 14
Baden, Switzerland
 ABB engineering company 11, 25
'Basel' door handle *153*
Basel, Switzerland
 see Administration Buildings
 Hochstrasse and Picassoplatz
 Apartment Buildings with Bank 13
 see Apartment Buildings
 Hammerstrasse, Riehenring and
 St. Alban-Tal
 see Apartment and Office Building
 Bäumleingasse
 Basler Versicherung 305
 First Church of Christ Scientist *85*
 Hochbergerplatz 30
 see Housing & Office Buildings
 Warteck Brewery
 see Kunstmuseum Basel Extention
 Leonhard-Gymnasium 99
 Migros Supermarket Eglisee 24
 see Novartis Campus Forum 3
 see Office Building Kohlenberg
 see Office Building Steinentorberg
 Residential Building
 Allschwilerstrasse 11
 Residential and Office Building
 Elsässerstrasse 14
 Row Houses Isteinerstrasse 30
 see Showrooms for Manor
 see Stücki Shopping Centre
 see Training and Conference
 Centre Viaduktstrasse
 see Vogesen School
Baumgarten, Paul 20
Bazzani, Cesare 199
Benjamin, Walter 153–4
Berlin, Germany

 see Apartment Buildings
 Parkkolonnaden
 BWB 11, 27
 Gauforum 155
 Ministergärten 307–8, 312
 see Museum of Natural History
 Office and Residential Buildings
 'Quartier 110' 27
 see Pergamon Museum
 see Swiss Embassy
 Office Building Spreedreieck *155*
Bern, Stuker Auction House 20, 21, 23
Bernoulli, Hans 9
Biel, *see* Centre Pasqu'Art
Bill, Max 160
Böhm, Gottfried 29
Bonatz, Paul 85, 283
Botta, Mario 150, 157
Braque, Georges 14, 189
Bührle, E.G. 273

Capraola, Italy, Villa Farnese 312
Casa A1 at the Olympic Village **246–9**
Centre Pasqu'Art 20, *21*, 23, 30,
 118–25, 142, *300*, 301
Christ, Rudolf 85, 283
Collection Rosengart 23, **188–91**
Cologne, Germany
 Gerling Buildings 27
 see Gmurzynska Gallery
Convention Centre 'ZürichForum'
 258–61
Cosenza, Luigi 199

Diener, Marcus 9, 302
Diener, Roger 7, 8–9, 9–10, 12, 13, 16,
 28, 149–55, 157–65 299–313
Drancy, France, *see* Shoah Memorial
Duchamp, Marcel 26

Eich, Günter 308–11
Einsiedeln, Switzerland
 see Music House for Instrumental
 Practice and Choral Rehearsal
Eisenmann, Peter 307
Eliot, T.S. 14
Essen, Germany, *see* Ruhr Musuem

Federle, Helmut 28–9, 145, 151–2
Frankfurt Book Fair *31*, **178–81**
Freud, Lucien 14
Fuller, Buckminster 150

Giotto 14–16
 Scorvengi Chapel, Padua *14*
 Annunciation to St Anne 15
Gmurzynska Gallery 10, 11, 14, 30,
 90–7, *161*, 162
Gotenborg, Sweden 141
 Law Courts 20, 312
Gropius, Walter 9

The Hague, Netherlands
 see Residential Buildings Ypenburg
Hauser, Arnold 301
Herzog, Jacques 150
Hitzig, Friedrich 141
Hoesli, Bernhard 157
Hoffmann, Ludwig 203
Hopper, Edward 15, 29
 New York Office 15
Hotel Schweizerhof, Migros Super
 market, Migros School 23-4, **126–31**
Housing & Office Buildings Warteck

 Brewery 13, *15*, 16, **106–11**, 305–7
Huet, Bernard 305

Kahn, Louis 31, 157
Kelly, Ellsworth 7, 17
 *Window, Museum of Modern Art,
 Paris, 17*
Kieren, Martin 100
Klee, Paul 23, 290
 Radiation and Rotation 214
Kleist, Heinrich von 165
Koetter, Fred 157
Kollhoff & Timmermann 133
Kunsthaus Zürich Extension **272–5**
Kunstmuseum Basel Extention
 85, 152, *154*, **282–5**

Lampugnani, Vittorio Magnano 231
Lausanne
 École Polytechnique Fédérale
 (EPFL) 11, 27
Le Corbusier 157
Léger, Fernand 29
Loos, Adolf 20, 31, 141
Losone school building 9
Lucerne, Switzerland
 see Collection Rosengart
 see Hotel Schweizerhof
Lyotard, Jean-François 9

Malmö, Sweden
 Biel Gas Works 12
 see Masterplan for the University
 Harbour
 see University Building
Marc, Franz
 Tierschicksale 290
Masterplan for the Maag Areal Plus
 25, **212–15**
Masterplan for the University
 Harbour 12, 24–5, **166–9**
Meiningen State Central Bank 29
Messel, Alfred 203
Mexico City 27–8, 231
Meyer, Hannes 9, 13
Milan, Italy, Bocconi University 27
Mobimo Tower **216–21**
Moser, Karl 9
Munich, Hypo-Bank 27
Museum of Natural History *22*,
 23, **286–97**, 301, *306*
Music House for Instrumental
 Practice and Choral Rehearsal,
 266–71

Nancy School of Architecture 11
National Gallery of Modern Art,
 Rome 22–3, **198–201**
Novartis Campus Forum 3
 27–8, *29*, 30, 31, **230–45**

Oechslin, Werner 158
Office Building Kohlenberg 10, 16,
 98–100, *162, 163*
Office Building Steinentorberg 10,
 11, **56–64**

Padua, Scrovegni Chapel
 Giotto's frescos 13–15
Panofsky, Edwin 14
Paris, France
 Museum of Modern Art 7
 Roquette Residential Buildings 18
 Tzara House 20, 141

Picasso, Pablo 14-15, 189, 190
 Houses on the Hill 14, *15*
 Women Running on the Beach 15
Pergamon Museum 22, 23, **202–5**
Posener, Julius 150

Residential Buildings Ypenburg **206–11**
Rigi Kaltbad
 Hotel Bellevue 24
Rome, *see* National Gallery
Rosengart, Angela 189
Rosenkranz, Karl 162
Rossi, Aldo 8, 9, 47, 149, 150, 157
 'Architettura per i musei' 312
 L'architettura della città 302
Rowe, Colin 157
Ruhr Musuem, Zeche Zollverein
 22, 23, **192–7**, 309, 311, 312

Salvisberg, Otto Rudolf 9, 85
Sansot, Pierre 16–17
Sartre, Jean-Paul 301, 302
Schinkel, Karl Friedrich 141, 162–3
Shoah Memorial Drancy **262–5**
Showrooms and Administration
 Building for Manor **65–7**
Snozzi, Luigi 8, 149, *150*, 157, 301
Steidle, Otto 247
Steinegger, Jean-Claude 157
Steinmann, Martin 48, 99, 152, 161
Stücki Shopping Centre **222–9**
Suter, Peter 104
Swiss Embassy *19*, 20, 23, 28, **140–7**,
 151, 152, 154, *303*, 311, 312
Swiss Re Headquarters **276–81**

Terragni, Giuseppe *151*
Ticino school 8–9
Tiede, August 287
Turin, *see* Casa A1
Training and Conference Centre
 Viaduktstrasse **76–83**
'Twogether' Prefab study 30

University Building, Malmö **170–7**

Vacchini, Livio 9
Vautier, Ben 35
Venice 157
Venturi, Robert 9–10
Vitruvius 158
Vogesen School **102–5**, *160*, 161

Weimar, Germany
 Halle der Volksgemeinschaft 308
 Residential and Cultural Buildings
 'Streichkan-Kaseme' 30
Westkaai 1 + 2 Apartment
 Buildings **250–7**
Wölfflin, Heinrich 158

Zeche Zollvern, *see* Ruhr Musuem
Zeugheer, Leonhard 127
Zola, Émile 302
Zschokke, Alexander 283
Zug, Residential and Office Buildings
 Rigistrasse 27
Zurich, Switzerland
 Athletics Stadium Letzigrund 29
 see Convention Centre 'ZürichForum'
 see Kunsthaus Zürich Extension
 see Masterplan for the Maag Areal
 see Mobimo Tower
 see Swiss Re Headquarters

Diener & Diener staff, Basel and Berlin, 1976–2011

Marnie Amato, Roberto Agnolazzo, Reem Almannai, Christine Anding, Haike Apelt, Alexandre Aviolet, Johanna Bade, Christine Baumgartner, Vera Baumann, Ruth Baumann, Susanne Bartholomé, Markus Bay, Susanne Bender, Petra Benthien, Pascal Berger, Maurice Berrei, Karl Betschart, Sven Bietau, Dirk Binert, Stephan Bischof, Roman Bitzer, Alexandre Blanc, Mireille Blatter, Severine Bloch, Jonathan Bock, Lorenzo Bonauch, Rebecca Borer, Oliver Boros, Frederic Borruat, Wulf Böer, Béatrice Bürgin, Roger Braccini, Monika Braig, Lukas Brassel, Anne-Christine Brehm, Eleanora Bressi, Christian Brunner, Piotr Brzoza, Oana Bucerzan, Kord Büning-Pfaue, Matthias Buser, Bruno Miguel Varejao Cardoso, Sonia Carvalho Taborda Barata, Adalgisa Cianci, Massimo Corradi, Christine Covas, Katrin Cramer, Philemon Dätwyler, Luisa Dazio, Stéphane de Montmollin, Fabian de Tomasi, Michael Deutschmann, Roger Diener, Dominik Dietziker, Claudia Dische, Kazuhide Doi, Adrian Dorschner, Régine Doutre, Reidun Dova, Markus Dreher, Martin Dubach, Laurène Dubuis, Bruno Eggenschwiler, Christian Eichhorn, Markus Elmiger, Jens Erb, Terese Erngaard, Federico Facchini, Colette Faehndrich, Leandro Fedele, Vanessa Fercher, Linus Fetz, Caroline Fiechter, Jürg Fink, Dominik Fischer, Norbert Föhn, Magnus Forsberg, Jens Förster, Laurent Francey, Ralph Franz, Josefine Frederiksen, Benjamin Frei, Isabel Frey, Thomas Friberg, Eva Maria Funke, Juan Tomas Ortega Garcia, Maria do Rosa, Garcia Goncalves, Dario Gasperini, Peter Gaub, Jan Gebert, Stephanie Gebhard, Linus Getz, Rita Gfeller, Kathrin Giesser, Hans-Peter Gilgen, Ben Gitaï, Hartmut Göhler, Nicolas Grandjean, Hans Gritsch, Andreas Grolimund, Michael Grunitz, Christoph Gschwind, Patrizia Guarnaccia, Stephan Gude, Lorenz Guetg, Andrea Guetg, Kornelia Gysel, Brigitte Gysin, Matthias Haldi, Isabel Halene, Anne Hangebruch, Guido Häring, Liqun He, Lars Heider, Thomas Heil, René Heinimann, Susan Held, Jens Hellmuth, Uwe Herlyn, Vera Hobrecker, Denisa Hoda, Marion Hofstetter, Karin Höhler, Aja Huber, Rosmarie Hüni, Ferdi Hufschmid, Rolf Hunziker, Yves Jaquet, Claudia Jeger, Gian-Marco Jenatsch, Anna Christina Jessen, Regula Joss, Vaiva Jundaite, Monique Jüttner, Christian Kaldewey, Gabriele Kalt, Oliver Kalt, Guido Kappius, Mark Kaul, Lili Kehl, Dorothee Kerbe, Florian Kessel, Fabian Kiepenheuer, Hiroyuki Kimura, Fabian Kirchner, Tobias Knaeble, Valerie Koch, Vanessa Koch, Daudi Kondoro, Barbara Krumm, Emanuel Kudris, Thomas Kühne, Cornelia Kunz, Michael Künzle, Markus Lampe, Melanie Langewort, Paul Langlotz, Aljoscha Lanz, Bianca Lauscher Besozzi, Florence Le François, Ursula Lehmann, Martin Leisi, Guy Leonard, Elvira Leu, Andrea Leubin, Stephan Leuenberger, Christian Lien, Gabriele Libera, Phung Long, Samuel Lindell, Anna Malin Lindholm, Patrick Loewenberg, Katja Lüneburg, Philipp Lustenberger, Claude Lüthi, Marcia Lüthi, Oliver Lütjens, Corinna Lutz, Katharina Mannhart, Michela Mariani, Frederico Marques, Carlo Martucci, Roberto Masoch, Sebastian Massmann, Marcello Mazzei, Wolfgang Meisl, Insa Meenen, Falk Merten, Paul Mihailescu, Philippe Mivelaz, Stephan Möhring, Alejandro Montiel Aguilar, Athos Morisoli, Nao Morohashi, Lisa Moser, Sebastian Mossman, Stefan Mühlemann, Jörg Müller, Mark Mulligan, Nathalie Nef, Delf Nickel, Christoph Niethammer, Lucio Nardi, Martin Neander, Christopher Ngahyoma, Jarno Nillesen, Philipp Oehy, Corinna Oesterle, Thomas Padmanabhan, Martin Palzenberger, Tibor Pataky, Valentina Patrono, Mathias Peppler, Judith Petz, Silvia Pfaffhauser, Jan Pfennig, Oliviero Piffaretti, Nelly Pilz, Guilherme Pires, Jacqueline Pittet, Annina von Planta, Sagar Prasad, Nina Prochotta, Jan Prosa, Daniel Rabi, Carlos Rabinovich, Mirjam Rahmen-Borer, Harun Rashid, Daniel Rebmann, Sara Reichwein, Heidi Reimann, Laurenz Reinitzer, Lars Reinhardt, Marcel Remund, Philipp Rentschler, Judith Resch, Tony Rhiem, Dieter Righetti, Franziska Ritzler, Katia Ritz, Henri Rochat, Carla Rocneanu, Yves Rogger, Mathias Rösner, Jan Rösler, Fabian Roth, Michael Roth, Andreas Rüedi, Renata Rüedi, Sandra Rumpf, Yvonne Rütsche, Emil Rysler, Parthena Sachanidou, Daniela Sammarruco, Béatrice Schaad, Wolfgang Schett, Christian Schibli, Birgit Schindler, Alexander Schmid, Tania Schmid, Asa Norman Schneider, Urs Schönenberger, Björn Schreiter, Silvio Schubiger, Thomas Schulz, Andreas Schürch, Marcellus Schwarz, Jörg Schwarzburg, Veronika Selig, Suzanne Senti, Can Serman, Marco Serra, Christian Severin, Henriette Siegert, Johann Simons, Susanne Sittig, Martina Soler Bach, Christof Sommer, Ursula Spitz, Christian Stamm, Daniel Stefani, Dieter Steinsberger, Rachel Stemmle, Markus Stingelin, Miroslav Stojanovic, Simon Stolze, Jürgen Strehlau, Benedikt Sunder-Plassmann, Nelson Tam, Stéphanie Thill, Nevena Torboski, Livio Tuccillo, Florian Ueker, Tiziana Ugoletti-Serra, Hana Vecera, Susanne Vécsey, Jan Verwijnen, Denise Vetter, Stefan Vetter, Marianna Deborah Vitello, Claudia Volberg, Georg Wagner, Timo Wahner, Marie Louise Walter, Anina Wanner, Lily Wanner, Anne Wehmer, Marion Weiler, Sebastian Weinhardt, Axel Wibbelt, Brigitte Widmer, Daniel Wili, Adam Wozniak, Andrea Wurm, Helen Wyss, Hanjun Yi, Sevim Yildiz, Dominik Zaugg, Yohan Zerdoun, Marina Zhurminskaya, Hanna Zielinska, Anna Zurbuchen

Picture Credits:

All images courtesy Diener & Diener Architects except those noted below. Numbers indicate pages, and the following abbreviations are used: 't'=top; 'b'=bottom, 'l'-left, 'm'-middle, etc.

Joseph Abram 13l, 13r, 29l, 29r; aeroGRID® PRO Graphics 252l; Gabriele Basilico 200; Basler Denkmalpflege 183; Basler Zeitung, Erich Meyer 223; Christian Baur 25, 215, 271; Tom Bisig 87; Werner Bösch 266; Hans–Jürgen Breuning 150l; CISA A. Palladio 272; Deimel + Wittmar 31, 178, 180; Simon Dickinson Ltd London 214; Hansruedi Disch 98, 108, 162; Electa 151m; ETH-Bibliothek Zurich Image Archive 212; Helmut Federle 20l, 28; Fonds Eugène Beaudouin 163; Frankfurt Bookfair 179; Roland Halbe 27, 112, 114, 115, 128, 129, 145r; Heinrich Helfenstein 56, 66; Institute for the History and Theory of Architecture (gta) 157; Gerry Johansson 170, 172, 175; Luuk Kramer 137; Kunstmuseum Basel, Martin P. Bühler 283; Landesbildstelle Berlin 141; Walter Mair 142r, 144; MoMA New York 15m; Musée national Picasso Paris 15r; Museum für Naturkunde Berlin, Carola Radke 290l; Erika Overmeer 245t, 245b; Regionalverband Ruhr 193; Christian Richters 22, 24, 84, 127, 132, 134, 135r, 136, 140, 142l, 143l, 143r, 164r, 174, 182, 184, 185, 190l, 207, 208l, 208r, 209, 216, 218, 219, 222, 224, 226tl, 226bl, 226br, 227, 232, 233, 234, 236, 243, 246, 248t, 248b, 250, 253, 254, 268, 269, 286, 288, 292, 296; Sammlung Hauser 130; César San Millàn 135l; SCALA Archives Florence 14, 15l; Ulrich Schwarz 145l; Ulrich Schwarz courtesy Galerie Dittmar, Berlin 20r, 151r; Luigi Snozzi Studio d'architettura 150r; Stadsarchief Amsterdam 133b, 163l; Stadsbyggnadskontoret Malmö 166; Bernhard Strauss 100, 104r, 106, 160r; Christian Vogt 10, 11, 57, 70, 78, 80b, 90, 92, 95, 109, 188, 190r, 152, 158; Ruedi Walti 64, 226tr, 230; Gaston Wicky 20, 118, 120, 122l, 122r, 123, 126; Lothar Willmann 203; Alo Zanetta 102, 104l, 160l

While every effort has been made to identify copyright holders, Diener & Diener would be grateful to hear from those who have escaped our notice.

Designed by Robert & Durrer, Zürich

Translations by Timothy Grundy, Sarah Robertson and Michael Robinson

Phaidon Press Limited
Regent's Wharf
All Saints Street
London N1 9PA

Phaidon Press Inc.
180 Varick Street
New York, NY 10014

www.phaidon.com

First published 2011
Reprinted 2012
© 2011 Phaidon Press Limited

ISBN 978 0 7148 5919 4

A CIP catalogue record for this book is available from the British Library.

All rights reserved. No part of this publication may be reproduced, stored in a retrieval system or transmitted, in any form or by any means, electronic, mechanical, photocopying, recording or otherwise, without the express written permission of Phaidon Press Limited.

Printed in China